PUBLIC ENEMY

ALSO BY BILL AYERS

Fugitive Days: Memoirs of an Antiwar Activist

Teaching toward Freedom: Moral Commitment and Ethical Action in the Classroom

Teaching the Personal and the Political: Essays on Hope and Justice

On the Side of the Child: Summerhill Revisited

A Kind and Just Parent: The Children of Juvenile Court

The Good Preschool Teacher: Six Teachers Reflect on Their Lives

To Teach: The Journey of a Teacher

To Teach: The Journey, in Comics (with Ryan Alexander-Tanner)

Teaching the Taboo: Courage and Imagination in the Classroom (with Rick Ayers)

Teaching Toward Democracy: Educators as Agents of Change (with Kevin Kumashiro, Erica Meiners, Therese Quinn, and David Stovall)

Race Course: Against White Supremacy (with Bernardine Dohrn)

PUBLIC ENEMY

Confessions of an American Dissident

BILL AYERS

BEACON PRESS
BOSTON

Beacon Press
25 Beacon Street
Boston, Massachusetts 02108-2892
www.beacon.org

Beacon Press books
are published under the auspices of
the Unitarian Universalist Association of Congregations.

16 15 14 13   8 7 6 5 4 3 2 1

This book is printed on acid-free paper that meets the uncoated paper
ANSI/NISO specifications for permanence as revised in 1992.

Text design and composition by Kim Arney

Library of Congress Cataloging-in-Publication Data
Ayers, William.
    Public enemy : confessions of an American dissident / Bill Ayers.
        pages cm
ISBN 978-0-8070-3276-3 (hardback) — ISBN 978-0-8070-3293-0 (ebook)
1. Ayers, William. 2. Left-wing extremists—United States—Biography. 3. Vietnam
War, 1961–1975—Protest movements—United States. 4. Radicalism—United States—
History—20th century. 5. United States—Social conditions—1960-1980. I. Title.
    HN90.R3A96 2013
    320.53092—dc23
    [B]
                                                                2013023310

To all those who've kept the faith as they've trudged toward liberation—teaching freedom, saving the earth, resisting the race to incarcerate and the steady descent into a brutal new Sparta,

to the aging radicals and the up-and-comers, the New Abolitionists and the old freedom fighters,

to the undocumented and the unafraid, the occupiers,

to the everyday people defying oppressive authority and rising in solidarity with the disadvantaged, the marginalized, and the despised—the wretched of the earth and our best hope for the future.

CONTENTS

Spring 2008, Chicago

It was a mid-April evening, the sweet smells of springtime upon us and the last light reluctantly giving way outside the front window, when my graduate seminar ended and everyone pitched in to clean up. A dozen of my students were spread out in our living room, cups and dishes scattered everywhere, small piles of books and papers marking specific territory. Until a moment before, all of us had focused intensely on the work at hand: thesis development, the art of the personal essay, and the formal demands of oral history research. As a professor for two decades, my favorite teaching moments often popped up during these customary potluck seminars at our home—something about sharing food in a more intimate personal setting, perhaps, or disrupting the assumed hierarchy of teacher authority, or simply being freed from the windowless, fluorescent-lit concrete bunkers that passed for classrooms at my university. But the seminar was done for this evening, and as students began to gather their things, a self-described "political junkie" clicked on the TV and flipped to the presidential primary debate, well under way by now, between Hillary Clinton and the young upstart from Chicago, Barack Obama.

ABC was broadcasting the debate to a record-setting audience, and the debate moderators Charles Gibson and George Stephanopoulos seemed to be doing their best to make a mess of things, avoiding anything of substance in favor of a kind of weird political cage fighting—bloody performance art—throwing up little bits of trivia and gossip and "gotchas," inviting snarls and cuts without any serious illumination or thoughtful reflection. I wandered in and out from the kitchen, muttering that no one watching would be the wiser for the time spent, but my students didn't pay me any mind. The only explicit response I got was from one of the youngest, who glanced at me impatiently as she emphatically shushed me. Everyone, it seemed, was captured by the theater riot beaming from the screen, political junkies all, fascinated by what was being framed by the big brains of punditry as a "historic contest." I stood near the back of the room.

Stephanopoulos, a former aide to President Bill Clinton, turned to Senator Obama and said, "On this . . . general theme of patriotism in your relationships . . ." The *general theme* in question was becoming central to the dramatic narrative spun by everyone now running against Obama, and Stephanopoulos was about to press him about his former pastor, the Reverend Jeremiah Wright, whose most impassioned statements about racism, war, and the American government ("God damn America!") had been widely disseminated and discussed.

"But do you believe he's as patriotic as you are?" he asked.

Obama replied, "This is somebody who's a former Marine. So I believe that he loves this country. But I also believe that he's somebody who, because of the experiences he's had over the course of a lifetime, is also angry about the injustices he's had."

Now Stephanopoulos was bearing down on the "general theme of patriotism in your relationships." "A gentleman named William Ayers," Stephanopoulos began. "He was part of the Weather Underground in the 1970s. They bombed the Pentagon, the Capitol, and other buildings. He's never apologized for that. . . . An early organizing meeting for your state senate campaign was held at his house, and your campaign has said you are *'friendly.'* Can you explain that relationship for the voters and explain to Democrats why it won't be a problem?"

I thought Obama looked slightly stricken, temporarily off-balance, and uncharacteristically tongue-tied. I was probably projecting, because I felt suddenly dizzy, off-balance, and tongue-tied myself. But I know for sure my students were thunderstruck. Their heads snapped in my direction and a few literally dropped to the floor, one with both hands over her mouth. Obama replied: "This is a guy who lives in my neighborhood, who's a professor of English in Chicago, who I know and who

I have not received some official endorsement from. . . . The notion that somehow as a consequence of me knowing somebody who engaged in detestable acts forty years ago, when I was eight years old, somehow reflects on me and my values doesn't make much sense, George."

He had us at "he's a guy who lives in my neighborhood."

An explosion of laughter ricocheted around the room. Some were genuinely amused, some disbelieving and a bit horrified; everyone clamored to make sense of the bombshell that had just dropped into our little seminar, and by extension, reverberated around the country and the world. I sat down, and the student who had shushed me a moment ago turned to me and said, "Oh my God, that guy has the same name as yours." Another explained to her excitedly that that's because we were indeed the *same guy*: "Bill's the guy, and we're in the neighborhood George is talking about!"

No one in our living room really heard Hillary Clinton raise the stakes. She was concerned about Obama's association with someone who, she pointed out, said in an interview published in the *New York Times* on September 11, 2001, that he didn't regret bombing government buildings even though, Clinton claimed, "in some instances people died," and "he was just sorry they hadn't done more," and that the relationship continued after 9/11. No one heard Obama match her poke for poke: Your husband, he charged, "pardoned or commuted the sentences of two members of the Weather Underground, which I think is a slightly more significant act than me serving on a board with somebody." Neither candidate really knew what they were talking about, and each seemed simply to be following fact-free scripts written by pollsters or aides assigned the dirt detail. Clearly, both camps had done some shabby opposition research, and each was busy, busy, busy spinning its particular phony narrative. Each candidate threw a few more chips on the fire before moving on, and no one listening or watching learned anything substantive from the exchange.

My students were amazed to see me cast on TV as some kind of public enemy, and even though I knew the connection was a story that had been percolating in the fever swamps of the right-wing blogs for months, I was amazed too. My partner, Bernardine Dohrn, and I had hosted the initial fund-raiser for Obama and uncharacteristically donated a little money to his campaign for the Illinois senate; we lived a few blocks apart, and he and I had sat on a couple of nonprofit boards together. So? Who could have predicted it would blow up like this?

"A guy around the neighborhood"—as funny as it sounded, I thought he got it exactly right.

Before Obama became a US senator and then a presidential candidate, Bernardine and I thought of *him* as a guy around the neighborhood, too. Even though lots of people have said to me something like, "Oooo-oooh!!!" remembering that he'd called me "a guy around the neighborhood," I didn't take it that way at all. After all we knew him then not as the huge, all-caps, super-accomplished, unbelievably successful, transcendent person he would become but as someone you might run into at the bookstore or the market. A guy . . . around the neighborhood.

Bernardine knew Michelle Obama as a smart, dignified, and community-minded advocate from the time they overlapped at a Chicago law firm, and when we later met Barack, she thought he was almost, if not quite, Michelle's match. He too was brilliant, "the smartest guy in any room he walks into," I said repeatedly, and later added, "Including the US Senate." And not only hugely intelligent but also kind and sturdy and compassionate—a great combination. No one could miss another quality either: political ambition. For years I said to Bernardine—in a real display of the low horizon of my own imagination— "Barack's obviously going places. . . . I think he wants to be the mayor of Chicago someday."

He and I served together on the board of the Woods Fund, a small Chicago foundation that supported community organizing in the belief that ordinary people have the keys to making a more just and joyful world for all. The people with the problems are also the people with the solutions, we said. Community organizing was the foundation of the Black Freedom Movement, the women's movement, and the labor and immigrant rights movements, the fight for safe workplaces and the forty-hour workweek, and much more. Barack came to the foundation because of his experience as a community organizer and as a lawyer at a civil rights firm. I came as an education professor and school reform activist, as well as someone who wrote about urban problems and city kids.

In our modest boardroom Barack was steady and cool, always a quick study and always a serious practitioner of conversation in search of common ground. Several of the grants we gave out were adventurous and unpredictable, and most of us felt that was exactly our job: to set a learning agenda and to provide teachable moments, times of disequilibrium where new and innovative solutions to old problems might emerge. That meant not all of our grants were successful in any conventional sense, and that board meetings were lively and sometimes contentious, even raucous.

At one meeting, the board split on a small arts grant to a theater group that performed plays challenging bias against gay and lesbian students, largely in schools. The young program officer who presented the grant was interrogated sharply by a senior board member, who said that it offended his personal moral views and his religious convictions. The younger man fought back quietly but bravely, defending it as a question of social justice and community ethics, and simply as the right thing to do. The grant passed, barely.

When we took a break, Barack pointedly told the program officer that he admired him for his steadfastness in a difficult situation. Then he stepped outside with the dissenting board member and told him he understood how hard it must be to see the value of this proposal through his own perspective, but that over time we would all be glad we had stood up against discrimination and for equal rights. Pure Barack.

When Bernardine and I were asked by our state senator, the redoubtable Alice Palmer, to host a coffee for Barack Obama as he launched his first campaign for public office, we said yes. Our home was always open for a rendezvous or two and for all kinds of gatherings, meetings, book talks, seminars, campaigns, salons, fund-raisers, discussion groups, get-togethers, play-readings, and round tables. It was a pretty routine Sunday afternoon: a few dozen folks—colleagues from the university, lawyers, Hyde Park neighbors—with coffee and cake and cookies. When Bernardine stopped the informal conversation, welcomed people to our home, and introduced Alice and Barack, the afternoon took on an unmistakable passing-of-the-torch vibe. Alice was stepping down from the Illinois senate to run for Congress, she wanted to see her seat go to someone who would continue in a progressive direction, and she thought Barack was the one.

Barack praised Alice for her work in and out of government, then spoke about the need to develop a bottom-up, top-down strategy for moving any progressive agenda forward. "Without organized power from the grassroots, nothing will advance; without political leaders who will respond wherever possible, those good efforts are stifled," he said. A South Side minister said a kind word about Barack's work, a couple of other politicians from Alice's generation agreed, and then Bernardine gave a modest pitch for donations—we raised a few hundred bucks. Obama won Alice's seat in the Illinois state senate, and the rest is history.

Of course, years later, on the night of the Stephanopoulos surprise, none of my students knew any of this, and no one in our living room could have seen this coming. By the time everyone settled down, the debate was done. My students stuck around for quite a while, a bit dazed, I think. Someone pointed out helpfully that I wasn't a professor of English, and someone else wondered aloud how this line of attack might impact Senator Obama's chances. Most were super considerate, asking what I needed and attending to me as if I'd been hit by a truck—which was a bit how I felt. How are you? Can I get you some tea? And then: how well did you know him? Are you thrilled to be associated like this? Are you scared? I think for some of them there was an abrupt awareness that, while they'd known me quite well a few minutes before, they had suddenly ceased to know me at all. That made sense to me, because for a moment I wondered who I was as well. When they finally trickled out, some still shaking their heads in marvelous disbelief, others smiling in wonder, each offered a hug or a handshake. It was a bizarre end-of-seminar moment, but quite tender.

The evening became even more surreal: no sleep, of course, and lots of phone calls from family and friends, lots of disbelief and laughter and support, as well as some sense of foreboding and apprehension. Bernardine and I held each other a little closer, trying to regain our balance and come to terms with the sudden sense that this cartoon character, *Bill Ayers*, who looked exactly like me and shared my name, address, and Social Security number, was about to become a punching bag in a presidential campaign, a character who might actually have an impact on the outcome of a national election. It felt altogether too big and, all in all, too strange.

Fantastic, unreal, crazy—*Bill Ayers* had been quiet and still, fermenting on a dusty shelf in an unused laboratory for decades, when he was abruptly plucked from a jar of brine. Suddenly, there he was, a little wrinkled, dripping and smelling of vinegar and garlic, but alive! And the Weather Underground, suspended in amber all these years, was reborn out of the blue, not only active and breathing fire but all of a sudden more menacing and dangerous—and far, far better known—than it had ever been before. Mouth-to-mouth resuscitation had been administered by the fringe, but its resurrection now lay in the hands of an opportunistic media and eager campaign staffs of the Right, the middle, and even the moderate Left.

Opponents had found it devilishly difficult to generate an effective blow against the smart and charismatic senator from Illinois, anything that might gain traction, score points, and derail this young, forward-charging politician. Hillary Clinton was blazing the trail that night, generating an attack with a murky story line built on a detestable political sleight of hand: old, reliable guilt by association.

Barack Obama emerged out of nowhere, she implied, as if in a dream. While he was certainly a man of charm, smarts, and skill, we should all have been asking, Who is he really? Admire the man's undeniable strengths, to be sure, but plant the doubt: he's an unknown with an "exotic background" and a strange name, a man who may knock everyone out but remains a mystery. The repeated and dramatic refrain came in the form of a question: "What do we *really* know about this man?" Uncertainty, innuendo, and the scent of fear: a long-standing poisonous brew in American electoral politics. And, of course, in the case of Obama, the venomous signifier of color—the smear that dare not speak its name—seethed and percolated just below the surface. Is he one of us?

A set of shadowy supporting actors added teeth and a little zing: an African American preacher with a Black liberation theology message, a social justice agenda, and a fiery style; an activist white priest identified with the Black community on Chicago's fabled South Side; a scholar with an Arabic name and a record of advocacy on behalf of the Palestinian people; and eventually an "unrepentant domestic terrorist." That last bit part would be played by me or my stunt double, and if I refused to cooperate, fading pictures of me recovered from my blazing youth would have to do. Each of us was cast as a public enemy, an opponent, and a treacherous foe of the decent people.

I had joined the civil rights movement in the mid-sixties, true. I'd later resisted the draft, become a full-time community organizer and antiwar activist with Students for a Democratic Society, and at the end of the decade, in the ashes of a Greenwich Village explosion that took the lives of three comrades, was one of the team that cofounded the Weather Underground. However, not only did *I* never kill or injure anyone, but in the six years of its existence, the Weather Underground never killed or injured anyone either. We crossed lines of legality to be sure, of propriety, and perhaps even of common sense, but it was restrained, and those are the simple, straightforward facts.

Never mind—Senator Obama, contaminated by his links with these dodgy characters, must immediately and repeatedly denounce, deny, and dissociate. The dramatic action involved selectively highlighting the histories and outrageous perspectives of these "un-American" eccentrics, ferreting out every secret tie and dangerous affiliation, and then insisting that the senator defend his associations. It was a war, and bloggers, commentators, and intrepid aspiring Jimmy Olsens on steroids began to man their forward outposts 24/7.

There had been a lot of chatter for several months on right-wing blogs about Hyde Park, the now-notorious "neighborhood," which was in fact a close-knit community on Chicago's South Side where folks actually knew one another; about the University of Chicago Laboratory Schools, the school that all of our kids had attended; and about the Woods Fund. Somehow, these scraps of facts were whipped into a toxic gobbledygook, including a story with growing traction in the self-referencing chat rooms of the Right that we were secret Muslims sharing a shadowy *masjid* in Hyde Park (proof: one of our kids was named Malik; one of theirs, Malia!), and another that I had ghostwritten his two wildly successful memoirs (proof: maritime allusions appear both in his book *Dreams from My Father* and in my first memoir, *Fugitive Days!*).

On Fox News, Sean Hannity quickly made me into a special project, asserting again and again that Barack Obama had blurbed one of my books and chalking that up as one of his many sins. In reality, the *Chicago Tribune* had run a feature in its book review section for many years in which they called people and asked them on the phone what they were reading. When Barack Obama was contacted, he was reading my book *A Kind and Just Parent*, and he had called it "a searing and timely account of the juvenile court system, and the courageous individuals who rescue hope from despair." Hannity never bothered to find out if the book was indeed searing and timely.

Hannity had thrashed around for a time, trying out a wide range of other fantastic plot points. I had written an editorial extolling the terrorist attacks of 9/11, he claimed, and I had killed several police officers. None of this was true. In the end, he simply adopted the story as it was crafted first by Hillary Clinton and eventually by John McCain and Sarah Palin: Barack Obama and I knew one another—no more than that.

Slightly more surprising was George Stephanopoulos's willingness to parrot Hannity's story. Stephanopoulos, an old friend of Clinton's, denied he was doing Hillary's or Hannity's bidding, but the day before the debate, in a radio interview, Hannity prompted him: "There are . . . questions that I don't think anybody has asked Barack Obama, and I don't know if this is going to be on your list tomorrow. . . . The only time he's ever been asked about his association with Bill Ayers, the unrepentant terrorist from the Weather Underground . . . David Axelrod said that they have a 'friendly' relationship, and that they had done a number of speeches together and that they sat on a board together. Is that a question you might ask?" Stephanopoulos's response: "Well, I'm taking notes right now."

Later, under intense criticism for the shoddy stupidity of the debate generally, Stephanopoulos defended himself, predictably claiming to "have been researching this for a while," and protesting that the "questions we asked were tough and fair and appropriate and relevant."

Hillary Clinton knew better, but wicked ambition apparently released the forces of opportunism, and she selectively forgot her own New Left leanings—research, writing, and friendships she could have been proud to claim. But nothing about her past affinities raises the question "Is Hillary Clinton a communist?" any more than Obama's association with me suggests that he was a Weatherman. Still, it's a long if sad tradition: Bob is a bank robber; Bob is close to Jesse; Clint is friends with Jesse; ergo, Clint is a bank robber.

The fallout for me was immediate and intense. Dozens of requests for interviews rolled in, as did an avalanche of threats from reactionaries happy to dispatch me to my final judgment right away—"Someone should shoot you in the head, you leftist fuck"—and lots of hate mail and denunciations from liberals who worried that I would bring Obama down simply by living. The weirdest of the liberal hate started that very night, a trickle that would soon became a flood of blogs, e-mail blasts, and mailers from a couple of other guys around the neighborhood. One was a longtime Communist Party organizer who had been to our house on a number of occasions for meetings and fund-raisers, and the other a former high school principal I'd worked closely with in the Chicago school reform efforts two decades earlier. Both urged voters to ignore the smears against Obama because I was a "distraction" and someone they suddenly regarded as a public enemy, a "dreadful person" who "had committed detestable acts forty years ago" and who, they were increasingly certain, had "no real links to the Senator."

It took work even for me—and I was motivated and focused—to keep it straight. The *Bill Ayers* introduced that night on television was a one-dimensional cartoon, while the other Bill Ayers was a contradictory, messy, three-dimensional flesh-and-blood work-in-progress putting one foot in front of the other as best he could, exactly like every human being I've ever met. While *Bill Ayers* may have been marinating up there on a shelf, I'd actually lived in the storm surges and the sunlight every day of those last forty years. I'd loved and changed and worked and built a house, and loved some more—every day. I was wrinkled, to be sure, and perhaps a little vinegary—I was then in my mid-sixties—but I was also living large and leaning forward, hopefully right up to the end. For a moment, I questioned why they'd selected *Bill Ayers* and wondered why they hadn't crafted a terrific-looking Weather avatar from his smarter, more radical, better-known, and more notorious partner of almost forty years, *Bernardine Dohrn.* I'd have chosen her. Well, that's not really fair—she was much too good for this.

I thought for a moment about pitiable Gregor Samsa, who awoke one morning after disturbing dreams to find himself transformed in his bed into an enormous cockroach. The metamorphosis was, of course, incomplete because Gregor was still Gregor inside himself—same mind, same memories, same consciousness—and he remained painfully aware of the revulsion he induced in everyone around him, including his beloved family. Poor Gregor. And I thought about the professor in Don DeLillo's *White Noise*, who experienced the shock of a major toxic event engulfing his small town, the panic spreading as a poisonous chemical cloud drifted overhead and people were forced to evacuate, and the weird dislocation he experienced when he was proclaimed officially, statistically dead in spite of being very much alive. What could he say to explain himself? Who would listen to him now? How could he adequately grasp his situation, split at the core of his being and stumbling through a familiar landscape unexpectedly made strange? I knew that I didn't want to be that professor; I knew that I didn't want to become some character from Kafka flailing around as I tried to set the record straight for a hundred years.

There was a lot of unexpected love from the start, too. The sweetest and quirkiest came from a colleague at the University of Illinois at Chicago who was a Democratic Party activist.

For several months, Espie Reyes had stopped by my office—right next door to hers—with the current gossip or insights or hopes or fears from the Democrats, and always with the latest combat from within her own family. She and her daughter were die-hard for Hillary, her husband and son-in-law equally strong for Barack. She suspected a deep sexist attitude in her husband, mysteriously undetected somehow in decades of marriage. I always listened a bit bemused: I'm glad I'm not a Democrat, I would invariably say. I can watch and not worry. She would smile impatiently. "It's Hillary's turn, Bill, and you know it. . . . Obama's so young, and he can come next," she'd say, or, "For women of a certain age this is a dream come true," or, "She can beat whoever the Republicans put up, but Obama's a kid and he'll get crushed."

One day she reported that the tension at home over the primary had finally reached a fever pitch and boiled over, and that John was now sleeping on the couch. I sympathized: Now I'm really glad I'm not a Democrat, I said.

I flew to California the morning after the Stephanopoulos moment to do some work with my brother Rick. When I finally got settled and could open my e-mail, I found four messages from Espie that she'd sent over a span of eighteen hours. The first was a magical note of friendship and love and sympathy for what she imagined I must be going through. The second, sent many hours later, was a copy of a long letter she'd drafted to Hillary Clinton detailing how much money she'd donated and how many weekends she'd devoted to organizing on her behalf, explaining who I really was in her "humble opinion," and encouraging, then demanding, that the campaign apologize to me personally and denounce the smears—or else she would have to rethink her commitments. The third letter was another copy, this one of a message fired off in haste and anger to the Democratic National Committee and its chairman, Howard Dean, in which she proposed a détente and insisted that Dean resolve the escalating warfare for the good of the party—oh, and apologize to me, of course. She attached a copy of my CV so that Howard Dean could see what a great guy I was—in her "humble opinion."

The fourth and final e-mail was sent after she'd had "a good night's sleep" and was just this, in full: "I let John come off the couch and back to bed. Hope you're OK."

Ah, love: I was at that moment happily beyond OK. All the attacks that had come, all the nonsense hovering just beyond the horizon, seemed for that moment a small price to pay for the ecstasy of reunion and the many blissful years ahead beckoning to Espie and John.

But when I returned to Chicago, I found that things had changed for the worse. The university had received hundreds of messages, mostly criticisms for having a public enemy in its midst, and heated threats to rectify the situation with vigilante justice as soon as possible. This was not the first time my notoriety had surfaced and stirred some creepy reactions, but it was more forceful and frenzied than ever before. My university assigned a campus police officer to stay close whenever I taught or had office hours. Officer Muhammad (true—his parents had been Black Nationalists and close to the Panthers back in the day) was a good guy with a happy heart and an open mind, and while he always wanted to walk with me on campus, he was never a heavy or a menacing presence.

The threats poured in, and I would dutifully turn them over to Muhammad. Eventually, he had a pretty fat file in his desk drawer. Once when he came by I'd gathered two gruesome notes that had just arrived into a folder. The first was signed by "The Waco Justice League," who said they would be in Chicago soon—they planned to grab me, take me to an undisclosed location ("already in operation"), and water-board me, the infamous torture technique employed by US forces at Guantanamo Bay and military bases abroad that painfully simulated the experience of drowning for its victims. The second, from the "Avenger," announced that I was already in his sights (my home address was listed as authentication) and that soon I would be "blasted front and back— dead before you hit the ground you piece of shit." Muhammad read them slowly, shook his head thoughtfully, and as he tucked them away put a friendly hand on my shoulder. He joked, "I hope the Avenger gets here first, Bill—you don't want to be water-boarded by the Waco

Justice League in that undisclosed location, only to come home and get shot. Better to get shot first." I, of course, agreed.

Muhammad sometimes followed me home in the evenings, and the police kept a car close by on the street. One morning I came out quite early, and a cop I didn't know was under my car with a flashlight. Years earlier, he might have been planting a surveillance device, or worse. But now he stood up, smiled, and shook my hand. "Just checking," he said.

ONE

A New American Revolution

Smoke and fire blazed up from decades earlier, ancient embers that had never been fully extinguished. For my students this was mostly vague and ancient history, but my road to becoming a public enemy in 2008 had begun when I was just about their age.

As the American-made catastrophe in Viet Nam was reaching full ignition in the mid-sixties, I was arrested with thirty-seven other University of Michigan students and one fabulous professor—my first defiant act of civil disobedience—for a militant, nonviolent sit-in at the Ann Arbor draft board. We had seized the ordinary looking office with its tidy files and typical clerks and standard procedures, because to us it had become an odious accomplice to war, issuing its toxic warrants to kill and to die in plain manila envelopes, bit by bit and day by day. When the police ordered us to disperse, we refused and locked arms, and the cops hauled us roughly down the stairs and into the police wagons one by one.

I'd returned to school from the Merchant Marines months earlier and had attended the first-ever teach-in against the war. I'd heard Paul Potter, then president of Students for a Democratic Society, end a talk on the necessity of agitation and dissent by issuing a challenge that echoes in my head to this day: "Don't let your life make a mockery of your values." I was twenty years old, and I signed up on the spot.

My brother Rick was a freshman, and we met up in the student union every day between classes to discuss life and love and politics with kids from all over the country and the planet—a rolling seminar fueled by coffee and cigarettes with a unity based mostly on frank questions and open argument, uninhibited analysis, solidarity, and rebellion. Most nights Rick would stop by my ramshackle rented garret to do homework, read, and talk some more. Leading up to the draft board sit-in, we focused urgently on whether we should participate, and we turned the idea over and over. It felt somehow necessary, but also in some sense way beyond our capacity. Was either of us really prepared for such a thing? And how did you prepare anyway? Was it too risky? The questions hung in the air until the morning of the action itself, when we met for an early coffee—I had decided to plunge in, and Rick got the tougher assignment: call our uncomprehending parents, defend and explain my arrest, and get me out of jail as soon as possible.

Rick and I had grown up in a place of privilege and prosperity, of instant gratification and seemingly endless superficial pleasures, of conformity and obedience and a kind of willful ignorance about anything that might exist beyond our neatly trimmed hedges. We were all anesthetized to one degree or another, all insistently sleeping the deep, deep American sleep of denial, but Rick, though a year and a half younger, was on to things early, and he had introduced me to the Beat poets and *Mad* magazine, for starters. My next steps were improbable, perhaps, but true.

Like Karl Marx and Friedrich Engels, Rick and I felt that we were defending not our short-term present privileges but our long-term future interests—a world free of the degradation of social classes. Like them, we were from bourgeois backgrounds, and like them we wanted to risk our privilege, or at least deploy it in the fight for liberation and justice. Too lofty? Well, that's where the similarities end, but we took heart as we abandoned our entitled standpoints—race traitors to Dinesh D'Souza, class traitors to Mike Royko—to place ourselves alongside Third World liberation, Black Power militants, workers, women, indigenous folks, the marginalized, the despised, and queers of all kinds. We went in search of a radically egalitarian world.

The war further illuminated everything: my country stood on the wrong side of an exploding world revolution, the hopes and dreams of people everywhere—for peace and bread and worthwhile work to do, for a world free of nuclear threat, for independence and self-determination, for dignity and recognition and justice—contested in every corner of every continent. The Black civil rights movement was the clearest expression of the world revolution inside the United States, and my own government was the command center of the counter-revolution both at home and abroad.

"Which side are you on?" began a traditional freedom song. I belted it out as I joined the movement—I wanted to usher in an era of racial justice and world peace, to end a war and demolish Jim Crow, and soon enough, I wanted to end the system that I figured made war and racism so predictable and so agonizingly inevitable.

When I was arrested that first time, the war was broadly accepted and even popular. We'd happily raised the banner of refusal, noisily urging all within our reach to join in, and we had the active support of hundreds of other students. But we had opposition from many more: Americans overwhelmingly supported the US invasion at the outset, and even on campus we were massively outnumbered.

So we got busy and invented a thousand different ways to organize and educate. War resistance mustered mothers and students, lawyers, returning veterans and union workers, churchgoers, teachers and nurses, and whole communities. Sites of protest included draft boards and induction centers, coffeehouses set up outside of military bases, ROTC offices on campuses, institutes conducting secret war research, Dow Chemical headquarters, the Pentagon, and appearances by every politician associated with the administration. The iconic images of the time are true—I took to the streets, marched and picketed and demonstrated and clashed with the authorities, who mobilized to put us down—but they were only a part of the story and a fraction of the action. Being arrested, beaten up, and tossed into jail quickly became a commonplace for me and for a lot of other activists, and I felt I could do it all standing on my head.

But there was so much more to do: we drew up fact sheets, created teach-ins, made spontaneous pop-up theatre, circulated petitions, and embraced music, dance, murals, and agitprop. I was in Detroit for two years with "Vietnam Summer," a concerted effort to knock on every door in working-class neighborhoods across America and meet people face to face in order to engage in a dialogue about peace. In a single day, Rick and I were called traitors three times, spit on and threatened with physical violence once, and invited in for coffee or cookies four times. One young woman burst into tears and came outside to sit on the front steps with us: her cousin Kenny, who'd grown up with her, had been killed a month earlier near Hue, and the family was still trying to understand all the specifics of his death and come to terms with their immeasurable loss. She talked, cried, and told us stories about Kenny for almost an hour.

Those front-door encounters were the most difficult and exhilarating thing I'd ever done. The more I tried to teach others, the more I learned—about the real circumstances of people's lives, and mostly about myself. Step by step, I became more and more radical, conscious of the connections between foreign war and domestic racism to start, between capitalist economic hierarchies and the hollowing-out of democracy, between the sexual exploitation of women in war zones to service the military and violence against women at home. Eventually I thought of myself as a revolutionary, committed to overturning the whole system of empire, and that was a decidedly two-edged sword: as an organizer I was learning to listen as well as to shout, but as a newly committed activist I was fired up and brimming with urgency.

The peace movement geared up to end the American invasion and occupation of Viet Nam, but as more and more people joined the effort, it seemed possible that we might not only end that single, despicable war but that we could prevent other such adventures—the invasion of Santo Domingo, for example, which was happening right before our eyes. At a certain point, it seemed to me that African Americans and the working class and, indeed, the majority of the American people stood in direct and deep conflict with the US government—a contradiction that could only be resolved in a second American revolution, a massive popular upheaval. It was a grandiose dream, to be sure, and a wildly passionate vision. The war enraged me—its brutality and horror—but the resistance to it inspired me—the sacrifices and steady victories of the Vietnamese; the courage of the anticolonial forces in South Africa,

Angola, Mozambique, and Guinea-Bissau; the audacity of the guerrillas from Cuba and all over Latin America. Live like Che!

Was it naïve? Of course it was naïve; the Tupamaros in Uruguay were naïve as well, and Che, too.

Did I misinterpret the conditions and the possibilities? Indeed, but who can gauge what's really possible in the moment?

Utopia beckoned, and we heeded her call—it was a Time of the Impossible, and the horizons of my imagination were expanding like crazy. I thought the violence of the world could be dramatically diminished, even if it took a fiery outburst from below to begin, and I held tight to the romance that ordinary people through their own self-activity have the capacity to eliminate the agony of exploitation and the intolerable suffering of the poor and despised—to achieve justice in the public square and establish a beloved community. It seemed it was all there within our reach—the revolution demanded everything of me and it offered everything to me. Much later, I cracked up at Mike Tyson's sharp observation: "Everyone has a plan till they get punched in the face."

By 1968 people had turned massively against the war, and at the end of March, President Johnson abruptly stepped aside. I was both surprised and overjoyed. *The war is over!* A million deaths, true and terrible, but at last it would end. I didn't stay hopeful for long. Five days later the Reverend Martin Luther King Jr. was assassinated in Memphis, and two months further along Senator Robert Kennedy was murdered in Los Angeles. Soon enough, a new Nixon/Kissinger administration doubled down, expanding and extending the war indefinitely.

And so it did not end, and it was back to the front, back to work, and back to the streets, but now with a determination edged with despair. Every week that the war dragged on, six thousand people were murdered in Southeast Asia. *Every week—six thousand lives extinguished*—with no end in sight. Six thousand human beings—massive, unthinkable numbers—were thrown into the furnaces of war and death—napalm and carpet bombing, strategic hamlets and tiger cages, My Lai and mass murder. We had tried everything, and everything had proved to be inadequate; the war was lost, but the terror continued. Everything added to the crazy sense that we were falling into the abyss.

None of us knew precisely how to proceed, for we'd done what we'd set out to do—we'd persuaded the American people to oppose the war, built a massive movement and a majority peace sentiment— and still we couldn't find any surefire way to stop the killing. Millions mobilized for peace, and still the war slogged along into its murky and unacceptable future, trailing devastation and death in its wake. The political class had no answers to the wide expression of popular will, and the ensuing crisis of democracy became a profound turning point for the peace movement as well—the antiwar forces splintered.

Some activists (including one of my brothers) joined the Democratic Party in order to build a peace wing within it. Some fled to Europe or Africa, while others migrated "back to the land" and built rural communes and intentional utopian communities to escape the madness. Some created tiny but humane and hopeful organizing projects, from women's health clinics to alternative newspapers, from gay pride marches to environmental action, from street theatre to underground comics—all of which would, surprisingly, change the culture. A few went into the factories in the industrial heartland to radicalize the unions, create a workers' party, and build toward a general strike to transform the country. And I took a different path altogether.

Malcolm X had called for liberation by any means necessary, and the Black Freedom Movement rose up and was met with escalating repression and police violence. Black Panthers were exhorting people to "pick up the gun"; Lorraine Hansberry, beloved and stunning author of *A Raisin in the Sun*, and Nina Simone, the dazzling jazz diva, urged Black people to arm up. After the assassination of Martin Luther King Jr., the idea spread like wildfire. The editorial board of the *New Republic* was at that moment debating the value and the efficacy of armed struggle, while the high-minded *New York Review of Books* featured an oversized depiction of a Molotov cocktail on its cover. A small group of us from the radical student movement—lacking experience and skill but compensating, we hoped, with determination and will—actually did it: we created a clandestine political force outside the reach of the FBI and the national security forces that would (we believed, but couldn't be sure) survive the approaching (we were sure) American totalitarianism and that could fight the war-makers by other means. In a great river of excess our words were surely excessive, but we were determined to meet certified state violence with a fierce eruption of our own, and for a moment a few of us—myself included—flirted with matching their official and systematic terror blow for blow. But we never did it; we drew back and reconsidered just what we were in fact willing to do, what our own reverence for life and moral outlook required of us for real, as well as what would be effective in the long run. Dramatic sabotage and precisely targeted vandalism as agitprop, yes; propaganda of the deed, always; but violence against people, no. I wondered: *When is an act of sabotage also an act of love?*

My brother Rick's activist odyssey included nonstop organizing, demonstrations, arrests, and the disruption of his induction physical. When they came for him to press him into the military, he ran to Canada, and this time I had the difficult task of explaining it all to our parents. There, he set up a station on the modern underground railroad, a halfway house for deserters escaping the war. After a couple of years, he convinced himself that his efforts were inadequate, and he returned to the United States and joined the army—now as an organizer for the banned and harassed American Servicemen's Union. When he was busted, he deserted, and we spent a decade together on the run.

A front page headline in the *New York Times* on March 7, 1970, declared: "Townhouse Razed by Blast and Fire; Man's Body Found." The story described an elegant four-story brick building in Greenwich Village destroyed by three large explosions and a raging fire "probably caused by leaking gas."

The body was later identified as belonging to twenty-three-year-old Ted Gold, a leader of the 1968 student strike at Columbia University, a teacher, and a member of what the *Times* would call a "militant faction of Students for a Democratic Society." Over the next few days two more bodies were discovered: both Diana Oughton and Terry Robbins had been student leaders, civil rights and antiwar activists. By

March 15 the *Times* reported that police had found "57 sticks of dynamite, four homemade pipe bombs and about 30 blasting caps in the rubble" and referred to the townhouse for the first time as a "bomb factory." These three were our comrades, and Diana, my partner, lover, companion, and much more—all suddenly gone. Their deaths became our irreplaceable loss and our shared sorrow—my hands never entirely cleansed, the grieving never done. And this was where and when the Weather Underground was born.

But that awful event also announced the existence of something weirdly original and brand new: a group of young, largely white, homegrown, "mother-country" Americans taking up arms in opposition to the war. Bernardine and I and a wider circle of partisans and fellow travelers were indicted by the Justice Department on two single-count conspiracies—we had crossed state lines, they charged, in order to foment civil disturbances and destroy government property. Bernardine was prominently placed on the FBI's Ten Most Wanted list, an inventory of J. Edgar Hoover's evolving obsessions that was quickly changing right then from a rogues' gallery of plug-uglies and terrifying gangsters to a catalog of appealing revolutionaries: Angela Davis, H. Rap Brown, and Bernardine. We were frightened, confused, and uncertain, to be sure, making it up as we went along, but we were also resolute and had no intention of reporting in federal or state court— too many other radicals, we thought at the time, got caught in a government trap that deflected their best efforts and reduced their political work to barricaded defense committees and occasional fund-raisers for legal fees. And so we took off and we lived on for more than a decade— on borrowed time, surely, and on the run from the law.

It was a revelation to me that pain can fade and that living goes on, moving ever more rapidly away from the dead. Survival was mystifying, but I had survived, and I thought if I was to live at all, it would from now on be for those who did not.

A few days after the townhouse explosion, Ralph Featherstone and William "Che" Payne, two "black militants" associated with the Student Nonviolent Coordinating Committee, according to *Time* magazine, "were killed when their car was blasted to bits" by a bomb police said was being transported to Washington, DC, to protest the prosecution of SNCC leader H. Rap Brown. Violent resistance to violence was as "American as cherry pie," Rap said at the time.

Time noted that in 1969 there had been sixty-one bombings on college campuses, most targeting ROTC and other war-related targets, and ninety-three bomb explosions in New York, half of them classified as "political," a category that was "virtually non-existent ten years ago." Suddenly, according to the FBI, from the start of 1969 to mid-April 1970, there had been 40,934 bombings, attempted bombings, and bomb threats, leading to forty-three deaths and almost $22 million in damage. Out of this total, 975 had been explosive, as opposed to incendiary attacks, and within that chaos and whirlwind, the Weather Underground took credit for some twenty actions over five years, causing maybe $2 million in damage, less than it had cost the United States to conduct its nasty war machine for an hour. No one was killed or harmed in any of them.

Our notoriety, then and now, outstripped our activity on every count, and who knows why? Perhaps because we couldn't shut up and issued long involved political statements with every action, or perhaps because of our familiarity as public student leaders, our white skin privilege, and our fortunate backgrounds. Perhaps it was the surprising American romance with outlaws on the run, or simply the power of metaphor. Whatever the reason, we made it clear that we intended to blast out our full-throated message to the heavens: I intended to fight and fight and fight on until I dropped dead.

Some felt that the actions of the Weather Underground were not only illegal and off the rails, but indefensible at best and even "detestable," and that case was not impossible to make. It was easy enough—and perfectly safe—to condemn us noisily for what we did, but just a bit harder to prove the efficacy of any other road taken—and impossible to stack against doing nothing. A prominent *Nation* columnist quantified her critique this way: "The Weather Underground didn't shorten the war by five minutes." That may well be true, but when I ran into her later and asked by how many minutes she figured the *Nation* had shortened the war, she said I was being ridiculous. I guess I was. Another old radical told me that if every person for peace had joined the Democratic Party at the same moment in 1968, we might have elected the principled George McGovern and ended the war. "Perhaps," I replied, "but if everyone had joined the Weather Underground in 1969, we might have made a revolution." "You're being ridiculous," he said, and we both laughed.

TWO

Up and Running

Eleven years after we'd plunged underground, Bernardine and I traveled to Chicago to surface—to turn ourselves in to the legal authorities who'd been pursuing us throughout those fervent renegade days. It would mark the loss of a special treasure for us—the good fortune of knowing precisely where we stood and finding a kind of paradoxical, fleeting fugitive freedom in a place of constraint and quarantine—our decade of living dangerously.

We'd thought she would return in relative obscurity—the war was long over and the Weather Underground quiet—but we learned later that someone in the state's attorney's office had told a friend that Bernardine had sent out feelers, and from friend to friend to contact to reporter, the story spread and grew. When we arrived at the Cook County Criminal Courthouse on Twenty-sixth Street and California, we were met by the rolling maul of a media scrum, something we'd never experienced before, and the pushing and rucking around caught us off-balance at first. Bernardine had resisted this moment mightily— "I'm not going to give up, and I don't want them to feel they've won even the smallest symbolic victory"—but now she held her head high, smiled slightly, and walked quietly and purposefully into criminal court.

We'd driven from New York to Chicago a few days earlier with Zayd, three years old, and Malik, not quite a year. We kissed and hugged them, and dropped them off that morning at our last "safe house," with friends who could be trusted—"You guys have fun . . . we're going to change our names," we told them. We met up with our legal team,

Michael and Eleanora Kennedy, and jumped into a cab headed down
to the gritty Cook County Criminal Court building, a place we once
knew well.

Eleanora, elegant and refined, was not an actual lawyer—she had
never gone to law school or formally studied the law, passed the bar,
or earned a license—but she possessed more raw courage than anyone
in any courtroom she ever graced with her presence and her laser-like
insights. Her fierce loyalty to Michael's clients—Los Siete de la Raza,
the Brotherhood of Eternal Love, the Black Panthers, the Irish Republican Army—was the stuff of legend and fiction. She could raise money,
write a press release, create an outfit, post bail, straighten a tie, clean
a wound, remove a splinter, do reconnaissance, find a weapon, light a
candle, say the Rosary, infiltrate the enemy, gather intelligence, run
interference, coordinate colors, move a family into her home, or plan a
great escape—all without mussing her make-up. "You can't wear that,"
she said critically, eyeing my bottom-shelf sport coat and khakis in their
hotel room the night before the big move, and she pulled out one of
Michael's suits and held it up in front of me for a serious appraisal.
Michael shrugged his shoulders and smiled knowingly—she dressed
him as well. "Wear this," she commanded. She was larger than life,
revered and feared, and in combination with Michael, her ferocious
pit-bull partner—who was possessed of the finest legal mind God ever
bestowed upon an Irish anarchist——she was an unparalleled advocate.
We were so happy they were on our side.

Michael had tried for weeks to negotiate a deal with the brand new
state's attorney, Richard M. Daley, son of the Old Man, but Daley had
refused, and so we were flying into the jaws of the beast a bit blind. I
worried even though we knew that the heaviest charges against us—the
federal conspiracies—had all been dropped because of gross govern-
mental misconduct and illegality linked to the FBI's COINTELPRO
violations, the fed's murderous counterintelligence program. I had
no legal charges outstanding whatsoever; Bernardine, though never
captured, had been quietly removed from the Ten Most Wanted list,
and while still notorious, her legal entanglements as far as we knew
amounted to eight aggravated batteries, a few mob actions, resisting
arrests from street demonstrations, and bail jumping. It was enough to

make me sweat, but Michael and Eleanora assured us that she would be back on the street by the end of the day.

Bernardine was taken into custody to be processed, and I waited outside the courtroom. One reporter came over to ask me if I thought this moment was "the end of the sixties at last." She sounded hopeful. I thought about how the so-called sixties had become completely commodified by then and sold back to us as myth and symbol. When had the so-called sixties actually begun? I wondered. *Brown v. Board of Education* in 1954? Montgomery in 1956? And had it ended in 1968, as *Newsweek* predicted at the time, or, as this eager intrepid reporter wanted to know, in 1980? In any case, I didn't remember anyone saying on December 31, 1969, "Oh, shit, it's almost over! I'd better get high." And I didn't know a soul who lived by decades—all of that was merely marketing. The sixties were neither as brilliant nor ecstatic as some wanted to imagine, nor the devil's own workshop, as others insisted, and whatever they were, they remained mostly prelude. We were still here, still living, up and running now. Scott Simon, a young reporter from local public radio, passed me a note on which he had simply written, "Welcome back." Later he told us that the media frenzy that morning matched the earlier coverage of public enemy and serial killer John Wayne Gacy—a dubious distinction to be sure.

I worried about Bernardine being shuffled around somewhere in the entrails of criminal justice, where I imagined two-way mirrors and good cop-bad cop routines in dingy interrogation rooms with the ghosts of torture victims wailing from the walls. I tried to picture what was really going on with her. I knew that if anyone could handle herself in bizarre and coercive conditions it was she, but I found it difficult to be separated at this precise moment when she was suddenly in the rough hands of the state she'd opposed so thoroughly. When Eleanora emerged to tell me that it was as routine and bureaucratic as it could possibly be, and that everyone was on best behavior, a couple of heavies watching from afar but several court workers excited to meet her and even asking for autographs, my troubled mind relaxed, and I breathed deeply.

Another young reporter said to me that this must have been a kind of Rip Van Winkle moment for us.

"No, actually it's not," I said. "After all, we'd never left the country, and we'd always lived inside the vortex of the everyday. We weren't some lost Japanese soldiers from World War II," I said, stumbling suddenly from a dense Pacific island jungle into the modern world.

He duly reported in the paper the next day that I had compared our situation to "some lost Japanese soldiers from World War II stumbling suddenly from a dense Pacific island jungle into the modern world."

Incredible, I thought, even as I sympathized: why let unruly facts get in the way of a sweet narrative?

Bernardine made a brief statement in court noting that her views concerning the nature of the system were unchanged, that she was in no way turning away from her revolutionary dreams, and that she intended to continue the struggle by other means. The judge smiled beneficently down from the bench and answered that while he disagreed with her analysis and her goals, he was nonetheless glad to see her back, and that he hoped she would now pursue her objectives through peaceful and legal channels. Like politicians of all stripes, the media from left to right, and the country as a whole at that time, the judge seemed relieved to forget that there ever was a place called Viet Nam with its attendant horrors and humiliations, and move on—the classic American selective amnesia: "Let's just remember the good things."

He smiled again, peering over his glasses, as he rejected the state's attorney's demand for a million-dollar bail, noting that he knew these Weathermen well. Bernardine was not about to plunge underground immediately after going to all the trouble of surfacing: "When they're gone, they're gone, and when they're back, they're back." Bernardine gave a press conference a few minutes later in a packed room. "This is no surrender," she said. "The fight against racism and war continues, and I will spend my energy organizing to defeat the American empire." Then she stopped in a neighboring courtroom to express solidarity with a group of prisoners known as the Pontiac Brothers facing death for leading a prison rebellion, before we were whisked down a rear elevator and spirited out of the building,

A few minutes later, we met up with our happy kids and a merry band of family and friends. My brother Juan, like our father before him, was a Chicago booster and chauvinist—he often ridiculed the Left

Coast and the Right Coast as he offered marvelous, personalized tours of the City of the Big Shoulders. Juan knew every back alley and hidden side street, and he haunted them all. Michael Kennedy had told Juan that he wanted to treat us all to lunch at "the best restaurant in Chicago," and Juan led a dozen of us to Nueva Leon on Eighteenth Street, a family restaurant in Pilsen, where we feasted on nachos dias, tostadas, tortillas con queso with three degrees of salsa, the best spicy guacamole any of us had ever tasted, and lots of celebratory toasts with Dos Equis and Mexican hot chocolate. When the check arrived, Michael was bewildered: "This is so small," he complained. "I'm a New Yorker, and I'm a lot more comfortable when I'm being ripped off."

My parents joined us at Juan and Judi's Logan Square apartment that evening, and there were tears of joy and sweet relief all around. When the doorbell rang, Bernardine and I tensed slightly out of habit until Juan returned with a gift for Bernardine from three University of Chicago law students: a maroon T-shirt with her alumni logo and the words "Bastion of Medieval Scholasticism."

A lot had changed in a decade, of course—Mom and Dad were overjoyed to meet Bernardine, whom they loved on sight, and ecstatic to know their two grandsons—but when Dad said to me over dinner, "Bill, you need a haircut," I realized that some things remained remarkably intact. I was thirty-five years old, the father of two young children, and had just surfaced from a decade on the run from the law for notorious—"detestable"—actions, and yet my dad mentioned none of it: "You need a haircut." I found that oddly heartening.

We four drove back to New York, to our tiny fifth-floor walk-up on 123rd Street and the cramped bedroom where we'd seen the face of God a second time when Malik was born ten months earlier, and to our welcoming neighbors and sweet friends. We returned to BJ's Kids, the dazzling child-care center where I worked and which our kids attended, to the playgrounds of Central Park, to Hunan Balcony and Zabar's, and to the work that had sustained us for the last few years.

Winnie, our apartment building super, had her all-seeing eye on the block from her window day and night, and when she spotted us pulling up she ran to the street to welcome us home wearing the same gray housedress, floral bathrobe, and bedroom slippers she wore all day, every day. She was short and as perfectly round as a bagel, buzzing with energy and ever loyal to friends and "good tenants": she had a pear and a colorful pinwheel in one hand for Zayd, a quick tickle and a coochie-coo for Malik. "I read all about you," she said. "You coulda knocked me over with a feather." But all of that was behind us now, and anyway, we were good tenants—"I made you a pineapple upside-down cake, and if you can come by the office at six, I'll get Jimmie and Hector and Ilene and Marta and we can have a little celebration." She had clipped the story from the *Times* and had our front-page photo proudly posted on the door to her little office.

All of our friends learned our names now, awkwardly at first. We set aside our *noms de guerre* in favor of Bernardine and Bill, and those names sounded jarring for a time, even to us. Of course, everyone now remembered or discovered that *Time* magazine and the New York *Times* had called us American terrorists in 1970, and that the word had been hurled in our direction from the halls of Congress as well. It was a definite disconnect for many, but for some it was too close for comfort. Two parents at BJ's Kids called a meeting—we were not invited—to discuss whether our presence created any vulnerability for the child-care center or for the kids. By all accounts it was a raucous meeting, some folks feeling personally betrayed by our deceit, some that we had, intentionally or not, put them at risk, others arguing the opposite: we'd been right to conceal our identities, for it allowed them all to be free from any kind of culpability or conspiracy. Bernardine and I felt bad for everybody, and especially for BJ, but when she called us late that night she was thrilled. "People needed to get it all out on the table," she said, "but I'm so proud of everyone for working it through, and I learned so much about how people think about politics and personal responsibility. And you two are really loved in this community." One family elected to leave, which was sad to me, but even that mom took me aside a few days later to tell me it wasn't personal but she was a frightened person much of the time, and this was just too big for her.

We picked up where we'd left off. I went back to graduate school and to teaching at BJ's, Bernardine proceeded to study for and pass the

New York State bar exam, each of us focused fiercely on raising our precious boys, and we both returned to open—"aboveground"—political work. The notoriety surrounding our return to the open world was short-lived, and the drama faded into the haze of memory as well.

The tempo of our lives echoed the rhythms of our two engaging boyos: early dinners and nightly baths, bedtimes with favorite stories, brown-bag lunches and healthy snacks for school, dance classes at the Harlem Dance Studio or art classes at the Y on Saturdays, trips to the zoo and the beach and the museums. From the outside, our earlier lives as student radicals, full-time activists, and then self-proclaimed revolutionaries and fugitives on the run from the law would seem a sharp contrast to this, but oddly it wasn't at all. In part this was because our daily lives—everyone's lives, after all, underground or aboveground, on the run or in the mix—were largely taken up with everyday matters: working, putting food on the table, paying the bills, cooking and cleaning, seeing friends, helping neighbors. Can you imagine a decade on the run without doing the laundry? The ordinariness of it was one of its most remarkable features. And in part it was because the extraordinary excitement of raising kids for anyone paying attention is more packed with purpose than anyone outside of it can possibly imagine—a life in miniature in one sense, but our days as vast and full and dense with drama, discipline, and commitment as they had ever been.

Bernardine and I were paying laser-like attention, and for the first few years the steady surprises—noticing one day that Zayd was studying our faces and looking from one to another as we talked, apparently taking in language long before he could speak; the first time Malik toddled over to a crying child and gently patted his back—occurred under the cloud of our vulnerability. We set up contingencies for their care if we were suddenly arrested, and we had a mantra that we repeated again and again to one another: whatever might happen now, he had a perfect birth . . . or a great day . . . or a wonderful first month . . . or year. We counted methodically backward and forward: whatever else happens, it's been great till now.

Leaving swim class one day, we were swept up into a raucous women-led march heading from Broadway and Fifty-ninth Street toward Times Square. "No more porn! No more porn! No more porn!" we chanted ecstatically, fists pumping and voices rising as we entered the pornography district. It was a feisty and colorful crowd, our attendance just a happy accident, but with Zayd cheerfully perched on my shoulders we were in high spirits and quite pleased to be in cahoots. Soon we spotted a pizza stand along the route, and Zayd was famished from swimming and ready for a slice, so we settled into a booth. Zayd reflected on the parade we'd just left: "That was fun," he said. "Why don't we want more corn?"

Our children were the hub and heart of everything, and the little daycare center became the nucleus of the everyday. Finding that magical place—three years before turning ourselves into the authorities—was one of those miraculous moments when choice and chance suddenly rhyme. Malik had not been born and Zayd was a year old when we first toddled into that enchanted spot. We were using a not-so-clever or imaginative underground moniker for him, simply the letter Z. I was called Tony Lee because Lee seemed to be the most common surname in the Manhattan phone directory, and Bernardine was Lou. Tony Lee, Lou Lee, and Z Lee—it had the rhythmic sound of three high school friends gathered in a garage with wildly inflated dreams of rock-and-roll glory.

We'd been in New York for just a few months then, living in a single shabby room in a Skid Row hotel near Times Square. The roaches were an unending scuffle with a temporary victory declared by us whenever the battlefield moved from our bed to the tiny sink under a bare light bulb in the far corner. The shared bathroom down the hall was a challenge, too, especially with a toddler to keep sparkling and clean, but the folks on our floor—old men with hard times etched into every crease of their leathery faces—were kind and accommodating, being sure to clear a shining path to the old tin tub or the toilet whenever necessary. "Love the kid," they'd say warmly, wrinkling into a smile or peek-a-booing to get a guaranteed happy response from Z.

Lou/Bernardine had worked a temp service job into a regular secretarial position at an office nearby, which allowed us to meet up at a diner for lunch—and a chance to nurse—every day. We settled into a suitable routine, heading out of the hotel and onto the street by 7:30 each morning, a quick coffee and bagels at the corner dive, and then Lou off to work, Z and I to the train and one of the several spots we'd found to be perfect winter playgrounds for him: the Metropolitan Museum of Art with its knights and armor room, Macy's toy section with the plush carpets and giant stuffed animals, the Guggenheim with its massive circular ramp rising into the sky, Shakespeare and Company with children's books galore. By ten we were back at the diner in Times Square, ready for replenishment and renewal.

I always rode the subway in those days accompanied by a shadowy memory from a nightmare that had startled me awake when we first arrived in the city. In that dreadful dream I entered the train with Z in my arms, swung him easily into a seat by the door, and suddenly realized that my backpack was on the platform, just out of reach. As I jumped off for less than a second to retrieve it, the doors slammed shut, and the train sped away. I woke up screaming.

When I began to look for work in earnest, we auditioned a couple of different babysitters we'd found through word of mouth, but neither was quite right, and nothing worked out beyond a morning or two. Perhaps we were overly critical or hypersensitive, perhaps handing over our precious one to someone else for the first time was too alarming, and being without him for more than an hour at a time a bit unbearable, or perhaps these two caregivers really were inadequate in some way. Perhaps we would let him out of our sight when he was twenty-one years old, we joked. Who knew? But because we were unsettled and unsure, and because we trusted our own instincts, we decided to keep on looking, unhurried and deliberate.

One Monday morning after a quick trip to the Natural History Museum and a visit with the giant whale suspended from the ceiling on the lower level, Z and I made our way up to Eighty-fourth Street near Riverside Drive—only a few blocks away but an authentic expedition for a toddler practicing the fine art and exciting skill of walking with his willing papa wobbling along behind, and with the New York City sidewalks filled with giant bags of garbage and fascinating objects fit

for close examination and deep exploration at every step. We were off
to visit with a woman who was just beginning a child-care center in the
basement of a brownstone.

A mom we'd met in a playground had referred us to "BJ's Kids."
"BJ is amazing," she'd told us, "and it's affordable, committed care."
Nice: affordable *and* committed. While we couldn't be sure what those
two words meant exactly, we figured they had to signify something specific; she could have chosen other pairs—"cheap, faithful" or "sparkling clean" or "tough love." To us, "affordable" struck an immediate
and essential chord, and "committed" meant so much more—it was a
stretch, for sure, but we imagined that somehow she might be part of
our extended and far-flung tribe, our very own beloved community.
And we weren't wrong.

When I'd talked to her on the phone she was super-friendly and
wide open, and she urged us to drop by anytime. I liked that—she
didn't need to clean up her act or prep for a performance. "Just come
down the front stairs," she'd said. "We're in the garden apartment."
Whatever we were about to see was just what we'd get.

Z and I jumped down the steps one by one to the garden apartment entrance—New York real estate folks had rechristened basement
spaces "garden apartments" years before, probably figuring that *base-
ments* are cousins to cellars and crypts and caves, while "gardens" are
a bit of Eden, all green and sunny with vegetables and flowers—and
rang the bell. We were buzzed into a small, delicious-smelling kitchen
and made our way to the big room beyond, which to my delight was
way more cabbage patch than crypt, a child's garden of color and light,
streaming with early childhood energy.

BJ looked comfortable on a sprawling green beanbag chair, swad-
dled in a tangle of toddlers. She smiled and waved to us and kept on
reading a big book about a mouse and a whale, best friends for life. Z
hurried off and began stacking blocks while I settled into a tiny chair
to watch the action.

She was about my age, maybe early thirties, her jet-black hair cut
into a pageboy that framed her perfectly round and pale face. She was
dressed for action—high-tops, rough-stitched fatigue pants, oversized

corduroy shirt sporting two big pockets—with no fear of tearing, wrinkling, staining, or mussing. She resembled a grown-up Buster Brown, the pretty cross-dressing comic book hero from the turn of the century whose charming demeanor hid a mischievous heart and a critical consciousness. Buster Brown's constant companion was his dog, Tige; BJ's roommate was a giant cuddly English sheepdog called Daisy. Like Buster, BJ was a living lovable contradiction.

The space was a perfect reflection of her personality—an enchanting jumble. There were books and book shelves everywhere, easels and paint supplies in one corner, wooden blocks in another, a large round table with eight little blue chairs in the middle, and a row of colorful cubby holes against one wall in the kitchen, each with a name, a few family photos, a change of clothes, and a favorite stuffy or snack or blanket. All the kids were part-time, so while there were only six kids in the space now, there were at least a dozen cubbies.

The toddlers were busy, busy, busy—someone scribbling wildly with big colorful chalk on the linoleum floor, someone else pushing cars up a ramp, others listening to the story—their natural narcissism on full display, and BJ, unruffled and at ease, finished the book, gently swooshed the kids from her lap to the table, and greeted me again on her way to get the apples and bananas she arranged at the table. The place hummed with the good anarchistic energy of toddlers at work, and BJ's Kids had the feel of a sweet if slightly screwball family with a surplus of very young children getting into everything in every corner. When we visited again with Lou/Bernardine later in the week, we all felt right at home and vowed never to leave.

BJ had no formal training, no college degrees, but she was an inspired early childhood educator right from the start with a burgeoning library about teaching toddlers, and anyone who watched her for a minute recognized something special. Perhaps it was her ability to communicate so easily with tiny people without a hint of patronization or manipulation, or perhaps it was the obvious delight she exuded, or her laser-like perceptions of what it felt like to be Lynnette or Little Jack or Z in full fury or crushing sadness or bursting bliss. She was one of a kind, and everyone knew it.

BJ's Kids was seat-of-the-pants as an organized enterprise, but Z felt safe and solid and fully recognized there, lighting up whenever we made the turn onto Eighty-fourth Street, and it quickly became his, and our, second home. Play-dates and picnics and outings followed, and little by little an entire community swung into view. I was parked there already when BJ hired me as an assistant.

Besides the hard work of taking good care of the swelling gaggle of kids, BJ was trying to manage her embryonic small business, juggling a blizzard of part-time schedules and the cash that flowed in and out daily. Tuition was based on an evolving, dynamic, and idiosyncratic hourly rate—unwritten, uneven, and unclear—that seemed to spring spontaneously and fully-formed from the head of BJ. My first payday was a marvel: BJ pulled her large shoulder bag from the top of the fridge as I was getting ready to leave and rummaged through the bills, emerging with a handful of crumpled up twenties that she handed over to me. "See if that's right," she said. I couldn't remember what we'd agreed on, but it felt OK, so I said sure.

BJ's Kids had a row of easels against one wall, a cozy reading corner with lots of books and pillows, a dress-up area stocked with hats and flowing scarves, colorful clothes and costumes, brief cases, handbags, cow-poke boots, capes, hats of all kinds, and milk cartons filled with specific items to create a make-believe hospital, pizza restaurant, shoe store, bakery, fire house, and more. It was home-like, hidden and impenetrable—a place to explore and experiment. And beyond this, there was clay, water, sand, and art materials set up and available in a corner near the sinks, a large collage table on wheels with a series of bins containing bits of cloth, shells, buttons, bottle caps, and corks. For Zayd, BJ's Kids was an infinite treasure-trove of discovery and surprise, and it was also the honey pot, a place to feast and fatten. The joy began each morning in the biggest collection of wooden unit blocks ever assembled—Build! Build! Build!—where Zayd moved in a matter of months from horizontal runways to vertical towers to bridges to archways to entire fantastical worlds complete with characters and action.

We earned some early childhood notoriety through what seemed to us a harmless enough innovation: we had a large juice and snack table near the sink that we kept stocked and available from the moment children arrived in the morning until the last one left in the afternoon. The table had little cups surrounding pitchers of juice that kids could pour for themselves whenever they liked—with all the attendant spills and stickiness—and paper plates and napkins for the taking, as well as larger plastic serving dishes with sliced apples, celery and carrot sticks, oranges and bananas, cheese and crackers constantly replenished by staff throughout the day. "Disgusting," said the director of a sister preschool. "You will have roaches and mice everywhere!" "This is bad practice," advised another. "The kids will eat all day and never learn the importance of meal time." None of this had occurred to us, and none of it made immediate sense, but we were a bit off-balance and unsure at the start. When a neighbor and friend—a therapist and a feminist whose practice focused on eating disorders—encouraged us to persevere, arguing that the main thing everyone needed to learn in relation to food was self-regulation, and that the operating question should always be, "Are you hungry?" the snack-on-demand table became a quirky signature we embraced.

This fit with a larger idea that guided BJ's Kids from top to bottom, beginning to end: kids need to be free to develop from the inside out, not the other way around.

We created a dazzling collection of good, solid children's literature by African American, Native American, Latino and Hispanic, Asian and European American authors; books that mirrored for children, culturally and personally; books that stretched them and opened them to different or unfamiliar cultures and situations as well.

My favorite books were the ones the kids made themselves, stories they dictated to an adult and then illustrated and bound. We had a vast collection about families, pets, monsters, baby sisters, grandparents, trips to the zoo or the museum, space travel and hospitals. One of my most beloved homemade jobs was an ABC book that BJ had developed by gathering the invented toddler-talk all around us into a compilation that arguably improved on the original words in several instances: N is for Nosey, a noun—those hardened bits of dirt and mucous one picks from the nose; B is for Blurries, a noun—sudden bursts of wind-driven blinding snow; R is for Repulsicans, a noun—it's the party of Ronald Reagan!

Over time BJ and I developed our own working early childhood education philosophy; we hatched as well a little set of grounded theories about kids, conclusions about how they grew and what they needed, coalescing in the middle of the muddle of our mish-mash classroom. We hadn't read or heard about any of this, and our observations were not confirmed for us by any research or authoritative sources whatsoever—but we thought putting a toddler in a walker was a form of abuse, asking a little kid to tell what a painting depicted a kind of censorship, and telling a child not to be angry a pathway to neurosis. As BJ would say, "If it's not true, I'll eat my shirt."

One mid-morning the front bell rang unexpectedly, and in swept Eva Wolfson from the New York City Department of Health—someone had ratted out BJ for running an unlicensed child-care center, and suddenly there was the distinct whiff of danger at the door. Eva was short and tough with BJ, reading her the riot act in her crisply accented voice, and the conclusion was both quick and apparently foregone: the place was substandard, second-rate, out of compliance, and would be "closed by order of the New York City Department of Health." The phrase evoked images of filthy kitchens and infestations of vermin—I wouldn't want to eat at any joint that had been "closed by order of the New York City Department of Health"—and the words themselves were tragically definitive and carried the chilling ring of irrevocability.

BJ's Kids was spontaneously, naturally homemade, and, of course, an uneasy fit with rules, straight lines, orderly regulations, or city codes. On that first visit Eva checked off the contradictions: improper files and inadequate record-keeping, sloppy documentation of attendance, unacceptable kitchen and bathroom sinks, no approved governors on the hot water faucets, insufficient square footage, inappropriate staffing, and no fully certified teacher. After she left and the kids went down for their naps, BJ cried for two hours, flattened momentarily. She didn't stay down for long.

By that evening BJ, who looked so mild and unassuming hours before, had organized a campaign to save the center that would have made

Patton proud. Parents were mobilized, politicians contacted, and an elaborate media strategy launched. Ken Auletta visited BJ's Kids a few days later and wrote a column for the *Daily News* entitled "Who's Afraid of the Big Bad Wolf," and both BJ and Eva were suddenly famous.

Thus began a complicated association. Eva was smart and capable and even, once she dropped that brusque bureaucratic pose, a good mentor for BJ; for her part, BJ was willing to learn and to search for the common ground between dream and reality. The swords were sheathed.

And within it all was an odd unintended consequence for me as well. I returned to school seeking certification as an early childhood teacher after fifteen years away from the classroom, to the Bank Street College of Education—a perfect fit, it turned out—where I would earn a master's degree.

I'd left college with a vengeance and vowed to never look back. School had felt increasingly irrelevant and superficial to me in 1964, and I was straining to escape, burning to dive head first into the real world to end a war and upend the system (this was a time before I'd discovered that all worlds can be real if you'll let them be, even the world of your imagination). Revolutionaries want to change the world, of course, and teachers, it turns out, want to change the world too—typically one child at a time. It wasn't as much of a reach as you might imagine: day to day, I had more adrenaline pumping through my veins as a teacher than at any other time in my life.

In any case, Bank Street quickly won me over and affirmed my basic instincts as a teacher: the learning child is an unruly spark of meaning-making energy on a journey of discovery and surprise, not a passive receptacle waiting for instructions; every kid is a whole human being with a mind and a heart, a body and a spirit, experiences and aspirations that must somehow be accounted for by an engaged teacher. But from this base my professors at Bank Street went deeper, showing me again and again that the work of teaching is infinitely complex and excruciatingly difficult—becoming a good-enough teacher (like becoming a good-enough parent) was a life project and not some easy fix or formula.

I learned to practice observing and recording, kid-watching, as a central activity—thick description and time-sampling, artifact analysis and tone-monitoring, and so on. I read Jean Piaget's stage theory and Lucy Sprague Mitchell's philosophy.

Doing some errands one Saturday morning, I said casually to five-year-old Zayd, "There's a guy named Piaget who says that kids like you think that people think with their mouths."

"What?" he said indignantly. "That's so stupid."

"Well, what do people think with?" I asked.

"People think with their brains, and people talk with their mouths," he said definitively.

I decided to interview Zayd for my class project, imitating the format that Piaget used with his own kids.

Piaget's insight was that young children are concrete operational thinkers, lacking the capacity for abstraction and inference, relying instead on the visible, the tangible, and the material. I was impressed that Zayd was as clear and confident as he was, and I figured as a modern kid his sophistication was way beyond what Piaget's kids had access to or knew.

"So," I said when we sat down a few days later, "you think with your brain?"

"Right," he said.

"And right now what are you thinking about?

"A TV," he replied.

"And where is the TV you're thinking about?"

"There's a tiny TV inside my brain," he explained.

Holy shit, I thought, concrete operational, as Piaget predicted. But onward: "Have you ever forgotten anything?"

"Sure, like when I forgot to tell Mom the joke from school."

"OK, where did that joke go?"

Without missing a beat Zayd said, "It went right out my mouth."

Wow! Piaget rocks!

From then on any assignment that came my way—child development, literacy, curriculum, teaching—drove me to my own little hands-on laboratory at home: snapshots of toddlers in motion, sketches of family life, representations of young children reaching deep within themselves and clamoring to learn and to grow.

For a class on art in the early childhood curriculum, I collected a portfolio of paintings and drawings by our guys, usually accompanied by dictated commentary transcribed by me. One morning I said to Malik, "Tell me about this painting"—a colorful set of big swirls and fat lines—and he replied, "That's me swimming with Zayd, and the river is cold." I wrote it down and added it to the file.

And for a course on teaching reading, I kept a diary of our kids' early language acquisition, writing about how Malik learned to read seemingly in one big gulp without much experimentation or trial and error. He grew up in a literate environment, to be sure, and he was read to all the time. But while Zayd had practiced and worked away at reading, Malik simply picked up a favorite book one day and read it through. Malik was the focus of a paper I wrote called "Perseverance and the Learning Child"—the picture of this little preschool guy self-pitching a whiffle ball hundreds of times in a row in an attempt to hit it onto the roof of the school with his plastic bat day after day is legendary—as well as a paper titled "Compassion in Young Children"—his finely tuned empathy and identification with others on display from the start.

I had to write a thesis to graduate from Bank Street, and that was hugely intimidating at first—too lofty and scholarly for me—but when my advisor suggested I write a series of brief portraits of teachers teaching, I was relieved and encouraged. I could do that, I thought, storytelling with my own people, a collective enterprise that would honor the work of preschool teachers. The first story I wrote was a portrait of BJ, and I loved it—close to the ground, engaged in practice, collaborative, and interactive. Perhaps you, dear reader—now that you know the phenomenal BJ a bit—can see why this was so much fun.

I was captivated. I liked college a lot this time, the pinheaded professors didn't get on my nerves so much, and my big passion became my modest teacher-portrait project. I joined a committee of students working to create a doctoral program at Bank Street so that we could stay on for a few years and keep going. When that effort fell short, a group of us reluctantly applied to Teachers College, Columbia University, and soon enough we started classes right down the street. TC proved to be no less seductive for me, and I jumped in with both feet with my preschool teacher-portraits deepening and strengthening as I trudged forward. TC was much more eclectic than the consistent and sometimes insistent philosophy that undergirded every course at Bank Street—the Bank Street "developmental interactive approach to teaching." Whew! A common joke among us was that TC *had* a chapel, where John Dewey once held forth from the pulpit, but that Bank Street *was* a chapel, with its comforting if limited dogma and Dewey as the resident saint. I loved them both.

I learned about qualitative research at TC, and I studied ethnography, alternative forms of representation, and collaborative, dialogic, and critical approaches, as well as oral history and all manner of scholarly traditions that used description, narrative, and interpretation to advance systematic inquiry. I loved foregrounding storytelling and story-listening as worthwhile endeavors—narrative suited messy me, but it also accommodated the noisy, idiosyncratic, complex, multilayered, dynamic reality of children themselves, as well as of schools and classrooms. It fit itself neatly to that reality rather than the other way round, hammering the natural disarray everywhere into a convenient if choked-off and clotted frame called research. All the while I was incubating and nourishing my portraits of preschool teachers, keeping them warm and well-fed and happy in the bulging backpack I carried with me everywhere—a teeming tropical rain forest of notes, sketches, and ideas.

I first got clued-up to the discipline of the desk by the Chicago author David Mamet, of all people, when I read an interview in which he said that he felt that he was only a writer when he completed the last line of whatever piece he was working on; every day before that he approached the desk knowing he was a failed writer. When he finally wrote that highly anticipated last line, well, then he was immediately cast out—he was now an ex-writer. You couldn't win—failed, former, ex—and yet I aspired to write, reaching toward something mysterious and elusive, and arranging words on the page became my discipline and my assignment every day.

My writing desk was the solitary table in our tiny fifth-floor walk-up—it only served that purpose when the dishes were cleared, the food put away, and the kids asleep—and my writing time was 4:00 a.m., when the phone was quiet and the hustle-bustle was on a temporary time-out. I'd pull out my backpack and the two canvas totes stored in a corner, spread out my notes, stack up my yellow writing pads, and go to work. I wrote long-hand, the feel of the words at my fingertips, with lots of crossing-out, re-writing, and arrows connecting new sentences and whole paragraphs with older bits, rearranging to make a point or to hear the words harmonizing a bit more clearly. It was cramped quarters to be sure, more than modest, but perfectly magical for three whole hours every morning.

Bernardine owned a first-generation Remington Electric Typewriter and yet—this is embarrassing—I couldn't type a word. She set down every line of my dissertation, and corrections were a huge pain. "This is some sexist shit!" she proclaimed early on, smiling patiently. "This joint isn't *Father Knows Best*, you know." She was altogether too generous, but she let me know that I was a jerk in need of some serious rectification.

BJ encouraged overalls for all from the start, work clothes over dresses, sweatshirts not dress shirts. "We're here to get dirty," she told parents, "to run and tumble and climb, to explore and get into as many things as we can." Her own outfit was built for action, and while she didn't want a uniform exactly, she didn't want anyone holding back for fear of wear and tear either. "Girls can do anything," was mantra and guiding principle as well as the title of a favorite and well-worn kids' book on the shelf.

When Lou/Bernardine had first come to visit and we all sat down on the floor to talk, she asked BJ how she chose her books for the center. BJ said that she had to rely on donations at that point and so she just took what was offered, never giving the library a second thought—books were books, and the child care was so new that she was focused on learning all she could about kids and kid development. Lou gently nudged her to think a bit about children's books reflecting our values, our diverse society, dignity for children, antiracist activity, and supporting girls in nontraditional roles. She pointed to a pastel poster on the wall of a little boy with his hand slyly on the behind of a little girl and noted that the poster was teaching that male supremacy was cute. BJ later described that as "my a-ha moment"; the poster was gone the next day. Children's books became her passion and her project, something she became known for in the early childhood community.

When she received a greeting card from Bernardine celebrating International Women's Day, BJ began to construct a large collage on one wall with pictures of women doing everything: a large color photo of the astronaut Sally Ride; Zaida Gonzales, the first female firefighter in New York, posed in front of a red and glistening fire engine; Rosie the Riveter; farmers driving trucks and tractors; pilots, cops, gardeners, and nursing moms in business suits. Families soon began to bring in pictures of their moms and grandmothers and aunts and sisters, working, cooking, singing in a church choir, riding a camel, and the collage became a living thing that grew like Topsy.

We delighted in a kind of preschool patois constantly being invented and reinvented by the kids but quickly incorporated into the culture of the place, words like *africot* (half a peach, half a plum, such a fruit!). We also all spoke a fun and sometimes funny feminist argot at BJ's: *firefighter*, of course, *flight attendant, cow-hand, waitron*! Our block area had the biggest collection of multicultural wedgies—the name we invented for these wooden wedge-shaped toys—ever assembled: a Black male nurse and a Chicana doctor, an Asian female cop and an African business person, on and on and on.

One day we went on a field trip, across the street to our local firehouse. A young recruit named Jimmie showed us around, letting kids try on the big hats, ring the bell, and sit in the front seat of the engine. It was totally awesome, until Caitlin, four years old, asked our new friend, "So, Jimmie, when are you going to get a woman firefighter here?" Jimmie exploded in mocking laughter. "A woman!" he cried. "I hope never! The neighborhood would burn to the ground! This is no place for women."

Caitlin was crestfallen and then furious. What did he mean? Why did he say that mean thing? Back at BJ's she dictated a letter to Mayor Koch about getting a woman firefighter up at Eighty-fourth Street:

"It's not fair," she declared indignantly. She concluded emphatically, "Women can do anything!"

BJ wanted to make a wide and deep space for a huge range of children, an early opening for each of them to find pathways to a life lived with courage, hope, and love, a life worth doing, and so BJ's Kids was always a work in progress. When Zayd asked if everyone who was heroic back then was dead we began to read the story of Rosa Parks each year on December 1, depicted a bus with chairs in two rows and acted out the drama, sang Freedom Songs and silk-screened T-shirts with Rosa's image behind bars. BJ wrote to Rosa Parks and invited her to the space, and lo and behold, she wrote back and encouraged BJ's efforts. When Rosa Parks came to New York to speak at an education conference, the organizers knew BJ's Kids celebrated Rosa Parks Day and asked BJ to pick her up at the airport. When they met, BJ asked Rosa Parks which children's book about her story she liked the best. Rosa Parks told her, "None of them, because they all say that I was tired from working all day and that's why I refused to give up my seat. The truth was, I was a political activist long before that day and I had said if I am ever asked to give up my seat, I will refuse because I am tired of being treated like I am not a human being. One day, BJ, I will write an honest children's book that you can read to your kids."

We took the kids to the UN and sang "Give Peace a Chance," and then we gathered the whole day-care community to march to Central Park with kids in red or yellow wagons for the million-person no-nukes rally; Pete Seeger read one of our kid's letters from the stage, and we all went a little giddy. BJ wanted the kids to feel that they and their families could stand up in acts of repair and hope, and that something could always be done.

One morning when Susan was dropping three-year-old Jemmie off at day care, she told us that she'd just learned that she would be laid off from her job as a nurse in a public hospital in Harlem in less than a week. Sydenham Hospital was slated to be shuttered by Mayor Ed Koch for budgetary reasons, and for Susan—as well as for many others in Harlem—it seemed that she and her neighbors were once again being treated, as Gwendolyn Brooks wrote, like "the leastwise in the land." Her spirits were down, but she was planning to attend a community rally later that evening.

Next day her spark had returned and she was on a freedom high: "The whole community is up in arms," she told us. "They rely on the hospital, and they care about us." The rally had been huge, filled with spirit and singing and determination.

Sydenham was a vital space—seven hundred beds in the middle of what was, without it, an effective health care desert. More than that, Sydenham had a storied history woven into the essence of Harlem: founded in a brownstone in 1892 to serve African Americans, Sydenham was the first US private hospital with both white and Black doctors on staff. Susan was trained in Jamaica and was one of thirty-two Black nurses whose jobs would disappear with a stroke of Mayor Koch's pen.

Each day Susan brought news from the hospital, and her accounts became a wildly anticipated and vivid "chapter book" shared at morning circle. She animated her stories with a colorful cast of characters, nurses and friends, community activists and ordinary folks, in a Dickensian slog through the empire city, life in excruciating detail, world without end. But the core of each installment was a clash of two titans: on one side, the Reverend Timothy P. Mitchell, leading critic and charismatic leader, beautiful, brilliant, and brave, rallying the community in heated demonstrations; on the other side, rankling all the good people, the scary and gnarly Mayor Koch, a lonely, barren soul whose foul deed had set the drama in motion. The Mayor Koch of Susan's story hated ordinary people—and Black people in particular—and was the embodiment of evil: the Wicked Witch of the West to the kids, Mistah Kurtz or Iago to the rest of us. Susan was in the thick of it, eyewitness reporter, participant observer, hero, sage, mom, and friend. She never mentioned the hardship of a no-pay payday—it was a children's story, a magnificent fairy tale.

When the ministers and their allies occupied Sydenham to keep it open, the kids were excited because, like Rosa Parks, they would not be moved. And when they escalated by announcing a hunger strike, the kids were electrified: "When will they eat?" "Are they sad?" "I'm hungry!"

"Let's bring them something to eat," Z said at snack time that day. Good idea! We baked for the ministers two big carrot cakes, decorating each with hearts and stars. And next morning, right after circle, Susan led the staff, kids, and a couple of other mothers on a field trip to bring carrot cake to the hunger-strikers at Sydenham Hospital—missing the concept a bit, perhaps, but wholly aligned with the spirit of the struggle. We wanted the ministers to be strong and successful in their righteous effort, we wanted Susan to keep her job, and we wanted to stand up for justice and against health care denied.

The bus dropped us a block from the hospital and we immediately heard the chanting and singing from down the street. We moved excitedly on, and when we got close Susan began greeting folks. She seemed to know everyone. The picketers cleared a path for us, smiled at the kids, and said, "Thank you, thank you, thank you," as we passed by. We were in the middle of the crowd when we spotted the famous Reverend Mitchell beaming at us. "Here you are!" he exclaimed, delighted. "Susan, come on up here."

And up we all went. Reverend Mitchell hugged every one of us enthusiastically, and spoke gently to each of the children, beaming. Z handed him one of the carrot cakes, and then allowed the reverend to pick him up. Holding the cake and the toddler aloft, Reverend Mitchell offered a prayer that stretched and searched beyond the available light, while TV cameras brushed the scene.

THREE

Learning to Walk

Zayd, Malik, and I walked and toddled and wobbled our way to Broadway and Eighty-sixth Street after school to meet up with Bernardine, shop for groceries, and head home for dinner, baths, stories, and bed—our regular rhythm and routine by now and the best two hours of every day. I was stopped short at the corner news stand by the front page of the *New York Post*, which featured a huge headline—"COP KILLER!"—and an oversized photo of a disheveled man bound in a straitjacket, his eyes swollen and his face bloody and bruised, being led by several cops into a police station. I'd heard fuzzy references on the news of a Brinks truck robbery near Nyack just north of the city, a car chase, and a shoot-out—typical train-wreck news as far as I was concerned, isolated and irrelevant, disconnected and distracting. But it was the photo that seized me, and staring at that picture, first in disbelief and slowly with a gathering certainty, things began to shift and the world flipped quickly upside down. I did a double-take and then another and another: David Gilbert, our sweet and smart and funny friend, was the person beneath that disfigured mask of pain in the photo.

Poor, dear David, he looked so badly beaten down and diminished in shackles—nothing like the beautiful man I knew—that I choked back a sudden sob. I wanted to cry out loudly and openly, but not now, not with the kids there. When Bernardine arrived moments later, it was clear she'd seen the same thing, and as we hugged she whispered in a tight voice, "Later." We sat on a bench and Malik nursed while Bernardine read a story to Zayd, and then we gathered ourselves and went home.

As soon as we could sit up and pay attention later that night, the terrible details zoomed into razor-edged focus: a group of armed men had stormed a Brinks truck at the Nanuet Mall and made off with over a million and a half dollars, killing a guard named Peter Paige (who we later learned was himself an activist, involved in Northern Ireland's liberation struggle against Great Britain), and severely injuring another, Joe Trombino, who managed to fire a single shot from his handgun before having his arm practically severed from his shoulder by the force of the gunfire he endured. As police converged on the mall and mobilized to cut off escape routes, the armed men drove to a nearby parking lot, where they quickly swapped vehicles and sped away. But someone across from the parking lot had called the police, saying she'd just seen "several armed Black men" piling into the back of a U-Haul truck, and moments later officers stopped the U-Haul at a road block on an entrance ramp to the New York State Thruway and all hell broke loose: as they leapt from the back of the truck the men blasted away with M-16 rifles, 12-gauge shotguns, and 9-mm handguns, killing two Nyack police officers, Edward O'Grady and Wesley Brown, and fleeing the scene. The driver of the truck and the front seat passenger were apprehended immediately: David Gilbert and Kathy Boudin were in custody, accused of murder. They were our friends and our comrades from SDS and the Weather Underground.

There was more that night, and much more to come—carjackings and car crashes, conflicting accounts of what had happened and how, escapes and more shootings, raids and round-ups, indictments, grand juries, and trials—but our interest was arrested right there: Kathy and David detained and living under the menacing cloud of being charged with murder. It seemed at once awful and improbable, so ghastly and so out of character. And it seemed altogether too big, a bloated and distorted caricature.

More than a dozen of our former comrades were still underground then—we'd returned to the open world less than a year before ourselves—but Bernardine had met their new-born son on the day of his birth just before we'd surfaced; we were certain then that they were about to take the same path, casting their baby's life-reel toward a hopeful and more realistic future. That's what Kathy had said, and they'd agreed that day to meet up soon on the other side.

Where's the kid? we asked in unison. Others would have to worry about the legal difficulties, the deeper meanings, the tragedy and its inevitable fallout. We set off to find Chesa.

The culture of our young family was shot through from the start with politics and activism—Malik and Zayd were born into picket lines and demonstrations, our lively little apartment abuzz with friends and comrades, meetings and political discussions, organizing projects and action plans, along with the ordinary dialogue of everyday family life. Because we refused to have a TV, conversation was the charge and current in the room—our kids' earliest words and phrases included "mama" and "dog" and "ball," of course, but also "Peace Now" and "No Corn." Even without a literal understanding of every detail or every cause, we tried to create a kind of loving, child-friendly, and joyful resistance in our daily lives, a sense that we always stood up somehow for "fairness." "That's not fair" had the same indignant tone, whether referring to the smallest injustice on the playground or some monstrous outrage like a police murder of a young Black man on the streets of Brooklyn.

Before the dizzying and defining moment of our children's' births Malcolm X had famously noted that Black people seemed forever to have an abundance of Washingtons and Jeffersons and Lincolns in their family trees, but white people didn't even have a twig or a leaf for Nat Turner or Cinque or Frederick Douglass or Harriet Tubman. Why, he asked rhetorically and pointedly, why the color line—even when it comes to naming the babies?

We chose to take Malcolm's observation as a practical matter, and so we named our first-born Zayd Osceola, to remember a Panther brother killed by the police and at the same time to raise up a Seminole leader who never surrendered to the US policy of relocation and extermination; our second Malik Cochise, this time in honor of Malcolm himself as well as a renowned First Nation legend, the great Apache guerrilla fighter.

Our children grew up on stories of freedom fighters: Zayd's changing table was adorned with postcards of Ho Chi Minh and a framed photo of Zayd Shakur, and above Malik's bed was a portrait of Malcolm X as well as pictures of Nelson Mandela and Walter Sisulu, South African revolutionaries imprisoned on Robben Island. Each of our kids started life with a home birth and an invented identity—is there any other kind?—outfitted with a false birth certificate and an assumed name as well as the more standard-issue Oshkosh B'Gosh overalls and tie-dyed T-shirts. Born on the run, they had their own youthful list of s/heroes: Robin Hood, Amilcar Cabral, Harriet Tubman, John Brown, Stuart Little, Jackie Robinson, Han Solo, Lolita Lebron, Che Guevara, Peter Rabbit. They liked outlaws. Kathy and David's beautiful baby—Chesa Jackson Gilbert Boudin—bounded into our family and crash-landed in our lives when he was fourteen months old with his name already attached, and it fit right in: Chesa, a Swahili word for dancing feet, and Jackson, taken from Soledad Brother George Jackson, murdered by prison guards at San Quentin. His prized T-shirt was a silk-screen portrait of Rosa Parks in dignified refusal.

Leonard Boudin, a prominent civil rights attorney, had rushed to his daughter the minute he'd heard the shocking news of the Brinks robbery, the killings, and her arrest. It was a troubling jailhouse reunion, he told us later—sorrow and remorse mixed with anger and accusation—but he left with one concrete assignment that gave him a sense of practical purpose. He hurried to the babysitter where Kathy had dropped Chesa a day earlier as she left for what she never imagined would be her last day of freedom, and he retrieved his grandson and brought him home.

We'd known Leonard and Jean Boudin for decades. Bernardine met Leonard first as a law graduate and organizer for the National Lawyers Guild; I met them when Kathy and I were community organizers together in the Cleveland ghettoes. Later we saw them often because their Greenwich Village home was a kind of center of left-wing social and literary life. Bernardine talked law with Leonard, poetry with Jean, and politics with all of us together. When we showed up on their doorstep after Brinks with our two little guys in tow and a shopping bag of baby clothes, they were still reeling from the tragedy of Kathy imprisoned and the consequences abruptly crashing down upon them, scrambling to pick up whatever pieces they could.

"Oh, my dears," Jean said as she answered the door, embracing us one by one, her dazzling smile in place, but her petite frame seeming even more fragile, her lively blue eyes brimming with tears now. "Thank you so much for coming." Leonard, too, big and handsome and exuding robust power most days, was strained and shrunken as we fell into an awkward embrace. For such a powerful man, such an influential man, to be unable to control an outcome when it mattered most was simply devastating.

They were in their seventies now, and Chesa was a handful—too heavy to carry up the stairs and too small to negotiate them alone, too full-tilt and too nonstop, too vulnerable and too needy. Everything was a challenge, from diapers to baths to bottles, and the energy it took just to keep up was backbreaking and mind-numbing for them. They'd had Chesa for less than twenty-four hours, but their elegant space was already messy, the two of them on the floor with a naked Chesa, completely spent.

We ate Chinese takeout from boxes, and then set the kids up to play on the rug with the few toys they'd quickly gathered from neighbors. As we talked quietly in the kitchen the two of them ricocheted wildly from tears to determination, anger to sorrow, grief for their daughter to astonished joy with their grandson. We were right there with them, bouncing uncontrollably from wall to wall. How can we help? we asked.

We came to visit every day, bringing clothes and books, stuffed animals and art supplies, and lots of homemade presents from Zayd and Malik for their new friend, Chesa—paintings, cards, collages, beaded necklaces. Within a week, Chesa was commuting each day from Greenwich Village to the Upper West Side with Lorraine from BJ's Kids, and soon after that, with agreement all around, he moved in with us—simple as that.

But, of course, it wasn't as simple as that; it wasn't simple at all.

Bernardine and I had had one long, long late-night talk right away walking down Broadway while BJ watched our sleeping kids, our thinking entirely in sync. We'd known and loved Kathy and David forever, and they were family—our brother and our sister—and, whatever else, family takes care of its own, especially in times of crisis. The pulse and measure of our lives was fully tuned to the complex rhythms of raising young kids, and here we were now, happily child-centered, fully immersed in the joyful noise of a chock-a-block toddler orchestra. Yes, there was room for one more. And if, God forbid, anything catastrophic ever overwhelmed us, our primal scream would be for our two precious boys, and who, of all the people in the world we could imagine, would we want to step up for them? We would want us.

We raised the possibility, gently, tentatively, with Leonard and Jean. They were torn into pieces, struggling to keep from drowning in tears and going mad with grief, frantic for some way out for Kathy, desperate to keep and raise Chesa, and eager for help—their heads said yes, but their hearts screamed no. Years later—long after Kathy had gone to trial and been sentenced to a term of twenty years to life in state prison, after we'd settled into our new family reality with us as Chesa's other parents (or "caretakers," as Jean called us for a while) and Jean and Leonard loving and engaged grandparents, and long after we'd moved to Chicago—I was back in New York for work and came to their home for dinner. "Oh, Bill, dear," Jean said, answering the door, reaching up to hug me warmly, smiling her warm and stunning smile. "I love you . . . and I hate you," just like that, completely matter-of-fact. She might have been channeling the common sentiment captured so simply by the conflicted and tormented Roman poet Catullus: "I hate you and I love you!" We both laughed, and I said, "Perfect!" and so she said it again with cheerful conviction: "I love you and I hate you."

That pretty much said it all, instantly recognizable as the mixed-up sentiment right from the start: she loved Bernardine and me for taking Chesa to our hearts and to our home, and she hated us for taking Chesa away. She loved us for helping Kathy, and she hated us because we weren't Kathy, and it was Kathy, and not us, who should be raising him. She would be fully satisfied only if Bernardine or I would trade places with her daughter immediately, if one of us would, please and thank you, go straight to prison and set Kathy free—the prisoner exchange of her dreams. Jean's deepest desire was to have Kathy released, and our inability to grant that bottomless wish meant that she would have to hate us even as she loved us. She said it, and we got it—the mashed-up feelings that were always on order, always right there, and sometimes on full display.

Visiting Kathy and David in those first days was dreadful for their parents: they'd been moved to an upstate jail, isolated and locked down with a breathtaking police and military presence on top of them. Jean and Leonard were scanned and searched and searched again before they could see them, and then only dimly behind thick mesh. Kathy looked desolate, while David, for all he'd endured, was unbowed and defiant.

When we could speak by phone we brushed lightly on what they had done, what had happened and why, and focused on Chesa—they were fearful for him, hungry for news, and worried about next steps. We broached the idea of taking him and they leapt as if at the last lifeboat pulling swiftly away. "Yes, yes, we will co-parent for a time, and when we get out . . ." Well, reality was still a ways off, but first steps—even if conflicted and ambivalent—were agreed upon all around.

When our guys heard that Chesa would come to live with us, that he would soon become a new brother for them, they accepted it as kids generally permit whatever weird proposition—visiting bizarre relatives, going on lunatic road trips, endorsing nutty and improbable religions—their parents put before them. But Malik, twenty months old then, had the gift of language well underway, and so before Chesa actually made the move, he circled the apartment with a steady refrain: "Chesa can't have my blocks." "Chesa can't have my ball." "Chesa can't have my bed." The ledger grew steadily, day by day, and one morning as Bernardine dressed him and Malik accumulated more and more items—"Chesa can't have my shirt; Chesa can't have my shoes"—he looked up steadily into her face and said forcefully, "And Chesa can't have my mommy!" Bingo! We all cheered and laughed, and Bernardine assured him that she was big enough to go around, and that she would always be *his* mommy no matter what, and that he would always be her precious bunny. It became a big happy piece of our family lore, Malik laughing along and delivering the punch line when needed. Bernardine taught him the phrase "sibling rivalry," and he busted that out for all occasions as well. But Chesa and Malik became best friends from that moment, Malik the older brother, holding Chesa's hand and teaching him to play ball.

Chesa dropped on our little family unit without the expected nine-months' notice and without any groundwork—suddenly, there he was, and what had been one thing quickly became another. Having a third biological kid, or even a planned adoption, would have involved warning and the possibility of preparation. This was not that. This was a bombshell from beyond the beyond, an accident of fate, a collision of chance and choice, and most of all a leap of faith and foolishness for us, and we knew it.

Bernardine and I checked in with each other morning, noon, and night about our observations and interactions, the latest developments, how he seemed to be doing, how the other kids were handling everything, how we were each holding up. From the start Chesa was an easy child, perhaps too easy—agreeable, eager to please, a bit compliant. Act your age, we'd think to ourselves and whisper to each other. He was never fussy, never demanding. But it was weird as well—his play lacked spark and his explorations of his world were rather reluctant; he watched his new brothers playing and painting from a distance, but only joined in when Malik reached out to him, and then only tentatively. This easygoing kid was suffering silently, and yet he impressed everyone, especially those with the least experience with toddlers, with what "a good kid" he was—no drama, no resistance. To us he seemed to display a troubling blandness: he never exhibited much enthusiasm for anything, and both his physical strength and his emotions seemed to be hovering at low ebb. And we didn't like the way he took to new adults, crawling immediately onto their laps—which they universally loved—without any wariness or toddler-normal stranger anxiety.

We talked and talked with each other, but never a peep of concern to Leonard or Jean, Kathy or David. They were in another world, a world of pain and pressure, and we wanted to reassure them that this was at least one place where they could feel safe and secure, that Chesa would be fine, and that we had everything completely in hand. It wasn't true, not even close, but when one of us would begin to feel overwhelmed or underprepared for this new family we now had, the other would try to buck up and rise to the occasion. Denial isn't just a river in Egypt, and we were both paddling as hard as we could to stay above water and on course.

When we took Chesa, we of course adopted an entire village—looking back it's so obvious, but at the time it came as a complete and not entirely welcome revelation—and a more far-flung, outsized, and bizarre village is hard to picture. At the center are two imprisoned parents, grieving or defiant for what they had done, aching merely to touch their child on their best days, and on their worst days filled with recrimination and guilt, begging to wake up from the nightmare and rewind life's clock. Next to them, four grandparents, all of them at an age when they should be sitting in rocking chairs surveying and considering their lives from a place of calm and relative comfort, thrust suddenly into an unwelcome place of dislocation and darkness, sleeplessness and necessary action. Frantic about the fate of their own kids and desperate to do the right thing by their newly discovered grandson, each was bombarded by a riot of emotions from anger and resentment to reconciliation and resignation. From there, it only got weirder.

Bernardine and the kids and I met Jean and Leonard at Shopsins Grocery and Diner often, or visited them in their Village home, and they trekked up to our fifth-floor walk-up when they could, bringing food or books and games. David's parents, too, living outside Boston, came when possible, and all four of them, while crowding at moments, became wonderfully engaged grandparents to all three kids. For us the loveliest surprise was Leonard, whom we'd known as a renowned radical lawyer, a powerful intellectual, and a forceful presence in any room he entered. Here, though, in this space and role, he was transformed into an affectionate and devoted grandpa—available and responsive, fascinated and connected, patient to the point of serenity, and remarkably light-hearted and fun-loving. He would slip off his coat and tie and pile all three boys onto his lap to read them a book, let them take off his glasses without complaint, or kneel down next to the bathtub (and get soaked), helping out before bedtime. He played catch with Malik for hours on end, and he introduced both Malik and Zayd to chess— Leonard, who loved the game, had famously played with Che Guevara in Cuba in 1963. He visited their classrooms and became something of a legend, taking on all comers, moving from desk to desk and defeating them all. He played marathon matches in our living room until, years later, Zayd and Malik could each finally defeat the old champion. It was a revelation to us, and perhaps at that time to Leonard as well: he was born to be a grandfather.

One Sunday morning soon after Chesa came to live with us, Leonard called: they were nearby, meeting friends for brunch, and could they grab us some bagels and stop up to say hello. Yes, of course, and within minutes a half-dozen people had climbed the stairs and were crowded into our living room watching delightedly as the kids played. It was all well-intended, to be sure, but it felt oddly like surveillance as well—the friends included the heads of the Horace Mann and the Bank Street schools, a child psychiatrist from New Haven, and a federal judge. Thus began a pattern that continued for years, acquaintances and associates parading up our five flights or assembling at BJ's Kids to get a glimpse of the Little Prince in his natural settings. And, of course, Leonard and Jean being who they were, early visitors included Letty Cottin Pogrebin, a visionary founder of *Ms.* magazine; Judith Viorst, the enchanting children's book author; Helena Kennedy, a radical "people's lawyer" who would later become a British MP; Corliss Lamont, the founder of the Emergency Civil Liberties Committee; I. F. Stone, the celebrated journalist and Jean's brother-in-law; Eqbal Ahmad, the Pakistani revolutionary and famous internationalist, and his wife, Julie Diamond, an education researcher and writer; Daniel Ellsberg; and Dr. Benjamin Spock himself. Had we been less secure about how we were raising our kids or how we were living our lives, this onslaught might have driven us over the edge, but we weren't and it didn't. It was a bit strange, and it could become a minor annoyance on occasion, like the first time Chesa got an ear infection—he was subject to every sore throat and ear infection that circled nearby in those early days—which we had dealt with adequately, we thought, by seeing our own pediatrician, only to have Leonard and Dr. Spock appear at our door for a "second opinion." It's an ear infection, for Christ's sake; do we really need Dr. Spock? But it was mostly fun and occasionally funny for all of us, and it was, after all, Ben Spock.

Our pediatrician, Dr. Catherine Lodyjensky, was a celebrity in her own right, at least in our neighborhood. Bernardine had given birth to Malik in our own bed just blocks from her office. When I called the New York Health Department to report his arrival a few days later, there was a long silence on the other end. "Where is the patient now?" the voice asked tentatively. There's no patient, I explained, just a baby and a mother, and I'd like to get a birth certificate. Pause. "Go immediately to an emergency room," she advised, and when I said that Bernardine was not going to a place for the sick and the wounded, she transferred me through a bewildering set of agencies and departments, landing me finally at the Office of the Visiting Nurse, the first person who didn't act as if I were entirely out of my mind. A couple of days later two lovely women climbed the endless stairs and registered Malik under his false name—the older one, African American and from the Deep South, surveyed our all-natural hullabaloo and settled in happily for tea and homemade oatmeal cookies, while the other, a recent immigrant from Haiti, kept a stiff distance. The younger one eventually asked Bernardine a series of prescribed questions and recorded the answers on a proper form, pausing at one point to ask me to leave the room, since the next few questions were quite personal. When Bernardine insisted that I need not leave the room, she read out with some embarrassment, "What was the date of your last period?"

We took Malik to see Dr. Lodyjensky a week after his birth—full head of dark hair and shockingly alert and active—and she peered and poked and probed and pronounced him perfect. And then in her lovely lilting Russian accent she added, "I see he has a *mano de azabache*," the tiny black hand worn around the wrist on a gold chain to ward off evil spirits, this one a gift from his Uncle Mickey, a Puerto Rican nationalist and *independista*. How do you know about the *mano?* I asked, thinking this is the hippest old Russian immigrant in all of New York City. "Oh, I remove them from baby's stomachs and throats all the time," she said calmly, smiling, and without another word Malik's *mano* was history, and we were on our own versus the evil spirits.

Shortly after Chesa joined our crew, Robby and Ellie Meeropol, friends from college, called to offer support and soon came to visit with their kids. Robby had been three years old and his brother Michael six when their parents, Julius and Ethel Rosenberg, were executed by the US government as communist spies at the height of the Cold War anti-communist frenzy. The boys were adopted by the songwriter Abel Meeropol (he wrote the Billie Holiday classic "Strange Fruit") and his wife, Ann. Years later Michael and Robby wrote *We Are Your Sons*, publicly and proudly acknowledging their biological parents as well as their brilliant second parents and reclaiming the full scope of their heritage.

"I have no words of wisdom at all," Robby said then. "You're doing a wonderful thing, but there's no road map to what's ahead for him or for you." He thought that Chesa looked great, but that he would probably be angry, depressed, and filled with questions in turn—as he himself had been—and that we'd likely all need some professional help down the road. Bernardine and I—born skeptics when it comes to "professional help"—were hugely grateful for their visit and concern. "His loss is bottomless," Robby said, "but who knows where that might take him?"

Later we spent a weekend with Bernardine's best friend from law school—twenty years beyond graduation. Flip, a brilliant, passionate, wildly funny, and hugely successful Boston lawyer brought T-shirts for everyone emblazoned with a motto he'd authored for the weekend: "Twenty Years of *Mens Rea*"—the Latin phrase meaning "guilty intent," the silent partner and evil twin of *actus reas*, or the "guilty action," both halves of which are necessary to win a conviction for certain crimes. We smoked too much and drank too much, we ate too much and we laughed too hard. Late at night, the talk turned to our kids, and Flip and Toddy, his partner and a genius high school teacher, began to share details of their lives with their middle child, just a few years older than Chesa. We sobered up fast, and all the noise and commotion and partying faded into the background. Their beautiful adopted daughter tended to be wary, disconnected, and low-keyed; she was often paralyzed by indecision, and she was practically pathologically accident-prone. All of it struck us as eerily familiar and as yet unspoken. We were riveted by Flip and Toddy, and felt that we might have entered some protective and intensely intimate embrace.

Flip eventually got rolling: "All those ads for adoption with the soft tones and the pink heart backgrounds, and those adorable faces looking directly at you like puppy dogs or cuddly kittens or Keane paintings, drive me right over the cliff—just too much bullshit, especially the mindlessly seductive tag-line: *All this child needs is love.* Are you fucking kidding? Of course this kid needs love; we all need love, but is that *all* she needs? That's it? Love, yes, and help, lots and lots and lots of help. And if you take that kid—don't be gullible, don't fool yourself—*you* will need help, too, and love, and then even more help." We realized later that we were joining a subculture that night, invisible to outsiders as most subcultures are, but as real as dirt to its members: the informal and hidden society of frantic adoptive parents. "I sit against the farthest back wall when we see her psychiatrist, taking notes," Flip said. "I hate it, but I'm desperate."

When Chesa's mild melancholy gave way, its successor was red-hot rage; the strange case of Dr. Jekyll conjuring the evil Edward Hyde came close, or the bland Dr. Bruce Banner morphing inexorably into the Incredible Hulk. Like Hyde and the Hulk, Chesa's transformations seemed beyond his control and, when the process began, irrevocable.

Two-year-olds' outbursts may be as common as mud, and the "terrible twos" a cliché, but a temper tantrum had about the same relationship to Chesa's furious transient madness as a peashooter had to a machine gun. The trigger could be a small transition (We have to start to clean up now), a common command (Let's get dressed before we go out), an everyday frustration (Oh, we're out of milk; we'll get more at the store later today), or something new and utterly unpredictable. What followed was awe-inspiring. Chesa's eyes narrowed as a storm cloud passed in front of his face, he clenched both fists and stomped his feet, and he sobbed *No!* Then he let loose, throwing himself on the floor without regard to hurt or harm, screaming and ranting, sweating, choking and vomiting, and he kept at a berserk high pitch past all previous records——twenty minutes, forty minutes, sixty minutes, or until he passed out from exhaustion. It was scary.

Scarier still was getting up early one Saturday morning and finding Chesa sitting on the floor in the corner of our little living room facing the wall and staring blankly ahead, banging his head repeatedly against the wall, holding himself and rocking back and forth. Autism, we said to each other, alarmed. We need help, we said; we need *professional* help.

What followed was an avalanche of appointments, interviews, evaluations, examinations, visitations, assessments, theories, analyses, and all the requisite accompanying meetings with psychiatrists, psychologists, brain scientists, learning specialists, speech therapists, shrinks and charlatans, some of whom we quite liked. When, in the midst of it all, Bernardine and I were sure we noticed an unusual pattern of rapid blinking, and when Dr. Lodyjensky confirmed our observation and pronounced it *petit mal*, and Dr. Spock concurred, off we went to a series of neurologists—all of them, regardless of age or gender, remarkably named Dr. Singh, and we thought for a moment we'd entered, not a specialty, but a secret camp—for scans and screenings and electro-encephalograms (we didn't even try to say it), and spoonfuls of bright pink medicine every night, and then, suddenly, a break in the storm, a clearing, and a plan of action. At three Chesa began seeing Dr. Berlin, a young psychiatrist of the Freudian persuasion whose shabby office was bare save for a large and lovely portrait on the wall behind his desk of a youngish Sigmund Freud looking curiously like Berlin himself—same beard and haircut, same glasses and tilt of the head, same waistcoat and tie. Coincidence? I'm no professional and so I can't say, but I don't think so. In any case it felt extremely weird facing the two of them in conversation, two big brains who together knew, well, everything.

Chesa looked forward to his sessions with Berlin, argued with him constantly, and then didn't want to leave at the end of the hour. I was in the room the first few months, and it taught me a lot—about listening better, rephrasing, or giving Chesa words for his feelings. But mostly it built my sense of empathy for Chesa, for what he was experiencing and how hard he was working to make sense of his life. Berlin was a great guy and a huge help, and I really loved him. Transference? Counter-transference? Who can keep it straight?

Bernardine couldn't help jerking his chain every time we met: when he offered strategies to get through the daily breakfast circus, she said, "Easy for you to say sitting here comfortably with Freud covering your back. Why don't you make a house call some morning at breakfast, and we'll see how smart you really are?" When he was alarmed to discover in conversation with us that all three kids sometimes ran terrified down the hall in the middle of the night and clambered into our family bed with us, he wanted to know what Bernardine wore to bed, and advised us that kids must learn to sleep alone to build independence. She responded, "They're independent all day long. Can't they have a little nighttime cuddling and connectedness?" Then she stepped way out of bounds: "What do you wear to bed, Doctor? Do you sleep alone to build up *your* independence?" She was trespassing and she knew it, throwing off the kind of question Berlin/Freud would never answer. But in spite of the teasing and questioning, and the alien cultural landscape of psychiatry and psychotherapy, we loved Dr. Berlin and credited him with saving us from sliding into serious despair. We were experiencing the hard truth that parents have had to learn through the ages: you are only as happy as your least happy child.

A few years later, when we moved to Chicago, Chesa met twice a week with Dr. Bennett Leventhal—a lifesaver for sure—at his open, sunny office at the University of Chicago. It was quite a contrast: family photos, games, toys, gardening on the roof and art materials everywhere, the walls decorated with children's drawings. My favorite was a giant, framed painting of a toddler-drawn tadpole person, thick-lined smiling face without a body, legs and arms dangling precariously from the head with the dictated words along the side: "Dear Dr. Leventhal, I hate you, I hate you, I hate you. Love, Aaron." Aaron somehow channeled every kid in crisis with a parent or a teacher or a shrink—he said it all—and it echoed Jean Boudin's painful proclamation: "I love you and I hate you." Leventhal was fully engaged and completely there for us. We met often, and he met as well with Jean and Leonard, talked on the phone and corresponded with David and Kathy, and even went to visit Kathy in prison once, well aware that he had inherited a hugely unique blended family. He was also a normal enough guy around the neighborhood—we'd see him at the market or the park, and always at Little League games because one of his sons was in Chesa's class and on the baseball team that Bernardine coached with our friend Rashid Khalidi.

Things got easier and better, and yet when Chesa was ten and Leventhal told us that his therapy could at long last come to an end and that the kid would be fine without it, we were nonplussed: Don't abandon us, I thought. Bernardine said, "I didn't know that therapy ever came to an end; I thought your professional code dictated that once you guys got your hooks into somebody treatment continued forever." We all laughed, but Leventhal added sagely, "Your family's been organized around having a troubled kid, and he's no longer troubled; for years, every relationship has had to bend toward that reality, but reality has shifted, and now every relationship has to shift along with it."

Soon after that Bernardine came home from work looking as if she'd been run over by a truck. All week she'd been interviewing kids locked in mental institutions as part of a class action lawsuit she'd helped organize on behalf of abused and neglected children, and all the interviews were heart-breaking, but she had spent two hours that day talking "with a kid who could have been Chesa." Their life stories overlapped eerily: both were ten years old, both had lost their parents at fourteen months, and both sets of parents were now doing life sentences in prison. But one was beginning to thrive and the world was opening up for him, while the other was trapped in a secured facility writing poetry in a tiny notebook, abandoned, fiercely making his own meaning, disappeared from the known world. Of course, the youngster she'd interviewed didn't have a relatively stable family to fall into as well as psychiatrists, reading tutors, speech specialists, neurologists, and a wealthy grandfather to pay for it all. But it was just too close for her that day, too harrowing and upsetting—a clear reminder, as if she needed one, of the fickleness of fate, and more to the point of her legal efforts, of the harsh and unforgiving face of the law and social policy when it comes to kids born into poverty and racism. It was an illustration as well of a fundamental contradiction that she knew all too well and that she dived into every day: love means nothing at all if it doesn't mean loving some particular person more than others; loving only a particular person and ignoring all others is a form of narcissism and barbarity. She loved Zayd, Malik, and Chesa specifically, and from that intimate space fought for justice—love enacted as law and policy and justice in the public square—so that all kids might have those choices and openings and privileges and possibilities.

I'll stop right there and bypass some of the most chilling ups and downs; I've said enough, perhaps too much. We would never have wished for the pain and suffering that brought Chesa to us in the first place, nor the difficult struggle we all experienced for several years, but Bernardine and I—and I think Zayd and Malik as well—were deeply and surprisingly grateful for the experience nonetheless. Knowing what I know and having witnessed all I've witnessed, accounting for the burdens he carried and the mountains he scaled, his trajectory seems all the more valuable to me. Chesa was fiercely protected by Malik and Zayd, but he didn't learn to read until the third grade, stopped seeing Leventhal in the fifth, regularly visited each of his imprisoned parents, and zoomed through high school in three years. Then he went off to Yale, where he won a Rhodes scholarship and attended Oxford University, lived throughout Latin America for years and traveled the world, published three books, and returned to Yale Law School. He was instrumental in the herculean effort that won Kathy's freedom from prison after twenty-two years inside, and he continues to fight tirelessly for David's release. I apologize for bragging about our own son, but he has become a person whose hard-won love of life has made him naturally open-handed and passionate, sensible and sympathetic, disciplined and driven, and hungry for every kind of freedom—a mensch among men.

Soon after Brinks and a few months after Chesa came to stay, all five of us came dashing down the stairs at 7:00 a.m. on a crisp New York

May morning, Bernardine in high heels and a business suit as always, on our merry ways to work and school, backpacks filled with snacks and lunches, books and art projects and notes. We careened onto the sidewalk at full speed into the spring air, admired the blooming magnolias, and were caught short by two men in matching brown suits and brown fedoras, white shirts and those signature scuffed-up brown shoes. "Ms. Dohrn," the taller one with the square jaw said, blocking her way and sticking an envelope into her hand. "This is a summons to appear in Federal Court next Monday at 9 a.m." There was no way to avoid him, to cut and run, and she simply looked at him coolly and said, "Oh, shit." "You've been served," replied the softer, plump-faced one, affecting a tough-guy swagger, and they were gone, leaving the intimation of peril and two gloomy silhouettes that suggested characters from a 1950s detective comic book.

Malik and Chesa missed it entirely, and Zayd simply asked, "Who were those men?"

"Just guys with a letter for Mom," I replied. And off we went.

Bernardine called Michael and Eleanora Kennedy, and met with them for lunch. She saw Leonard right away too, and then gathered half a dozen friends at our apartment later that night to talk strategy. She was in high gear. We half expected it. A federal grand jury had been impaneled to investigate the Brinks robbery, subpoenas were in the air, and given Bernardine's history and the fact that the US attorney was casting a wide, wide net in hopes of turning up anything at all, she had apparently made the list—but even so, when the blow was delivered it spun us around. "Let's go underground," I suggested. "Not funny," she said, but smiled nonetheless.

Grand juries are oddities descended from English common law, established originally to provide a buffer for the ordinary people against the unchecked power of the king, but in modern times turned into their opposite: star chambers where prosecutors alone wield powerful weapons and act on their own authority, virtually unchecked. Bernardine would be required to enter the chamber alone, without counsel, without representatives of the free press, without a public gallery. She would be asked to answer questions without benefit of context, without being told what evidence was already before the panel, without knowing if she herself was the target of an investigation, and without being able to face or contradict or cross-examine any possible witnesses or accusers. I reminded her that when John Brown was indicted by a slave-loving grand jury in Kansas, members of the panel ended up dead. "Please shut up, honey," she said. "Please and thank you." "Just a joke," I said, but again not funny, and I did shut up, of course, very politely and quite contritely.

Though famously also refusing to talk to the media since we had come aboveground, Bernardine gave an interview to CBS reporter Chris Weicher in Central Park, noting the unjust and unconstitutional uses of the grand jury throughout US history and explaining her pending refusal to cooperate, despite her disagreements with the Brinks robbery. She highlighted other grand jury resistance, including the scores of people who had refused to cooperate with grand juries seeking information about the Weather Underground. When she spoke about defying the subpoena as the most difficult decision of her life, given her young children, she teared up and ended the interview.

We'd stayed close together that whole weekend, lots of quiet time and calm and familiar pleasures: baking cookies with the kids, walking to Broadway for pizza and ice cream, playing in the Eighty-fourth Street playground and picnicking under flowering cherry and apple trees in Central Park. Bernardine knew from the start that she would never talk to the grand jury, and she knew, too, that she would likely be jailed for that refusal. She explained to the boys that she would be going away on Monday, but that "Poppy will be here to take care of you," and that BJ and all their friends would be here too. It was all a bit abstract. They all knew that their momma would be in jail for a while, but jail was already familiar to all three because of visits with and phone calls from Kathy and David. Chesa had enough prison visits in his life, so we planned for him to see Bernardine infrequently; Malik and Zayd could visit her every week and talk to her on the phone and write letters to her every day. Malik and Bernardine clung hard to each other, but none of it made Monday morning any easier.

We stuck to our routine, and after breakfast dropped Malik and Chesa at BJ's Kids—the good-bye hugs lasted longer, Bernardine's backward glances were heavier, and her tears were just barely in check. How could she leave them? How long until she saw them again? We were scared and we were miserable, but we wanted to be strong, to assure the kids that their lives would be OK, that we would be OK. BJ as always rose to the occasion, kissed us all and wished us good luck, and then quickly swept the kids up and away into a project making papier-mâché masks and cloth capes for a dramatic play.

Zayd wanted to see what would happen, and Bernardine always talked to him about everything anyway, so he came along with us to the anticipated nine o'clock collision. We would stay together as long as possible, but my first responsibility was to him, to be sure nothing scary happened for Zayd. As the three of us held hands and mounted the imposing staircase to the federal courthouse, a media mob descended, cameras flashing, reporters shouting questions, and Zayd looked up and said, "They're excited." Not much got past Zayd, even then.

Bernardine was swept up to the grand jury chamber while Zayd and I joined Michael and Eleanora Kennedy for toasted raisin bagels and cream cheese. We rejoined her shortly, this time in the courtroom of federal judge Gerhardt Goettel. Michael asked the judge to release her from the subpoena, and certainly to reject putting her in custody, explaining that she was the mother of three young children and that the judge was not permitted to punish her for her silence. Goettel rejected Kennedy's plea, saying he wasn't punishing her, but simply compelling her testimony. "You have defied the law before," he noted. "And this time the law compels you."

When invited to address the court, Bernardine said, "Judge"— none of the usual "Your Honor" bullshit for Bernardine in this situation—"I will remain silent not as a Fifth Amendment matter but as a First Amendment principle." She argued that freedom of speech had no practical meaning if the state could force someone to speak against her will, that she had nothing to say, and that her silence was protected. "Nonsense," Goettel replied. He ordered her locked in the Metropolitan Correctional Center "until such time as you are willing to respond to a lawfully constituted grand jury." He added an inelegant phrase that he would return to each time Bernardine appeared before him: "The keys to your cell are in your mouth." As she was taken from the courtroom in handcuffs she turned to smile at Zayd and me. Zayd blew her a kiss and waved bye-bye.

The days and weeks and months dragged on, and because her imprisonment was indeterminate—"The keys are in your mouth"—we couldn't plan or even pace ourselves. She could talk and get out, or she could stay silent and spend what felt, day by day, like life in prison. And although she had nothing to do with the Brinks robbery and faced no criminal charges, she would refuse on principle to cooperate with a fishing expedition of the state: "It's an abuse of state power, and it gathers greater and greater strength every time people cooperate," she said. Eventually, a total of one man and sixteen other women—also refusing to speak on principle—were locked up in the federal detention center in downtown Manhattan for resisting the Brinks grand jury. Bernardine felt unsure about a lot of things, but completely resolute on just this: Don't talk! Ever! She'd likely be locked up for quite a while.

The kids and I went to a print shop on Broadway with a photo of the three of them sitting on the hood of a car in just their swim shorts eating big ice cream cones, and we ran off hundreds of postcards with Judge Goettel's address on the back side. It made a sweet card, and they each sent one every day to Goettel—their very own Sheriff of Nottingham—with a personal plea to let their momma go. We also handed them out liberally to friends and associates and anyone who attended the meetings that were organized to fight grand jury abuse. When we heard later that as the flow of cards increased his irritation in chambers escalated as well, we felt that at least we were finally visible, which cheered us up.

We were trying, without great success, not only to get Bernardine and the others who'd been swept up by this marauding witch hunt out of jail, but also to build, if not a movement, at least a wider and deeper awareness of the dangers of unchecked government might. We got only fleeting coverage in the press, with one notable exception: Phil Donahue got permission to bring a whole film crew into the MCC, where he taped an hour-long interview with Bernardine for his TV show. It was great, and she was stunning.

By and large, it was a daily slog. She endured the isolation and helplessness of being caged, the despair of being disappeared and its accompanying sense of insignificance—as if being cast out of the open world had gone unnoticed and left not a mark——and mostly the crying anguish of being separated from the kids. "The keys to your cell are in your mouth."

I worked all day at BJ's Kids, day after day, and then took the train downtown to see Bernardine. I tried to be with the kids every morning and every night, and with my sweet partner in life and in crime every late afternoon. I got a lot of help from BJ and other friends, including Peter M., a lovely teaching assistant at BJ's Kids by day and a flamboyant gender traitor and fabulous sexual outlaw by night. Peter moved into our apartment with us, became a lifelong friend to our boys, and joined the growing list of lifesavers.

I slept less and less, and relied more and more on Coke—the diet kind and the real thing—just to make it through. My admiration for single mothers spiked right then, as I realized that beyond the physical demands of parenting was the pervasive weight of emotional and psychic responsibility with no breaks and no downtime, an all-encompassing sense that *you were never off the clock*. Even if the kids were OK and Peter had them at the playground while I jogged in Central Park, I still had to be on. I was completely shot.

Zayd and Malik went separately to visit Bernardine every week in the federal remand center. "I want to be all-there, and it's just altogether happier one on one," Bernardine would tell me. Chesa's assignment was already too much: he took long trips—by car with Leonard and Jean, by bus with BJ—to see Kathy and David regularly, and while it was necessary to maintain a connection with Bernardine, it seemed nuts to add him to this new dance card very often. BJ, the resident genius in all things young children, was the mainstay of the system, the godmother of our visiting mafia, juggler and helper, and she took it on with characteristic thoughtfulness and passion, making each trek to lower Manhattan its own field trip for Malik or Zayd, something special to plan and anticipate with the kids and then pull off as an exciting, immense journey.

The Metropolitan Correctional Center was a tense, angular tower, all brick and steel and glass, squeaky clean on the surface and stinking of sterile antiseptic toxins deep down. The visiting ritual began with BJ registering and showing an ID at the front desk, then making her way with Zayd or Malik to the waiting room—overcrowded, hot, and full of irritable children—where they would stay until their names were called. The guards weren't mean in any overt way, but the casual and bored bureaucratic coldness incensed her. "For us, every minute lost was stolen treasure," she said later, "and their apathy or exaggerated lack of concern just grated on me." They could be kept waiting anywhere from fifteen minutes to two hours to see Bernardine.

BJ would snuggle the kids on her lap and talk about all the highlights from the week that they would want to tell Bernardine when they saw her in a few minutes, so they would have news about their day-to-day lives fresh in their minds. BJ also wanted to distract them from the inevitable tantrums going on around them—no bottles, diapers, or toys were allowed, and kids were hungry, thirsty, wet, or just crumbling under the stress of separation and waiting.

When they finally got to the visiting room, a bare, square space with metal chairs up against the wall, there was another wait. BJ initiated a ritual that became the indispensable start to every visit: the kids hid under the chairs or behind BJ or in back of the opening door, and when Bernardine walked in and asked, "Where's Malik?" he would pop out and leap into her arms. BJ got the idea for this when she was first figuring out how to do these visits as well and as stress-free as possible, and she read in *We Are Your Sons* that the Rosenberg kids had initiated the same game. "Children have no control over being separated from a parent," she said. "And just this tiny thing, hiding, gives them a little agency about when they see them again." A lot of other kids began to do the same thing.

Good-byes were always tough, but here too BJ developed a custom that the kids looked forward to—they walked to a far corner on Park Row and looked high up to the women's floor. Bernardine would blink the lights off and on in her cell, and they would wave wildly and blow monster kisses. She would blink some more, and then it was over.

Bernardine, Kathy, and David were all learning together how to be with their kids in these terrible circumstances, and in time Kathy became the most creative and wisest person I'd ever known around practical ways to parent from a distance—applicable to hospitalization and divorce, forced migration and military deployment, but in our cases, applied to the separation of prison. She became more and more honest with Chesa about what had happened and her own responsibility, but always following his lead on how far to go and what territory to enter. She was unstinting and unambivalent in communicating to him her support for us as his other parents, and she took a lot of time and spent enormous energy working on art and story projects that would last over time and could be done by phone or mail as well as up close and personal. She was a mentor to us all.

Bernardine wrote long, intricate chapter books for each of the kids, soliciting advice and counsel from them on the phone about the direction of the next week's installment. She created a growing catalog of riddles and knock-knock jokes for Malik, and made a crossword puzzle every week for Zayd based on a theme of his choice: favorite foods or best fruit, Central Park and dogs, baseball, and mommies coming home.

I made an appointment to see Viola Bernard, a renowned New York psychiatrist and a leader of the orthopsychiatry movement, who for decades had been an outspoken champion of humanistic approaches to therapy, racial justice, and mental health reform. Viola was in her eighties and had become a friend. I told her I was losing it and needed to talk to someone—perhaps she could refer me to a colleague. We met after dinner in her cluttered and overstuffed office on the Upper East Side—I ran into Woody Allen in the elevator on my way up—and I settled into a huge leather chair with a warm cup of tea and a little plate of cookies. "I'm depressed," I began, and we talked for over two hours about the kids and Bernardine, the Boudins and Kathy and David, work and prison visits, fear and loneliness, exhaustion and apprehension. At the end of our time she reached across from her chair and took my hand. "Bill," she said warmly, "you're rarely sad or even upset, but now your life is pretty terrible; you have these appalling burdens to bear and an awful lot to be sad about. But sadness is not the same as depression. You don't need a therapist, Bill. You need to get your wife out of prison."

I felt much better.

A few months in, my senses badly battered and beaten down, Bernardine asked me to marry her. I was shocked—she'd been the most vocal opponent of state-sanctioned marriage I'd ever met. Of course, I agreed. She was locked up, seemingly forever, and what could *I* say— where are your principles, Darling? Her rationale was that if she were indicted or if I were to be subpoenaed, this might offer a thin layer of protection. Far-fetched, perhaps, but being behind bars hurts and messes with your mind. Goettel granted permission, and while Bernardine was interviewed by the prison priest, minister, and rabbi, and approved, I ran around to get the official papers. At the last minute, the judge granted a two-day furlough. We were married on Central Park West in the home of Judge Elliott Wilk and Betty Levinson, two cherished friends from the Lawyer's Guild. A dozen other friends bore witness, and Brother Kirk of the SNCC Freedom Singers brought the beat.

Lots and lots and lots of lawyers had gone in to see Bernardine in the MCC—friends, colleagues, associates, students, even judges. One crazy visitor was Don Reuben, a high-powered attorney from Chicago and as unpleasant a person as I'd ever met. "I like your father," he told me on the phone, "and I feel bad that he's suffering." He'd be in New York in a few days, he told me, and he had a plan to get Bernardine released that he wanted to discuss with me.

We met for an outrageously expensive upscale dinner at the Quilted Giraffe, a restaurant whose owner-chef coincidentally had graduated from law school with Bernardine—Don's treat. "I know Bernardine won't talk to the grand jury. I get that," he said when we sat down. "So I'll get her released to my custody." Goettel had been Reuben's college roommate, and Don was a cocksure SOB. "I'll put her on a lie detector, ask her the same questions, and then *I'll* testify."

"That's it? That's the plan? It'll never happen," I said. "It entirely undercuts the principle she's stated a thousand times and so she'll never agree. Plus, it will never work; and it strikes me as rather stupid."

"So you're a lawyer?" he said. "You know more than I do? Do you tell your surgeon where to make an incision?"

Actually, yes, sort of, and I reserved my deepest skepticism for every kind of expert, but I spared Don the details.

He went to see Bernardine the next day with Judge Harold Tyler, a colleague of his with an independent and ethical streak, now retired from the federal bench and returned to big firm practice. She listened politely, then explained to them that she could not go along with their scheme because it would violate her values and beliefs, that it was clever but unprincipled, and that if she did it, it would undercut her entire stance. Reuben told me on the phone later that day that we were idiots who deserved whatever pain was coming our way, and left New York steaming.

The Kennedys had a brainstorm then that lit us all up: we would set about collecting affidavits from everyone—especially all the lawyers, even Reuben and Tyler—who had visited Bernardine, each one saying whatever the hell they wanted to say as long as they made a single point clearly, simply, and forcefully: having met her in lockup, and having discussed her thinking and the issues with her fully, it was abundantly clear that Bernardine Dohrn would not talk to the grand jury under any circumstances, period. She was completely defiant and would remain silent, and the feds could lock her in a dungeon for five or ten or twenty years and it would make no practical difference—her testimony would never, ever be compelled. If everyone made that particular point, Michael Kennedy would pile them all up and provide the conclusion: keeping her behind bars no longer served the purpose of compelling her to talk; it had become a punishment for her silence. And he'd try to sell it to the judge, while the rest of us crossed our fingers.

We went before Goettel after having submitted the collected bushel of affidavits. "Most of these are from ACLU types," the judge began, making the common mistake of painting anyone to the left of Ronald Reagan with a broad brush and then affixing a convenient if inaccurate label. In fact, some were indeed ACLU attorneys, but most were members of the National Lawyers Guild or her law school classmates from the University of Chicago. "But I see here that Don Reuben of Chicago and Judge Harold Tyler have also seen fit to sign an affidavit." He proceeded to read one weird and, to us, highly entertaining sentence from Reuben: "Bernardine Dohrn suffers a kind of martyr complex, fancies herself a modern-day Joan of Arc, and will therefore never talk, preferring prison in the service of some delusional principle." I was interested that Reuben, so insistent at our dinner of the importance of professional expertise when it came to the law, now fancied himself a psychiatrist as well as a lawyer, but never mind.

Goettel asked the prosecutor for a comment, and the prosecutor dismissed the affidavits as political propaganda and meaningless before the law. Goettel then noted that the government had been seeking handwriting samples from Ms. Dohrn, which she had, of course, refused to provide, and yet he, the judge, had routinely received written letters and petitions that she had submitted to the court—describing the unjust handling of the women prisoners there, the fire danger, and arbitrary treatment by guards—and that he had always forwarded them to the prosecutor. "What about those letters?" he asked the prosecutors. "Are you still in need of her handwriting?" Apparently unaware that the judge had fresh copies of her handwriting, the prosecutor stumbled momentarily but recovered to argue nonetheless that they wanted her to write specific words and statements that would not be contained in the petitions, were they able to locate them. Michael Kennedy leapt in: "Specific words and statements? How about 'I'm guilty'?" Goettel gave the prosecutors one week to find and analyze the handwriting, and at the next court hearing, released her on the spot. The strategy had worked. The judge was convinced that her testimony could not be compelled, and the law was clear that short of that, he must let her go.

I raced uptown and rounded up the kids, and then raced back down to meet Bernardine coming out the door. Ecstasy! We all waltzed and pirouetted and rock-and-rolled to Eleanora's favorite family-style spot in Little Italy, just a couple blocks from the MCC. Michael bought bottles of champagne and sparkling apple juice along the way, and we piled into a huge booth in the back and celebrated with heaping platters of homemade lasagna, pasta puttanesca, penne primavera, fettuccini Alfredo, and warm bread fresh from the oven slathered with extra virgin olive oil, mashed garlic, and diced peppers—Italian peanut butter, Eleanora told the kids. When the Italian ices were ordered—peach for Chesa, lemon for Malik, and very berry for Zayd—I headed to the men's room.

Frankie, the owner, who'd introduced himself when we arrived, stopped me in the wood-paneled hallway. "Yo," he said, our eyes level, his face close to mine. "What's the celebration?" His salt-and-pepper hair was slicked back, his body broad and muscled, and he had no neck. It was an uncomfortably narrow hallway. But his tone was curious and friendly, not the least bit menacing, as if he wanted some reason to join in and share the collective joy. I hesitated, wanting to avoid Brinks, the Black Liberation Army, and the Weather Underground just now, swallowed hard, and settled on an abbreviated version of the truth. "My wife just got out of prison," I said. "Federal lockup."

"No shit!" he said, his eyes bulged as his voice lowered to conspiracy-level. "That lovely lady over there?" He cocked his head toward Bernardine, covered with kids. "Yes, that's her," I said. "What was she in for?" he asked, wrinkling his brow, curious and quite friendly still, and then, apologetically, "that is, if you don't mind my asking."

I swallowed hard once more and plunged on but still in short form, avoiding the content of the case. "She refused to talk to a federal grand jury," I said. "She refused to cooperate."

"No shit!" he repeated emphatically, astonishment mixed with awe. The content seemed to matter not a whit to him. "No shit!" His voice rising in admiration, he added, "Beautiful! Good for her! She's a real stand-up chick!"

"Yes, she is," I said.

And Frankie picked up the check.

There was no accessible mass movement sweeping us forward and illuminating our demands for peace and justice at that moment, no unifying focus, nor any widespread, palpable sense that if we could just muster ourselves up and storm the heavens, another world was in fact within our reach. But Bernardine and I agreed with our old friend Myles Horton, who'd always said that in every social movement there were bound to be valley times as well as mountain times. During mountain times, the popular struggle is visible, explosive, and the momentum of the movement creates a range of spaces to enter and to participate; the challenge of the slower and seemingly silent valley times is to prepare for the inevitable propulsive upheavals to come—and they *will* come, they surely will come.

But those were valley times, and we dug in.

Our political outlook was what it always had been: still opposed to imperialism and its evil twin, white supremacy; still believing that capitalism had exhausted itself and was in its dying moment and most dangerous zombie stage; still certain that the political class was corrupt and without a single answer to the gathering crises. All of that combined with a strong reserve of romance and idealism—not the dreamy sort, but an idealism edged with pain and urgency; not a barricaded retreat, but a living sense that there are ideals worth striving for in this wicked, wounded world. I was still hopeful for a freer and more peaceful future, a world more joyful and just than the one we'd inherited. We were also now a lot more agnostic about how to get there, and because we were unsure, Bernardine and I divided up our forces and attended every demonstration, every meeting, and every conference of the Left. You take the kids on Saturday and I'll go to the organizing meeting, or I'll take the kids to their swimming lessons and you go to the conference, or let's pack a picnic and take the kids to the rally in Washington Square Park. And so it went, day by day.

One day I stood right outside the front gates of Stateville Correctional Center as the State of Illinois willfully murdered John Wayne Gacy Jr. I'd come to witness and protest the execution.

John Wayne Gacy Jr. had been projected onto our collective screens as a monster of mythic proportions, and at the time of his state-sanctioned murder was the reigning poster boy for the wisdom of the death penalty in Illinois. Serial killer, violent rapist, sociopath, fiendish slayer of at least thirty-three teenage boys and young men over the period of a decade, Gacy had buried twenty-six of his victims in the crawl space of his home and discarded the remains of his last four known victims in a nearby river. He had run his own construction business in suburban Chicago and dressed up as an affable clown he called Pogo to perform at charitable events and children's parties. He was a lurid nightmare come to life, so when the ogre was finally trapped and condemned, the cheering crowd, led by the media and the political class, was unrestrained.

Bernardine and I didn't join the mob; we'd been instinctive abolitionists forever and the identity of the perpetrator/victim changed nothing for us. The death penalty was legal, it's true, and also intentional, deliberate, calculated, and considered—planned, premeditated, and purposeful—all of which made the killing that much more barbaric and inexcusable. It was well known that public hangings did nothing to prevent the acts of a psychopath or the murderous outbursts of spontaneous passion. The bad guy—in this case, the monster—was already captured and caged; no more harm was anticipated or possible, so the authorized execution merely added to the coarseness and cruelty of our already violent culture. The elaborate machinery of death, finally, served only one purpose: it fed our repulsive penchant for vengeance. It was morally indefensible.

We were sickened for days by the gleeful anticipation of Gacy's appointment with death beaming through our radio, and when the day finally arrived, Bernardine and I looked at each other and quickly agreed that one of us had to go down that night to bear witness and stand in opposition.

After the kids were asleep, we made a cardboard sign—"Thou Shalt Not Kill"—and drew straws. I won, and Bernardine sent me off to Stateville without a plan or any idea what to expect.

As I drew close to the prison, traffic on the two-lane highway thickened and then clogged up, so I pulled onto the shoulder and parked in the middle of a tangle of cars and pick-up trucks. I joined the crowds surging toward the prison as rock music blared from boom boxes: "Pray," "I'm Too Sexy," and "Hold On." There was beer and marijuana everywhere, and young people carried homemade signs and stretched painted banners from trees to trucks: *No tears for the clown*, said one. *Who's laughing now?* said another. I kept my little counter-sign folded under my vest as I made my way for over a mile toward the front gates, the party intensifying and the chanting increasing with every step: *Burn, baby, burn! Burn, baby, burn!*

When I finally arrived, my natural crew was easy to spot: nine elderly nuns with candles standing in a circle singing "We Are a Gentle,
Loving People." Two lawyers were there as well: Larry Marshall, a colleague of Bernardine's at Northwestern School of Law, and Michelle
Oberman, a brilliant feminist legal scholar teaching at DePaul. I pulled
out my sign and was welcomed into the round as I joined the singing.

I'd felt marginal and lonely and practically invisible in my dissent before, but this was as severe an instance as I could remember: thousands of
people rallying in support of a popular court decision and the mandated
action of the state, and perhaps a dozen of us standing up to say NO!

Sometime after midnight, Gacy's death was announced. A massive
cheer went up as the nuns kneeled to pray. I said good-bye and headed
for home. There'd been no calculus of success in my presence nor in
the presence of the other protestors. There was no expectation of victory that had drawn any of us to that place on that night—Gacy would
die, some sick bloodlust would be served, the mechanics of criminal
injustice would grind forward, and we would return home and resume
our lives.

And yet . . . even though lawmakers wouldn't know we'd been there,
even though the general population might not notice, and even though
the death penalty would go on and on forever, it seemed, being there
was somehow essential. I knew who I was then, I knew where I stood.
I knew that in a society that legalized murder, I'd refused to go along.

I drove home feeling sad but honorable.

And within a few months, a miracle: Larry Marshall won the first
wrongful conviction action for a Death Row inmate and the floodgates
opened. Activists like Alice Kim united with parents of inmates and
began to organize a movement, journalists from the *Chicago Tribune*
and Northwestern's journalism school took up the serious task of in-
vestigating and shining a light into that darkness, and Larry and his
colleagues began to win case after case. Soon the die was cast, and our
corrupt and mildly right-wing governor became an abolitionist and
emptied Death Row. But none of that was on the table as we stood in a
circle of candles, singing softly against the storm.

FOUR

Fugitive Days/Fugitive Nights

When I published *Fugitive Days*, my memoir of the wretched years of the American war in Viet Nam and the sparkling resistance that blossomed in response, it felt like all hell broke loose. I woke up before dawn on September 11, 2001, the official publication date, in Ann Arbor, Michigan, the second stop on a scheduled thirty-five-city book tour. I'd begun the journey the night before in East Lansing with an overflow crowd at a spirited independent bookstore. The book had been generously endorsed by Studs Terkel, Edward Said, Rosellen Brown, Scott Turow, and Tom Frank, who told me with a wink, "If the New York *Times* gives it a positive review, we can't be friends anymore." The first reviews were already in—delightfully, amazingly positive. Zayd, now an artist and playwright beginning his career, had warned me to ignore the reviews, and never, ever try to analyze them. "If they're positive, just figure someone liked your book for whatever reason," he cautioned. "If they're negative, someone didn't like it so much. Those are the only two choices, and everything else is autobiography—don't get into motives, don't try to explain or defend, just move on and write your next book." I remembered a story about the actor Kirk Douglas working in mid-career with the older, renowned Sir John Gielgud and telling the old man that he'd gotten to the point in his career where the criticism no longer devastated him. Gielgud replied, "You're almost there; now don't let the praise seduce you." Good advice, no doubt, but those first reviews felt wonderfully seductive, and so I read each one twice.

Hunter S. Thompson had offered his endorsement months earlier in a tightly packed, handwritten love letter and screed with long rants and plenty of ellipses as well as unforgettable HST phrases like "More chilling than being held hostage in a Mexican whorehouse" and "an orgy of enthusiasms, and a dangerous invitation to a CIA-hit." His letter ended on a positive note: "Tell Ayers to stop by if he's ever in the neighborhood—he can bring the heavy stuff; I've got the firearms." He was kidding, I think, but a few months later I did stop by—without anything volatile—to meet the legend. I'm still recovering from an evening in his fun house.

But the book was generating a lot of hopeful buzz for my publisher right then: the *New York Times* would review it for sure and run a feature in its Arts section. The *Chicago Tribune* would run a front page review and a cover story in its weekend magazine. I'd be a featured writer at the Chicago Public Library, the Chicago Humanities Festival, the South Carolina Humanities Festival, and the Los Angeles Public Library, among others. And I was scheduled to be interviewed by Scott Simon, Terry Gross, Tavis Smiley, and Bob Edwards. The paperback rights had been sold to Penguin a few days earlier, Steppenwolf was talking about film rights, and, based on early sales figures, the book was already scheduled for a second printing. The evening in East Lansing was pulsing with good energy. Up, up, and away.

I bought the *Times* around 6:00 a.m. and headed over to a campus coffee shop. I opened the paper, and there on the front page of the Arts section was a big picture of Bernardine and me sitting on our front steps in Hyde Park—she looked elegant as always, and I, well, I looked as usual like her porter or her driver, and damned lucky to be there at that. The article was by Dinitia Smith, who had interviewed each of us extensively, and had even come to our home and met our roommates, Dorothy Dohrn, Bernardine's mom, and Florence Garcia, her steady caregiver. I liked Smith even though she repeatedly referred to Florence as our "housekeeper" and showed decidedly less interest in the people in the house than in the house itself: "The ceilings are so high," she remarked several times. "Yes, they are; it's not Manhattan, you know." "You certainly don't live like Weathermen," she said. I wondered what Weathermen lived like. The reporter who interviewed me from *Chicago* magazine had told me that I didn't "look anything like a *real* Weatherman." I asked her what a real Weatherman looked like, and we laughed together. She reported that, for Weathermen, Bernardine and I had raised three remarkable young men, though I was unsure what parenting skills and dispositions distinguished the Weatherparents from anyone else. The title of the *Times* piece was pretty dopey: "No Regrets for a Love of Explosives." "No Regrets" had been the headline of the *Chicago* article about the book the week before, and Smith had stayed in the home of the *Chicago* writer and editor on her overnight to interview us—they had high ceilings too, she told me.

The article seemed OK to me, but when I called Bernardine an hour later, she didn't think it was OK at all. "The headline is not *dopey*; it's *disturbing*," she said. She read aloud a single sentence: "Even today, he finds 'a certain eloquence to bombs, a poetry and a pattern from a safe distance,' he writes." This supports the "love affair with bombs" thesis, Bernardine pointed out, but "it's completely dishonest—you don't write that *you* find any eloquence in bombs." True: I'd written that the American war-makers—the cozy corps of Dr. Strangeloves and Brigadier General Jack D. Rippers—seemed to hear a joyful noise while bombing villages from forty thousand feet, and that that was perverse and disgusting. But no matter—let people read the book and see for themselves, I said.

It was all a little silly and forgettable, mildly irritating, and sure to quickly fade away. I was wrong, of course, for the known world was about to blow up, and *love of explosives* and *no regrets* would be infused with fresh meaning and new urgency.

I returned to my reading and my coffee, but the background buzz in the coffee shop escalated suddenly, and the place got noisy. I looked up as everyone crowded around a man at a table in the center who was pointing at his computer screen and shouting, "It's not a film . . . this is real, and it's happening right now!"

Everything suddenly cracked open, brittle or broken, and frighteningly out of balance. We were already living in a post-Holocaust, post-Hiroshima, post–Viet Nam world, and we'd taken the measure of mass terror perpetrated on innocents more than once before. But what was this? In those early hours and first days, no one knew for sure. The images played over and over—an airliner slicing into the tall building, smoke, disbelief, the second airliner going at full speed into the smoking tower, bodies tumbling to the ground, the two massive towers collapsing in slow motion as thousands of people fled. It was incomprehensible, horrifying, and sickening, and eventually numbing. Bits of information emerged every hour; the air vibrated with rumors and speculation and theory. But no one knew what had happened, or what was to come.

At the reading in East Lansing the night before I'd joked about American politicians and their media allies sweating and fretting in public about how threatened we were ("Security precautions for the Super Bowl are elaborate and more costly than ever!"), while the US military scorched the earth and US power menaced the world. It was generally true, but suddenly, weirdly miscalibrated in the dawn's early light.

"Come home," Bernardine said when I reached her an hour later. She had talked to Zayd, who was studying in Boston, and to Chesa, who was in school in Santiago, Chile, and demonstrating on the anniversary of the US-sponsored coup and assassination of Salvador Allende. She was with Malik, whose flight back to California and college that morning had taxied out and then returned to the gate, grounded.

"I can't come home yet," I said. "I've got this event tonight."

"Cancel it," she said.

I walked over to Shaman Drum, where I was set to read that night, and sat with the bookstore staff in a troubled knot watching the coverage on a laptop for several hours. Should we cancel the reading? I called my publisher and editor, and she agreed with me and most of the folks gathered at the store: people need a place to gather, a place to talk no matter what. "Go on with it," she advised.

Bernardine weighed in on the other side: "Come home! Come home!" she repeated.

I wobbled, unsure, and asked if Major League Baseball had canceled games. By midafternoon, baseball shut down, and so did Shaman Drum. "We'll sort things out from here," Bernardine assured me. No planes were flying, the whole book tour was put on hold, and I reluctantly drove back to Chicago, the sound track of all-news radio accompanying me on my solitary slog, hyperventilating and speculating, deeply disoriented and confused, uninformed and struggling to catch balance. In those early hours, we were all feeling a huge hole blown through our collective consciousness, but the rupture presented such an unruly range of dimensions that no one peering uneasily into that smoldering crack saw exactly the same things. It was a tumultuous but desolate drive.

I dissolved when I saw Bernardine—exhausted and relieved—and I held onto her for a long time, weeping—so much unrecoverable loss and so much unnecessary pain. But I was home at last.

Mona Khalidi called right away, insisting that we come for dinner, and of course we would, we must. On this night of all nights, I thought, people would be reaching out to friends and family to touch and talk, to try to make sense, yes, but mostly to find some solace and salvation in our simple connectedness—the preciousness of one another, the sanctity of modest gestures, and the vastness of small affections. The world was in flames, the West was burning and the oceans rising, but we would not so easily collapse into the conflagration, and so we gathered ourselves.

We'd met Mona and Rashid Khalidi by chance years earlier, just before we moved from New York. They had three kids the same ages as our three, and their babysitter happened to be one of my students. When the babysitter introduced us, she was certain that Bernardine and I would hit it off with the Khalidis. "Same relaxed approach to raising your kids," she'd told me, "same crazy politics, same everything." When a few weeks later and within days of each other, our two families rambled to Chicago from the Upper West Side of Manhattan, she was sure it was destiny, a match made in heaven. "Karma!" she said happily as she waved good-bye. "You guys will love each other."

She was right. We lived only a few blocks apart in Hyde Park, and now we began regularly looking after one another's kids after school and going to the beach or the movies together on weekends. Bernardine proposed having dinner once a week at each other's houses, but soon we were having dinners on alternate nights at one or the other of our homes, and it grew into a new big blended family tradition—dinner four or five times a week at seven o'clock for at least ten people, and often fourteen or sixteen or more, as one or another kid brought along a classmate or we invited friends and colleagues and elderly parents or folks visiting from out of town or one of the many Khalidi "cousins," an indistinct but vast and expansive collection of relatives just passing through. "The diaspora is far-flung," Rashid would note with a wink whenever a "cousin" was en route, "and Samer is the second cousin of my great-aunt's brother-in-law." "It's well known," he would continue, "that we Semites—and not exclusively the wandering Jews—are tribal and nomadic peoples, drifting here and there in search of our land." He would then pull out a series of maps in order to trace Samer, for example, from UCLA back through Detroit to Lebanon and Jerusalem, and the high desert beyond.

Mona, wooden spoon in hand, pot bubbling on the stove in the background, stood at the center of the shimmering multitude—organizer and scheduler, comrade and companion, advisor, critic, agitator, busybody, provocateur, reporter, newsmonger, nudge, nag, fixer, Arabic coach, cheerleader, librarian, yenta, lover, healer, nurse, community psychologist, schemer, social worker, earth mother, and cook. She was elfin, but there was nothing diminutive about her presence—she had a huge heart, a colossal spirit, a big brain, and a supersized opinion about everything. Something was always cooking at Mona's because food was not only nourishment, it was also love and therapy, rehab and remedy, the perfect medium for problem solving or political discourse, homework help or healing. Feeding people was Mona's default position, no matter what, and so whether things were fast-paced or slow, happy or sad, urgent or relaxed, she insisted that whatever else was on your agenda, you had to eat, so stop by "just for a bite." Once ensnared, you didn't dare refuse a second helping for fear of unleashing the ferocious Semitic inner mother lurking in the centuries-old well of accumulated cultural memory: "What, it's not good enough? You don't like my food, or you don't like me? Which?" Still, hers was the lap every wounded child desired, the ear every troubled teen sought out, the essential table for serious conversation.

Our communal kitchen quickly took on the tone and spirit of a lively and eclectic salon—we designated the Khalidi kitchen Club-K, and our house B and B's American Café. Over time, it felt that we were feeding the wide, wide world, one memorable dinner at a time, our very own movable feast. One night a few regulars joined a coincidence of visitors, and the extraordinary scene led Mona to suspend a standard rule. Edward Said, the literary scholar and Palestinian rights activist, had been staying with the Khalidis, and Jaqui and Homi Bhabha, colleagues at the University of Chicago, had come for dinner with their kids; Edward called his friend Daniel Barenboim, maestro of the Chicago Symphony Orchestra, who then called Zubin Mehta of the Los Angeles Philharmonic, who was in town for the day, and each brought partners and special friends. Brandy flowed, Turkish pastries and tangerines were consumed, and when Daniel said, "Mona, would it be all right if I had a cigar?" she didn't hesitate: "Of course, Daniel, please." All the regulars were shocked—Mona in the thrall of the maestro had become a pushover. Everyone lit a cigar, and we sat around the table blowing smoke toward the ceiling.

On September 11, Mona served her signature tabouli with its surprising amounts of mint, finely chopped green onions, and gallons of olive oil and lemon juice, chicken with yoghurt (and about four heads of smushed garlic and a dusting of sumac) over white rice, and Khubz Arabi (what Americans call *pita*), but the table was unusually somber and subdued. Sim Sim, the last of our collective six kids, had left to begin college three weeks earlier, and it was just the four of us together, with Malik quickly off to see his local friends, and of course everything was in a muddle. No one had much of an appetite for dinner that night.

Everything but Mona's food felt bizarre, beyond reason or logic, murky and clouded with wild reports of armed men on the Washington Mall and warships in New York harbor. The constantly ringing phone—kids checking and rechecking in, friends and colleagues calling from New York, London, Cairo, Jerusalem, and Los Angeles to share information or to speculate about what the hell had just happened—added to the turbulence. All we knew for sure that night was that four passenger planes had been hijacked: two had flown into the

World Trade Center towers in New York—the sickening images captured on film and playing over and over—one had hit the Pentagon, and one went down in a field in Pennsylvania. We were groping in the dark, all of us, across the country and the world, but we couldn't help wondering: what would come next? Retaliation and revenge were in the air, but what shape would they take? What forms of violence loomed ahead? Was a huge war inevitable? Who might the United States strike now? And who later on?

Our conversation ricocheted rapidly around the room, moving from the well-being of our kids to politics and global power, our work, the fragile condition of our parents, the craziness of a story about Bernardine and me being featured in the *Times* on this day of all possible days, my shattered *Fugitive Days* book launch, and back to our kids. "I worry most about Sim Sim," Mona said. "He's been away only a couple of weeks, and he can't have many friends yet. This must be hard for him no matter what he says." Bernardine was relieved that Malik's plane hadn't got off the ground that morning. We agreed that in a day or two, depending on what unforeseen events popped into view, the four of us would drive to Macalester College in Minneapolis to spend a day with Sim Sim. I was so happy right then to have one another and to be here together, and to have a plan to do something, anything concrete. We would eat, and we would drive. Good enough.

Shortly after 8:00 p.m., the doorbell rang. It was Adele Simmons, the president of the MacArthur Foundation and an occasional member of the communal kitchen, who'd driven from Lincoln Park to check in with Mona and Rashid. "I've been worrying about you all day," she said. "Who knows what's coming next, but there's already a whiff of anti-Arab sentiment in the air. I want to help." Just as most liberals were poised to duck, cover, and disappear, coming to Mona and Rashid's side was the sweetest and savviest thing she could have done, and so very typical of her.

I got an anonymous phone call at home after midnight: "Do you support the bombing of the World Trade Center?" a man's voice asked angrily. I was astonished. "It was a monstrous crime," I said, and added that I wished he would, whoever he was, call me at my office during the daytime. He replied in a suddenly subdued tone, "OK, thanks."

The *New York Times* piece with its off-kilter headline was on newsstands and porches around the country as the buildings fell, and through that bizarre coincidence of timing I became linked in the minds of some to the overwhelming event itself. The calls and e-mails, letters and messages, threats and warnings escalated wildly over the next several days, and I was accused of being one of the evil ones, a mass murderer, and a terrorist. One e-mail said, "I admire your tactics, and I plan to show you exactly how much." Another said simply, "Hide . . ." Bernardine was often mentioned and singled out for threats of sexual violence—vile, vivid, disgusting stuff. "Screw you, cunt!" and "Fuck you and die, Bitch" were pretty typical.

The hate mail rolled in:

Are you an American?

You get rich spewing hatred of America, and then live the high life which for you is obviously the whole point.

You're a traitor and a terrorist in spite of your accomplishments and good qualities.

You should be shot for treason.

Go live in Russia.

You should be jailed and hanged for using your American freedom to undermine that freedom, and then you will rot in hell you filthy bitch.

My eighty-six-year-old dad got anonymous calls, too, from men who berated him for raising me. "I just listen calmly," he told me later, "and when they run out of steam I say, 'You're wrong,' and I hang up on them." Good old Dad—I felt rotten that he had to go through all this. Florence—such a lovely person, and caring for Bernardine's mother, Dorothy, so creatively—left meticulous messages on the little island in our kitchen: "Bill, Someone called at 8:40 and told me you are a murderer and deserve to die, but he didn't leave a name or a number. Love, Florence." No name or number? How can I call him back to thank him? And what did poor Florence make of this entire tumult and hullabaloo? I felt terrible for her, too.

An editor from *Newsday* called to ask if I could write an op-ed about terrorism. "Why me?" I asked. "You know, just write something about terrorism." No thanks. Then a Chicago paper wanted me to do a story about life underground. Nope. Before long I was besieged by reporters and editors wanting my take on Al Qaeda, on the psychology of fanaticism, on wanton violence. I declined every one. I don't have any particular insight or information about that, I explained.

History was shuddering in front of our eyes, pain and suffering falling from the sky and etched into the landscape, US military power thrashing wildly out of control. The pettiness of my personal challenge was fully illuminated, the fate of my little book—which had been my focus and my obsession on September 10—suddenly and definitively overshadowed by the fate of the earth. Thousands of people were dead; rumors of war were in the air; troops were mustering, battleships and warplanes converging; US flags were rolling out of the mills in record numbers. The absurdity of launching a book tour at that moment added to the surreal shroud that enveloped me.

Yalah! Let's go!

We hurried into the car, reluctantly dropped Malik back at the airport where he would return to college and his eclectic cohort, happy no doubt to be away from our stifling obsession with the news, turned north, and jetted toward Minneapolis for one night just to have a quick sighting of Sim Sim, to take him out to dinner and then breakfast, and to hang out together on a road trip. I brought all the newspapers I could gather, Bernardine and Rashid brought books mainly, and Mona schlepped the food—olives, cheeses, tangerines, and Khubz Arabi for the road, a massive emergency Palestinian care package of *manaeesh*, lemony lentils, white rice with olive oil and small broken strips of sautéed vermicelli, olives, cheeses, *ful muddamas*, *labneh*, and *mouloukhiyeh* for "poor Sim Sim."

Labneh is thickened yoghurt strained in a paper towel overnight, and *ful* are simply fava beans, cooked and mashed with lemon, garlic, and olive oil; *mouloukhiyeh*, or "green slime," as Zayd called it at first sight years before because of its deep forest-green color and wondrously thick and saucy texture, is a vegetable "you find only on Sixty-third Street from the nice Arab grocer"; and *manaeesh* is a flat and flaky biscuit slathered with olive oil and sprinkled heavily with *zaatar*, a seasoning similarly available "only from the nice Arab." Mona's magic got a special lift from Sixty-third Street.

"Sim Sim can find olives and rice in Minneapolis," Rashid ventured.

"Not these olives," Mona shot back.

We roared out of Chicago on the interstate beyond the airport and on past Madison, the Dells, and the rolling Kettle Moraine, past Eau Claire and the green trees just starting to flame yellow and red as we raced into the land of ten thousand lakes toward the frozen North Country. Rashid was behind the wheel—a demon driver, focused, attentive, and under control but with a heavy foot on the accelerator going fast-fast-fast—talking a mile a minute, zooming toward his son.

All of us were raw and roiling emotionally, struggling to make sense of all that was unfolding and upon us, looking uneasily at what lay ahead. I was miserable, of course, but everyone was miserable in his or her own way. My misery was miniscule. The fate of *Fugitive Days* seemed sealed—there was a long article in *Publishers Weekly*, I think, about several books, including mine, that had had the misfortune of being born into the chaos, a time when the only book that was selling was the Holy Qur'an and no one was reading anyway, everyone, including us, mostly staring at TV screens. And every review of my book post-9/11 echoed a theme from the *New York Times*: whatever virtues the book might have had, in the aftermath of the terrorist attacks that killed thousands of people in Lower Manhattan and at the Pentagon, the Weather Underground actions are impossible to forgive. The connection seemed sketchy to me at best, but it stuck. Anyway, it was just a damn book, and on the scale of suffering all around, hardly a blip. I struggled to move on.

Sim Sim was OK, but we were all super happy to see him in the flesh and pleased we'd made the trip. We rounded up his roommate and another new friend and took them all out to dinner at Babani's, a family-style Kurdish place. A large homemade sign with a hand-drawn American flag was taped up on the front door of the restaurant: "We are Americans," it read, practically pleading. Inside were empty tables mostly, and the Babanis, a lovely couple in their fifties, jumped up and greeted us with aching enthusiasm, both of them near tears. That, too, was a sign of the times, and also heart-breaking.

The book tour was revamped and restarted; I was determined to make every stop and fulfill every commitment, but it was not to be. The first to cancel was the Chicago Public Library, where I was scheduled to speak in a distinguished author series that included Salman Rushdie and Alice Walker. I was told by a top librarian that Mayor Daley himself had called and told the commissioner that I was not to appear under any conditions in light of the raw feelings and reactions following 9/11. The head of the Chicago Humanities Festival called me directly to tell me my talk there had been canceled as well; American Airlines was a key sponsor, she told me, and while she was embarrassed and apologetic, she had to withdraw my invitation or the airline's funding and sponsorship would cease. I felt wounded. "You have to see the big picture," she said. I replied that I thought she had a sacred responsibility to the humanities—not to me—to resist the bullying and to call American Airlines on it. "There's a picture even bigger than the big picture you have in mind," I said, and she said, "I understand how you feel, and I'm sorry, but my hands are really tied on this."

When the skies opened up I was on the first (United!) flight out of Chicago to the West Coast. Everyone was still a little jumpy and tentative, the airport itself eerily empty. The pilot strolled the aisle and spoke to every passenger, reassuring us, thanking us for flying, and repeating "God bless America" over and over.

I made my way from Seattle down the coast to LA, back to the Midwest, and then to New York, Boston, Washington, Atlanta, and many points in between. I spoke at universities, on local radio and television programs, and mainly in independent bookstores.

At a bookstore in Iowa, more than two hundred people crowded into a space that could comfortably hold thirty. I read briefly and took a few questions: Why did you resort to violence? Was it a reckless or a sensible thing to do politically, and was it in any sense the right thing ethically? Was it effective at all? The conversation turned to the events of 9/11, its consequences and implications, the responsibilities we had as citizens and as human beings. An entire class from a local Quaker high school was there, and the event turned into a two-hour teach-in on politics, peace, the world situation, and the limits and prospects of protest—a teach-in led by the kids. What role does the United States play in the world and what should it be? What is the truth of our history, and how do we learn from it and teach it? Is "American exceptionalism" defensible at all? I was merely a witness and a happy participant.

Everyone had seen the vicious attacks at the World Trade Center in vivid color, over and over, less illuminating and more deadening with each viewing. There was a dreadful break in the world—we'd seen it all together, a collective image and a shared experience—but over time it was clear that no one had seen the exact same thing. What did it mean? There was an uncharacteristic openness and curiosity for a moment, and it seemed there was a chance that we would search for real answers, all of us, and that America might seize the opportunity to join humanity: the Netherlands and Spain knew atrocities and attacks on their people, after all, Italy and Great Britain, too, and, of course the whole world from Viet Nam and Sudan and El Salvador—on and on—to South Africa and Indonesia and Afghanistan had all been bombed and hurt. Solidarity beckoned. But powerful voices from Washington were taking up a huge part of the available space, shouting through their expanded megaphones and imposing their own self-important narrative everywhere. This is war, plain and simple, they intoned. We are under siege, and we will invade, occupy, and punish at will. Our pain is entirely unique and unprecedented.

But that fiercely promoted narrative was widely contested and deeply unstable just then. People were clearly eager to gather together, to talk and exchange ideas, to wonder and question in a public space, and just as clearly the sense of urgency was not tied in any way to my book. The book and the event were an excuse to assemble in a public space in order to conduct the business of democracy: dialogue, argument, investigation, exchange. That really moved me, and this became the defining feature for those few months: a voyage into the new and unfinished, a rolling teach-in on politics and the responsibilities of residents fired by an aching desire to meet in a public space, to face one another without masks, and to ask unexpected questions.

In October, when David Schwartz of Harry W. Schwartz Bookshops got a tsunami of calls and letters urging him to cancel my reading in his store, he offered this eloquent defense, the text of which was widely circulated in the publishing world:

> I myself grew up in Wisconsin during the McCarthy era and witnessed firsthand the attack on civil liberties and civic life that crippled America at that time. My father was accused of running a Communist bookshop by many people just because he thought it important to stock and promote books which were unpopular in the political climate of the time. I also was engaged in the movement against the Vietnam War and had some opportunities to view the Weathermen in action. I decided that I was politically and intellectually opposed to their positions on most matters.
>
> Now to the specific issue of whether or not Bill Ayers should be allowed to be one of the twenty-six authors who will visit our shops in October. It seems to me this is what America is about: listening to many freely expressed viewpoints so we can decide for ourselves the truth. America's brilliance and enormous distinction from other democracies is that it truly believes in the democratic process. Letting Bill Ayers speak is a part of that process. I hope customers who disagree with Bill Ayers and his views will attend this book reading so you can question him about his ideas. That's another part of the process.

And in response to a rabid customer who threatened to boycott his store if he permitted me to speak there, Andy Ross, the president of Cody's Books in Berkeley, wrote,

> Cody's has lots of authors with lots of points of view. Frequently they are offensive to one group or another. We have sponsored

events for Noam Chomsky which led us to be accused of being dupes for Saddam Hussein. We also had an event for Zev Chafets who was Menachem Begin's press secretary. We were bombed during the Rushdie Affair. So we are quite sensitive about silencing people's voices.

Which is why, as the event ended that night in Iowa, it occurred to me to ask everyone to please buy a book. "Not my book necessarily," I said, "but please buy any book at all as an act of solidarity and support for this precious little independent bookstore, this uniquely and universally important place that both creates and defends the public square."

Everyone I saw in those raw first days was feeling wounded and aggrieved; everyone in my close circle of friends and family was shaky and unsure, each of us unsettled. At that moment I was never so grateful to be a teacher, because teachers, whatever else and no matter what, show up—simple as that. Confident or confused, off-balance or on, prepared or not, I always knew I had a place in the world to be and an appointed time to be there. The days after 9/11 were no different. I made my wobbly way to class on time to meet my students.

Years earlier when I was supervising teachers in an elementary school on the South Side of Chicago, a fire broke out in the kitchen just before lunch. The school was evacuated, the big trucks came, the firefighters in their distinctive peaked hats, long black coats, and big noisy boots raced into the building hauling their rough equipment as we all watched in excitement, and within an hour the fire was out and everyone was back in class. In the afternoon a few teachers tried mightily—and without much luck—to get back "on task," to return to normal and to the prescribed, planned lessons for the day as if nothing had happened. Most saw the folly in that, since the day could not return to a time before the fire or be made normal in spite of what we all might hope, and many recognized the teachable moment that had so spectacularly presented itself. The kindergarten kids were making pictures and writing stories about the fire and the firefighters, some of which included dramatic rescues on ladders and flames leaping high above the roof—records of meaning-making and fear and imagination way beyond any observable facts on the ground. One third-grade class was writing thank-you notes and generating questions for the firefighters—How did you learn to put out fires? Why did you decide to be a firefighter?—and making plans to deliver them to the firehouse in person. And a group of sixth graders was researching the latest advances in fire safety and fire-fighting equipment and modern techniques for fighting urban fires.

I had no concrete plan for how to proceed with my graduate students on that First Night after the Fire, and all the more reason to focus on meaning-making and soul-searching. We could draw pictures, write stories, conduct research, and ask questions—just like those schoolkids years ago—and we could recognize this as an unprecedented and extravagant teachable moment, and resist, then, any easy answers or any gestures toward self-righteousness or certainty.

I wanted students to examine and interrogate the world as it really was and to look beyond the endless mystification and ideological fog that shaped options and put well-policed limits on our imaginative horizons, to shake off what Bertrand Russell called the pervasive cloud of comforting convictions that moved along with each of us wherever we went like flies on a summer day. But I didn't want the propulsive flash of the newest insight to become its own comfortable and well-lit prison. The burden was always the weight of honesty, and my preferred pedagogical signal mostly dialogue and asking the next question.

We faced the danger of doctrine and the danger of neutrality in the face of profound human catastrophe, the danger of easy belief and the danger of turning away indifferently in the presence of preventable human suffering. I wanted to be a teacher who pursued the unanswered questions and the unresolved stories, a teacher who was agnostic in some areas, skeptical in others, engaged to be sure, but contingent in most things.

When we were all assembled around the seminar table I suggested that we begin by each drawing a freehand sketch of Central Asia. Only Nikki could do it—and with breathtaking speed and accuracy—but it wasn't fair since she was European and European children study geography in school. More specifically, she was Cypriot, from Cyprus, which, she pointed out, is the last divided country as well as the easternmost country in Europe (who knew?), hovering around the Middle East and awfully close to Turkey, which borders Iran, which borders Afghanistan. No American came close—so we asked ourselves a bit uncomfortably, "Where in the world are we?" And then, "Who in the world are we?"

"Good questions," Nikki said in her heavily accented but otherwise perfect English. "Everyone I know loves Americans—not your government so much, but Americans themselves—and everyone also thinks you act sometimes as a spoiled child, whether willfully or innocently unaware of others. You're also famous the world around for being geographically challenged and basically clueless when it comes to history." I was immediately reminded of a great Motown hit from my youth about the power of teenage love to make the world a wonderful place in spite of not knowing much about history and even less geography. Nikki might have added that we were tone-deaf to languages and cultures—the rock song relishes ignorance about French—but she was being restrained, I think. I loved that Motown song as a kid, and felt all warm inside humming it to myself then, but I had to marvel suddenly about an anthem of my adolescence that was also a joyful and hypnotic celebration of know-nothing narcissism.

One of my grandchildren made a recent drawing—two equal-sized amoebas floating near one another on a large piece of white construction paper, one a squiggly blue, and the other a wobbly red. The red one was labeled "America"; the blue one, "I don't know." And so it goes.

I pulled out a couple of world maps from Doctors without Borders that I always carry in my backpack, and we spread them out and gathered around to have a look. Nikki opened her handy map of the whole Mediterranean Sea and showed us her beautiful Cyprus, where, she pointed out, Lazarus died, Saint Peter was flogged and jailed, Shakespeare set *Othello*, and Richard the Lionhearted left his betrothed as he set off to sack the Holy Land. That's a lot, and it turns out there's more. One student dug up an old atlas and a globe in a classroom down the hall for closer study and a different perspective. People had at least heard of Turkey and Iran and Saudi Arabia, but finding them was quite a challenge. And then there were all kinds of new places to discover and marvel at: giant Kazakhstan, medium-sized Uzbekistan, and little Tajikistan. Nikki told us of a study she'd recently read in which a group of eighteen- to twenty-four-year-old Americans were asked to fill in the names of countries on a blank world map: 80 percent couldn't find Israel-Palestine, 80 percent missed Iraq and Iran, 50 percent couldn't recognize Great Britain, and 15 percent could not identify the United States itself. Everyone laughed at that last one because, damn it, we could find the United States, but the laughter became hollow fast when it dawned on us suddenly that anything beyond the United States was pretty much outside our consciousness. Since we were all also teachers, we also realized that buried in that study of young Americans was an indictment of American education and of ourselves—how could we be so blank and so blind?

A couple of years later, I was in Rwanda with Bernardine and her law students at the tenth anniversary of the genocide there. We visited a high school in a refugee camp on a dusty hillside fifty kilometers outside Kigali. When the refugee students learned that we were from Chicago, one fifteen-year-old boy went to his work folder and, smiling broadly, brought Bernardine a colorful painting he'd done of the United States. He pointed to Chicago and said through our translator that he lived on the Great Lakes of central Africa, just as we lived on the Great Lakes of North America. That classroom of the displaced highlighted my own ongoing myopia and abiding ignorance: I didn't know anything about the Great Lakes of Africa.

Nikki happily helped us lift ourselves up as we searched and sorted previously clouded or entirely unexplored features of our environment. She embraced us with humor, bringing us a silly block of cartoons from the *New Yorker* under the heading: "Americans See the World Anew." In one, a person looking slightly baffled says, "I just don't see how they can spell Al Qaeda without a U," and in another two men are striding confidently down a New York avenue as one says cheerfully to the other, "I just love the sound of it—Jalalabad, Jalalabad." Seeing the world anew has its limits, of course.

. . .

The attacks of September 11 were—no doubt about it—pure terrorism, indiscriminate slaughter, crimes against humanity carried out by
reactionary thugs with fundamentalist fantasies dancing wildly in their
heads. These right-wing zealots, filled with awe and obedience, were
absolutely determined to impose their arid ideology on America and
the world. And in the immediate aftermath Americans experienced, of
course, grief, confusion, compassion, and solidarity, as well as something quite rare: uncharacteristic soul-searching, questioning, and political openness. But not for long.

There was palpable grief and a shared incredulity in all my classes
from the start, and everywhere sudden outbursts of civil-rhetorical
patriotism too: flags and signs proliferated, people lined up at blood
banks, and pilgrimages were organized to "Ground Zero." Given the
pale American palate, reaching for the flag seemed to mean sympathy
and solidarity for most people in those first days.

George Packer, one of my most helpful mentors and teachers from
my days as an MFA student at Bennington College, published a piece in
the *New York Times* called "Recapturing the Flag" in which he claimed
that the terrorist attacks "made it safe for liberals to be patriots." I
wrote and asked him pointedly when it was unsafe (and where was the
threat coming from?) for liberals to be patriots. Where was there any
evidence of *that?* In the piece, he went on to say that the assault "woke
us up to the fact that we are part of a national community" and that
"patriotism has nothing to do with blindly following leaders." I disagreed noisily: Couldn't the attacks have awakened us just as easily to
the fact that we are part of an *international* community? Isn't patriotism typically a space where nationalists manipulate their neighbors
into seeing events or actions like torture and bombing civilians as good
or bad, not on their merits, but exclusively according to who com-
mits them? Wasn't he imposing a kind of imperative patriotism that
demanded mindless conformity?

George is an accomplished writer—his long-form journalism and
personal essays and thick descriptions of people and events have been

widely praised—and I admired his accounts of his work in the Peace Corps and teaching in Togo. Whenever I read a newly published piece by George, I'd send a note or a letter congratulating him, sometimes adding just a word of criticism, and he almost always responded.

His political commentary was a different matter altogether, because no matter the subject, it was always framed by an exacting liberal ideology that could as easily blind him to evidence or actual argument as any other totalizing dogma—"communism," say, or "Freudianism" or "neuroscience." "Recapturing the Flag" was a case in point. George was a leader of the so-called "liberal hawks," a loose collection of New York academics and writers who were social democrats and often identified as "doves" by day, but who could in a burst of patriotic fervor be rather easily enlisted in a nationalistic war effort when the sun went down. The Socialist Party shamefully supported the United States in World War I, and socialists like Michael Harrington and Hendrik Hertzberg had justified the US invasion and occupation of Viet Nam for years because Ho Chi Minh was a "Stalinist," the greater evil.

After the attacks, George proclaimed that the United States was at war, and he feverishly promoted the invasion of Afghanistan. When I said that 9/11 was a crime against humanity and that a crime required a criminal justice response, not a war response, George responded, "Are you saying we should send the Chicago police after Bin Laden, or maybe the Keystone Cops?" I said that a criminal justice reaction might be forced by circumstances to mobilize an army, but that the goal would be to solve a crime and bring a perpetrator to justice, not to occupy a country and overthrow a government. I pointed out what to me seemed obvious: it was always easier to start a war than to end one, and that the "war on terror"—or, as the BBC called it helpfully, "this *so-called* war on terror"—was a metaphorical war: how would anyone know which nations the United States was fighting against or how much was enough, or when the goals were reached? When you unloosed the dogs of war, I said, it was almost impossible to rein them in. Our argumentative correspondence spooled forward for months. "You're either being deceptive or you're delusional and dangerously naïve," he wrote.

During the years of my student activism, George had been a young-ster growing up in Palo Alto. His dad was a dean and then provost at Stanford when students took over the campus there to protest the war; he'd suffered a devastating stroke a few days into the occupation and committed suicide a few years later. The excesses of the radicals and the blood of the liberals were themes etched deeply into George's heart—and who couldn't understand that? As his student, whenever I wrote anything for him that veered toward politics—and most every-thing did—George's red pencil was wielded like a sword, and his mark-ings bled all over the page. He challenged me to rely on evidence, not opinion; on solid argument and not easy belief. I was grateful: George had been a terrific writing teacher for me precisely because he was an ideological (as opposed to a knee-jerk or default or vaguely multi-culti) liberal. His ideas were firm and well-formed, and his political outlook fierce. He was generous and yet tough—I couldn't get away with a thing—and George was exactly the teacher I needed.

I ran into George years after 9/11 at a bookstore in Manhattan, and he had all but forgotten his strident advocacy for the failed in-vasion of Afghanistan. We went out for a beer, and I reminded him that we had corresponded about it for several months and that he had feverishly promoted the invasion of Afghanistan as a moral impera-tive, as well as the price of the ticket for even the cheapest seats in the national community. He'd led a chorus insisting on agreement with the Bush-Cheney team, but war unity proved to be weak and wobbly, as it often does, hobbling along on broken legs and slippery ground, and it didn't last.

"You were proven wrong," I said. "Admit it."

"I don't remember you and I arguing about any of this," he said.

"Memory is a motherfucker," I said, even though my recollections are vast and indelible, and we shared a laugh—being a liberal hawk means never having to say you're sorry.

A headline in the *Onion* got it partly right: "Unsure What to Do, En-tire Country Stares Dumbly at Hands." Actually, Dick Cheney, Donald Rumsfeld, and John Ashcroft knew exactly what to do, and they did it—they reached down to the bottom drawers of their desks, pulled out and dusted off their most ambitious plans and began to hurriedly remake the world to their liking, mobilizing a new and unapologetic American empire, suppressing dissent, bailing out the airlines and transferring $20 billion without safeguards or benchmarks from public to private hands in a matter of days with a single no vote in the Senate, scuttling aspects of the law that checked executive power, and delivering the country, in the words of Arthur Miller in his essay "Are You Now Or Were You Ever?," "into the hands of the radical right, a ministry of free-floating apprehension toward anything that never happens in the middle of Missouri." Not to be too hard on the middle of Missouri, but I got his point: the ideologues filled up every available space with their fantastic interpretation of events, rode out under the inflamed banner of "American exceptionalism," donned the mantle of patriotism to defend their every move, and demanded obedient silence, shouting down anyone with the audacity to disagree.

Stanley Fish, my colleague at the University of Illinois at Chicago and the dean of liberal arts at the university, wrote an op-ed in the *New York Times* pointing out that all the popular mantras of the moment—we have seen the face of evil, the clash of civilizations is upon us, we are engaged in a war against terrorism—were not only inaccurate but entirely unhelpful, failing for the lack of shared meanings, coherent definitions across wildly disparate contexts, or mechanisms for settling deep-seated disputes. In other words, they could only make sense to those who already agreed or had drunk the nationalist Kool-Aid. An American exceptionalist could easily embrace the idea of a war on terror—its vagueness evaded by grief and anger and self-referencing platitudes—but anyone else might wonder how the war on terror was like or unlike the Revolutionary War or the Civil War, World War II, or, for that matter, the war on drugs or AIDS. As battles go, how does it compare to a war on anxiety or a war on scheming?

Stanley and I were unlikely friends, but we were friends nonetheless. He'd been a controversial celebrity scholar for decades before UIC recruited his partner, Jane Tompkins, to be a professor in the College of Education and Stanley to be a dean. Bernardine and I had attended gatherings and receptions for Stanley and Jane, and became part of the informal wooing team—our pitch emphasized the impact they could have late in their careers on this amazing urban public university, and the joy and challenge of living in the most exciting city in America. I loved Jane immediately for her romantic spirit and generous heart, and because we shared a deep regard for the humanizing potential of teaching; I admired Stanley for his intellectual courage, his irreverence, and the mischievous smile and bad-boy glint that still sparkled in the corner of his eye. In spite of the ferocious criticism (some of which I made myself) that followed him everywhere, I liked Stanley a lot.

Stanley was a literary theorist, a legal scholar, and a public intellectual widely recognized for his research and writing on John Milton and *Paradise Lost*, but also identified as a central figure in importing French postmodern philosophy to these shores—an honor (or a charge) he rejected. He was pilloried by the Left and the Right for being "unprincipled," "sinister," and a "hypocrite," and for espousing views based on "extreme relativism" and "radical subjectivism." He wrote books with titles that seemed designed to drive other academics nuts, like *There's No Such Thing as Free Speech . . . And It's a Good Thing Too*. And that's a major reason I liked him: whatever ideas were laying heavy in the halls of the academy, whatever everyone seemed settled on, whether free speech or students' rights or diversity, Stanley had a way of sticking his finger in its eye, reminding everyone to beware of the new orthodoxies. We went toe to toe on a lot of issues, but he was so much more fun and interesting than colleagues who shared a vague but unexamined agreement on the issues of the day, sleepwalking across the campus. To meet Stanley for the first time created an overwhelming sense of cognitive dissonance for most people—he was mild-mannered, soft-spoken, and elfin: where is the giant monster? That's him, over there, the little gray-haired guy in the expensive suit, standing next to his Jaguar. Really? Yup, that's Stanley.

After 9/11 the attacks on Stanley ramped up: he was targeted as a destructive leech on the American way of life and told by commentators and pundits and politicians alike to apologize for his postmodern devil work of forty years. Of course he was not alone: *The Boondocks*,

Aaron McGruder, and Bill Maher came under steady attack, too, and Susan Sontag and Edward Said were told to shut up, give up their jobs, and, by implication, retreat to their caves with their terrorist soul mates. I was getting pummeled publicly and pretty badly as well. The threats and hate were at a disturbing fever pitch when I got an early morning phone call from Edward Said: "Of course it's painful for you personally, but cringing and going quiet is the worst thing you could do at this moment. Your kids are watching you and your students too and a lot of others. Don't let them down." I was electrified and energized by that five-minute talk and heartened to be in the company of all the other targets. It dawned on me that when the White House noisily attacked Said or Sontag or Maher, the real audience was not those individuals, but a larger collective of listeners and onlookers: if they could silence people like them, what chance do the rest of us have?

Whenever I ran into Stanley Fish on campus in those days, we would compare notes on the latest attacks on each of us. I was happy when it was him and not me getting publicly flogged on the front pages and the nightly news, and I urged him to keep writing op-eds so that I might fade into happy professorial obscurity. He chuckled and asked me if he could edit my next op-ed so that the attackers' sights would refocus on me. One day, looking amused and clearly having given the matter some thought, he stopped me on the way to class: "Why don't we call a joint press conference at UIC," he said. "Each of us can denounce our sordid pasts and our life's work. You can defend me and I'll defend you, but each of us will insist on breast-beating and full confessions." I laughed as he imagined matching headlines: "Ayers issues a full apology for everything he ever did or thought—more required" and "Fish ironically announces the death of postmodernism—millions cheer."

The *New York Times* began publishing a special section about the terrorist attacks and their aftermath entitled "A Nation Challenged," and I was quickly captivated by a feature within it called "Portraits of Grief," small sketches of individuals who had perished in the disaster. I read every word, and when I brought the first issue to class, two other students had had the same idea, and so we passed the sections around and read a few aloud. It felt more real, more connected, and finally more painful as well to have a glimpse into the specifics of a single lost life—"Outspoken and Maternal," "Committed to His Daughter," "A Poet of Bensonhurst," "Helpful Was Her Only Gear," "'The Rock' of Ladder 3"—than was possible in the aggregate. A snapshot of George Llanes or John White or Margaret Mattic illustrated the extent of the tragedy more fully, I thought, than the recounting of large numbers ever could. The vastness of the heartbreak was in the tiniest details of each individual life.

This became a class ritual for the whole semester—reading every word, imagining a specific life, discussing a portrait in depth each week, and connecting as individuals.

The ritual had something of the feel of the sacrament Bernardine and I tried to attend every year at Fort Benning, Georgia. Now in its thirty-fifth year, the demonstration targets the School of the Americas at Fort Benning as an accessory to murder, war crimes and crimes against humanity, torture, and genocide. The school trained practically every thug in a uniform across Latin America for decades, and we gathered under the banner of peace and justice, led by a Jesuit priest, Maryknoll nuns, and the Catholic Worker community to bear witness and to object: Not in Our Name.

In the beginning, demonstrators were met with hostility, harassment, and even acts of violence. But in recent years, the community has seen at least some advantages to a weekend when tens of thousands of peaceniks flock to town. The motel we stayed in last year had two messages side by side on its marquee: We Support Our Troops! Welcome SOA Demonstrators!

After two days of workshops and strategy sessions, concerts and connections, the peace forces mobilized on the main street of town, arm in arm, twenty abreast, and, as a lone singer on the stage sang the name of a single person killed as a result of the bad work of the SOA, the thousands sang back to her, "Presente," and we would advance one step: "Jose Lopez, twenty-six years old." "Presente." Step. "Haydee Cruz, fourteen years old." "Presente." Step. We wanted to acknowledge each

specific life lost, and we wanted to remember that each person had a
mother and a father, someone who loved or cared for them, some hopes
and dreams and aspirations not yet fulfilled. We wanted to place blame,
and we wanted to atone. The desolate tone, the relentless rhythm, and
the persistent echo were mesmerizing. It was transcendent.

The *Times'* "Portraits of Grief" aroused a shared impulse and had
a transcendence of its own. It felt just as necessary, just as urgent, to
share the mourning with everyone in reach and to perform this simple
act of Kaddish.

Over time, the sketches began to merge and collapse into one another, and the homogenizing began to seem artificial and stylized—no
one was a drug addict or a drunk, a crummy partner or a cheat, and everyone was a hero in life as well as in their shared victimhood. I thought
of Lenny Bruce's savage bit about the caption of a *Life* magazine photo
of the Kennedy assassination that claimed the First Lady was clamoring onto the trunk of the speeding limousine in order to get help. Not
at all, said Bruce. She was trying to get the hell out of there just like
anyone else would.

Still, I read on, compelled to continue.

"But," said Nikki late in the term, "the lists are also incomplete."
Some portraits were missing. She evoked the catastrophes of ethnic
cleansing in Cyprus, the invasion and occupation of 1974—all open
sores and part of a living memory. "There is no monopoly on suffering." True, true. I kept on, nonetheless, reading every word.

And then a terrible shock: on December 31, in a long list of the
known dead that ran above the portraits, was the name Joe Trombino,
the guard who had been so severely injured two decades before in the
infamous Brinks robbery.

Somewhere along the way I got a bad cold that turned into a persistent
and disabling cough. When I went to my Chinese doctor for herbs and
needles, she said decisively in her cheery and colorful metaphoric language: "Ah, lungs . . . grief!"

Indeed.

It was inevitable, I suppose, given the odd public moment that
emerged with such chaotic force, that the professor, although nowhere

on the syllabus, would become a subject of the class, and soon enough I was part of the substance being picked over and examined and debated in seminar. In week one, a student asked me to sign *Fugitive Days* for him, and by the second week everyone had a copy in their gym bags and backpacks. Several students had seen the *New York Times* account of the book, and those who hadn't were quickly brought up to speed by their classmates.

As for the *Times* piece about the book, which had run on September 11, I'd expected nothing nice. Janet Malcolm had long ago starkly portrayed reporters as seductive betrayers locked in an uncomfortable but firm embrace with their subjects, who will inevitably be wooed and then jilted, and Stanley Fish had pointed out in a *New York Times* op-ed that this kind of reporting "can only be unauthentic, can only get it wrong, can only lie" because writers of these fictions will necessarily "substitute their own story for the story of their announced subject." I knew that talking to the *Times* was a bargain with the devil, but what the hell? I'd give them a story, they'd do whatever they do, clouded of course with that irritating superior air of comprehensive examination and considered judgment, and whatever it was, it would help publicize the book, which seemed at the time a reasonable transaction to me—if not to Bernardine—and well worth the hassle.

I'd met the *Times* reporter, Dinitia Smith, almost two decades before, when she approached me on a Manhattan street corner as I waited for our children to be dropped off from summer day camp. She proposed then that we collaborate on the story of the Weather Underground, but I declined, saying that I didn't have the time or distance to tell that story yet, and doubted in any case that I would want a collaborator. Back in July, when she'd interviewed Bernardine and me in our home in Chicago, Smith proved to be a particularly resolute interrogator: she insisted on confidentiality and an exclusive interview; she embodied both the good cop and the bad cop, cajoling and flattering one moment, threatening in the next; and she relentlessly invoked the authoritative power of the *Times* to make or break the book, implying a kind of collaboration—"Remember, don't talk to anyone else until my piece runs"—and inviting dependency. In spite of everything, I liked her.

From the start, she had questioned me sharply about the bombings, and each time I referred back to *Fugitive Days*, in which I'd discussed the culture of violence so central to the American experience, my growing anger with the structures of racism and the escalating terrorist war, and the complex, sometimes extreme and despairing, sometimes inspired choices I made in those terrible times. She pressed on: "Well, when you bombed the Pentagon," she began on three separate occasions, and each time I interrupted her and said, "But I didn't bomb the Pentagon." A running joke between my publisher and me began, "How should I plead when the Smith piece appears?" "Just confess," she kidded. "It won't hurt. Whatever she says, just smile and say, 'I did it.'"

Smith didn't disappoint, and her angle was captured perfectly in the headline: "No Regrets for a Love of Explosives." Her piece quoted me as having said, "I don't regret setting bombs. I feel we didn't do enough." Did I actually say those words? I probably did, because something like it appears in the book—in what I hoped was a denser and more layered treatment, reminiscences about effectiveness, not tactics. I also said something close to it in 1998 to Connie Chung on a special report about 1968 and again on a MacNeil/Lehrer broadcast.

Smith and I had spoken a lot about regrets, about loss, about attempts to account for one's life. I had said at one point that I had a thousand regrets, but no regrets for opposing the war with every ounce of my strength. I told her that in light of the indiscriminate murder of millions of Vietnamese, I still thought the Weathermen showed remarkable restraint, and that while we tried to sound a piercing alarm in those years, in fact we didn't do enough to stop the war—no one did, and the evidence is clear: we didn't stop it. We might have been smarter; we should have been more focused; we could have been more effective.

Bernardine had worried all along about whether the book was a good idea—she didn't want her current work disrupted or derailed or put on hold because I was dredging up the deep past. Plus she knew, as few others do, the special rage reserved for well-known women of the Left—Angela Davis forever and Jane Fonda at a moment. Bernardine had held a uniquely prominent place in J. Edgar Hoover's Rogue's Gallery thirty years before—he saw her as public enemy number one and called her "the most dangerous woman in America" in 1970, reprising a phrase he'd attached to Jane Addams at the start of his career; later he said she was "La Pasionaria of the Lunatic Left," drawing a neat comparison to the ardent leader of the resistance to fascism during the Spanish Civil War, an association Bernardine found flattering.

Bernardine had been the object of a low-key but persistent letter-writing campaign led by Charlton Heston to have her fired from Northwestern University long before *Fugitive Days* was published. Heston was the president of the National Rifle Association and a former president of the Screen Actors Guild, a Northwestern alum, and a major donor to the theater program. After 9/11, the campaign against Bernardine ramped up, and Heston told the student newspaper that he was shocked and appalled that "an unrepentant terrorist like her" was on the faculty of the law school and was the director of the Children and Family Justice Center. He said he would reconsider donating money to his alma mater and urged other alumni to join him in pressuring the administration to fire Bernardine.

There was a growing firestorm around *Fugitive Days*, too, in Chicago and beyond. Steve Neal of the *Chicago Sun-Times* effectively took out his own little fatwa on me and Bernardine, demanding that we not be allowed to speak or teach anywhere any longer. Neal noted that the *New York Times* article was published on 9/11 and claimed that I'd "made comments supporting the bombings on the morning of September 11." Not true. He attacked as well anyone who'd endorsed the book, calling Studs Terkel "the village idiot." Scott Turow told me later that it was the first time in his life he had received hate mail for reviewing someone else's book favorably. The mood was turning ugly.

Isabel, one of my brilliant graduate students, brought in the Neal piece, and soon a class "smash-book," a collection of reviews and commentary, was under way:

The Nation: "Don't tell me, as Ayers does, that you had to be there to feel the Weather's rage."

Jonah Raskin: "Ayers offers a highly romanticized view of life as a fugitive."

David Horowitz: "[Ayers] wallows in familiar Marxist incitement."

The New York Times: "[Ayers was] playacting with violence."

The Chronicle of Higher Education: "[Ayers is an] unrepentant New Leftist."

Todd Gitlin: "[Ayers committed] absolutely, I mean literally, incoherent and reckless acts in the name of nonsensical beliefs."

Commentator after commentator offered evidence of my screwballness, and insisted that anything I might say now should be discounted because of what I did then. I thought about Ralph Ellison writing in *The Invisible Man*: "These white folk have newspapers, magazines, radios, spokesmen to get their ideas across. If they want to tell the world a lie, they can tell it so well that it becomes the truth." These white folks! As the fragments and phrases were echoed and repeated, reverberations bouncing around and around, any possibility of explaining, contextualizing, or reinterpreting narrowed and then disappeared.

A favorite demonizing story about the Weathermen in 1969 held that we ate cats in the collectives. We were American dissidents, and like dissidents here and everywhere throughout history we were ignored, ridiculed, marginalized, beaten, and jailed (but not assassinated as were our Black dissident comrades—the legacy of white-skin privilege), all the while being deemed crazy by all the established powers. We were pretty goofy and weird in those days, it's true—and I don't claim to be completely free of traces of eccentric nuttiness today—but it was a weirdness I tried to honestly portray in *Fugitive Days*. I'll say it here once and for all: we were often wrong or off base, but we never killed or ate a cat in the collectives. I'd heard the story so often from so many different people, not all of them hostile, that I began to wonder, and so I called a lot of comrades to be sure. No cat snacks, no cat-on-a-stick, and no cat barbecue that anyone would admit to. But the cat story endured, and packed a little power—they eat cats for God's sake; what could they possibly think or say or advocate that's sane? Try to provide evidence of nonindulgence in the cat feast, or to prove you don't even like the taste of cat, and the trap tightens: I sounded like a complete idiot flailing with shadows.

Todd Gitlin, a sociologist at Columbia University and an early president of SDS, was a steady and consistent critic. Todd seemed to be the first name in every reporter's Rolodex or computer file for all things sixties, and he popped up in every story of a notable anniversary, every reference comparing current events with the olden days, and every obituary of a prominent character from the movement—and that right there could provide a strong motive to stay alive, just to keep any remembrances Todd-free. I borrowed an irreverent idea from my teacher Philip Lopate, who had written about a certain commodifying of Holocaust literature into "The Holocaust, Inc.," and began to think of Todd in his later incarnation as the unofficial, self-appointed CEO of a small business that might be called "The Sixties, Inc." His steady string of op-eds and articles and books and appearances in the press read like the work of a scrivener defending the enterprise's most profitable "patents."

Whenever I ran into Todd on the street near Columbia we exchanged friendly greetings—we'd known each other since the early days in Ann Arbor—but little more. I made Todd uncomfortable in part I think because my existence challenged a revisionist theory he promoted wildly that "the sixties" was a bifurcated decade: the early or "good sixties" all participatory democracy and sacrifice and the beloved community, the later "bad sixties" all stormy Weather and nationalist Black Panthers and revolution. I was—along with Ralph Featherstone and Stokely Carmichael and Kathy Boudin and Dottie Zellner and Tom Hayden and thousands more—part of both. I still embraced the beloved community, and I saw no necessary contradiction between that and movement-building or making a revolution.

Todd and I were both public people, and our politics were too well-known and too knitted into our identities to make for much easy banter—Todd, an insider in the liberal wing of the Democratic Party, hosting fund-raisers for the likes of John Kerry and Wesley Clark; me, allergic to military men by nature and still searching for the revolution I knew we needed.

Bernardine and I did have one face-off in public with Todd, on a national radio show shortly after 9/11. The interview and conversation began cordially enough, with long stretches of agreement among the three of us about the horrors of war and the importance of dissent and opposition. But after several minutes, Todd disrupted the surface calm, saying, "We're being overly polite and deferential here, and we're acting as if our disagreements are cultural when in fact our differences were deeply political." Yes, yes, we agreed quickly—let's talk politics and let's go deeper.

"Let me read you something that these two folks wrote in 1969 that they apparently believed at the time," I recall Todd starting, "which is absolutely insane." Bernardine and I exchanged a look. Oh, God, brace yourself, I thought. Our rhetoric, while very much of the time, was regularly off the rails. We each held our breath and waited, her eyes shining in anticipation as she sent me a telepathic message: What does Todd have in his back pocket? Eat the cats? Off the pigs? Kill your parents? Eat your parents? Eat the pigs? Todd read: "To a large extent the wealth of this country—certainly the wealth of Standard Oil and General Motors and Coca-Cola—already by right belongs to the people of the world."

Yes, yes, go on. We still believe all that; get to the crazy part.

I was waiting for the other shoe to drop when he said, "You see what I mean? This is absolute political madness."

"Wait, wait! That's all you've got?" Bernardine relaxed with an amused smile and asked Todd calmly what part of anti-capitalism and anti-imperialism he didn't understand.

The cats-for-snacks tale was small potatoes (an appetizer, so to speak) next to the notorious, persistent, and fictional story of Bernardine's abiding love affair with Charles Manson. She was reported to have said in the middle of a speech at an SDS meeting in 1969 in Flint, Michigan, "Dig it! First they killed those pigs and then they put a fork in their bellies. Wild!"

I didn't hear that exactly, but the words were close enough I guess. Her speech was focused on the murder just days earlier of our friend Fred Hampton, the Chicago Black Panther Party leader, a murder we were certain—although it would take decades to prove beyond a doubt—was part of a larger government plot, the Gestapo-like tactics of a repressive police force. Bernardine linked Fred's murder to the murders of other Panthers around the country, to the assassinations of Malcolm X and Patrice Lumumba, the CIA attempts on Fidel's life, and then to the ongoing made-in-the-USA terror in Viet Nam. "This is the state of the world," she cried. "This is what screams out for our attention and response. And what do we get from the media? A sick fascination with a story that has it all: a racist psycho, a killer cult, and a chorus line of Hollywood bodies. Dig it!"

So I heard it partly as political talk, agitated and inflamed and full of rhetorical overkill, and partly as a joke—tasteless, perhaps, but a joke nonetheless. Hunter S. Thompson was making much more excessive, and funnier, jokes about the fascination with Charles Manson then, and so was Richard Pryor. I thought again about my protest outside State-ville prison on the night the State of Illinois executed John Wayne Gacy and immediately saw the conspiracy and the connection: they eat cats, they love Charles Manson, and they're in cahoots with John Wayne Gacy. Yes, yes, yes: "Unrepentant terrorist supports serial killer!!!" It fed a stuttering but established plot point, while piling on additional color and spice—one could envision Charles Manson, John Wayne Gacy Jr., Bernardine, and me all settled in to our own little satanic psycho cell with the grilled cats.

Not only was it an apocryphal story, it was irrefutable—every attempt to explain, including possibly what I've just written, was held up to further ridicule as deeper dimensions and meanings were slipped into place and attached to the story. Elizabeth Kolbert of the *New Yorker*, for example, after a three-hour conversation, reached out and touched Bernardine's arm and said, "I just have to ask you about the Manson quote. It's my duty as a journalist." Bernardine responded in full, explaining the context, the perverse humor of it, Fred's murder, the savagery in Viet Nam, her own meaning-making, and her sense of its meaning to insiders and outsiders alike. She said pretty much what I wrote above, but it made no difference: Kolbert reported the received story intact without any mention of any part of their exchange. One of her colleagues at the *New Yorker*, Hendrik Hertzberg, looked over her piece. Since he'd been in the Trotskyite Left back in the day and was a popularizer of the Manson myth, perhaps it was him and not Kolbert who tacked on this added fiction: "The Manson murders were treated as an inspired political act." Not true—not even close. A lie on every level. And we didn't eat cats!

Two months later, Steve Neal, playing off Kolbert, wrote: "The Weathermen idolized killer Charles Manson and adopted a fork as their symbol." What's the use? By the end of the year a *Time* magazine essayist called me an "American terrorist" and, echoing the *Times*, said of me that "even today he finds 'a certain eloquence to bombs.'" It was an endlessly repeating story, and the echo grew and grew as it bounced off the walls.

Two of my students started a project to count up the number of terrorist events in the modern world and tally them by category: religious group, political sect, individual, established government. Two others examined high school history textbooks and began a chart of the "good terrorists" in US history (Christopher Columbus, George Washington, Andrew Jackson, George Custer, Teddy Roosevelt, John McCain) and the "bad terrorists" (Geronimo, Joe Hill, Lolita Lebron, Rafael Cancel Miranda, Oscar Lopez, Reies Tijerina, Mabel Robinson and Robert Williams, the Earth Liberation Front, Weather), with the textbooks conflicted and the jury still out on John Brown and Harriet Tubman. One of my conservative students created on poster board a large and elaborate portrait of me crafted from torn newspaper clippings; diagonally across its front, he had taped a fat piece of yellow police tape and scrawled in thick black marker the words PUBLIC ENEMY! I think he was being ironic.

FIVE

The Revolution Will Not Be Televised

It was late, and Bernardine and I were ready for bed. We found ourselves instead in the Press Room at the Sundance Film Festival, facing journalists, critics, editors, and columnists in a series of radio interviews, TV spots, and brief Q and A dialogues. Minutes before *The Weather Underground* documentary had screened for the first time to a warm response—this was Park City, Utah, after all, on the eve of the unpopular US invasion and occupation of Iraq—and a thumbs-up and a wink from Robert Redford, who was sitting near the front of the theater. The two young filmmakers who'd midwifed the project for years, Bill Siegel and Sam Green, were rapturous, a tidal wave of relief sweeping through them, cleansing and joyful and over the moon. Their baby was finally born, and all the labor, sweat, and tears seemed worth it after all. But ambitions were now expanding and expectations naturally rising; getting into Sundance was great news and reward enough a few months before, but now a commercial release, financing for their next project, maybe an Academy Award loomed on the horizon. The sky's the limit! Bill and Sam had invited us to join them and their families and crew at Sundance, and now they looked to be on the far side of giddy—happy-exhausted, adrenaline-fueled, and bouncing blissfully off the walls.

A young entertainment reporter for the *Los Angeles Times* asked Bernardine and me a couple of questions about our lives and experiences underground: How had we stayed together for over three decades with

all the chaos and madness in our lives, and did we really think a revolution was possible in America? Then she said, "You seem so everyday
normal, and I wonder why you didn't follow the nonviolent path of
King and Gandhi and Mandela." We were always asked about violence,
an obvious and essential question when it came to anything Weather,
but her question had an interesting twist. "Mandela?" Bernardine and I
asked in unison. "Yes," she repeated, "King and Gandhi and Mandela."

"Do you know why Nelson Mandela was in prison for twenty-seven
years?" Bernardine asked.

"Well, for opposing apartheid," she replied.

"Yes, that's true," Bernardine said, "and for organizing and leading
an army—armed struggle, sabotage, the whole difficult deal. If you're
really interested, you ought to read his 1964 statement from the dock at
the opening of the defense case in the Rivonia Trial, where he admitted
and defended all of it."

"I will," she said.

It made sense to put Nelson Mandela in the front lines of some
imaginary League of Justice Heroes—his struggle for freedom
throughout his life was exemplary, righteous, brave, and laudable. And
because he had achieved hero status by then inside the United States, it
made some sense to conflate his work with others and to imagine him
as a nonviolent saint. For Americans, the world becomes less messy if
we don't have to think too hard about complex choices and if our heroes are all good and without contradiction.

At his trial, where he stood as first accused in a vast conspiracy
against the state, Mandela reviewed his biography and the dreadful
situation for Blacks in his homeland and quickly claimed to have been
one of the main organizers of Umkhonto we Sizwe, the armed wing in
the fight against apartheid. He argued that years of nonviolent struggle
had brought nothing but greater repression and exploitation, and that
the people demanded they answer violence with violence and develop
new channels toward liberation. The apartheid state never missed the
opportunity to call Mandela and the ANC "terrorists," even though
the Rivonia trial made it crystal clear that "the violence which we chose
to adopt was not terrorism." Mandela made the case for choosing

sabotage on government buildings and other symbols of apartheid as a way to inspire people without injuring or killing anyone. And he freely admitted his attraction to building a classless society, influenced, he said, by reading Marx and from admiring the structures and organization of early African societies, in which there were no rich or poor and there was no exploitation. The Rivonia speech was required reading for us in the late 1960s, and I had several passages memorized.

The Reverend Martin Luther King Jr. admired the ideal of a classless society too, and while the mythological King led a boycott, had a dream, won a Nobel, ended racism, and made us all better people, the real King was a spirit-based, pro-democracy activist and a deep analytical thinker, a loving pastor, and an angry pilgrim on a quest for social justice in his time. He evolved and became more radical with every campaign he led, every resistance he encountered, and every step he took. When his journey and his mission led him to link racial justice to economic justice and global justice, he called for an end to the three great evils—racism, militarism, and materialism. He urged activists and creative dissenters to call the nation to a greater expression of humanness, echoing the blunt-talking Fannie Lou Hamer, leader of the Mississippi Freedom Democratic Party. When Hamer had been asked if she wanted full equality with the white man, she said that she didn't want to go that low but sought instead a real democracy and a rebirth of freedom that would lift a newly enlightened America out of the morass in which it was stuck.

The real King repeatedly condemned the US government as the greatest purveyor of violence on earth—his heated sermons bring Jeremiah Wright into clearer context—and argued within the movement for nonviolent direct action as a principle for himself and as a necessary approach for the struggle as well. As he wrote in *Where Do We Go from Here*:

We had neither the resources nor the techniques to win. . . . The question was not whether one should use his gun when his home was attacked, but whether it was tactically wise to use a gun while participating in an organized demonstration.

If anyone looked closely at the photos of King and his family during the legendary bus boycott, they could just make out the background figures of Black men in chairs with shotguns on their laps—the legendary Deacons for Defense of Justice. King's home was armed, and Fannie Lou Hamer, too, let everyone know that she had an adequate arsenal near her bed. There was nothing passive in King's pacifism, nothing docile or immobile in that nonviolence.

Gandhi, too, is more difficult to embrace in reality than as the cardboard cut-out we are urged to admire and emulate unquestioningly. Most Westerners who evoke Gandhi are thinking of the activist who led the struggle that brought the British Empire to heel—what's not to love!?!—not the religious zealot who was willing, by his own account, to let his wife or a child die rather than provide the medically indicated but religiously proscribed food (chicken! milk!) or who said in 1938 that the Jews of Germany should commit collective suicide to alert the people of the world to Hitler's violence. After the war, Gandhi defended himself, noting that the Jews had died anyway, and that they might have died more significantly. And again, in 1942, he urged nonviolent resistance to a Japanese invasion, conceding that it could cost millions and millions of lives. Gandhi's orthodoxy—like any dogma—was at least dependable; his consistency, however, was something that few would ever endorse or practice. Most of us who considered ourselves radicals or peace and justice activists struggled for more peace and more freedom at the moment, more democracy and more fairness and more justice *now*—a more human world right here.

None of this detracts in any way from the greatness of these struggles or the power of those lives—if anything, reckoning with the contradictions they faced and the activist commitments they embodied makes each of them even more admirable to me and to Bernardine. Their nonviolence showed the power of love and by design exposed the hidden violence lurking in the everyday. But it was their activism, not some vague armchair pacifism, that animated them, and it was the popular movements they inspired and led that defined them. Each was part of a massive social upheaval, each took risks and acted in the world without any guarantees. As the legendary Ella Baker said of King, "The movement made Martin rather than Martin making the movement."

On a beautiful spring day I left home early to catch a flight from Chicago to western Canada, where I was scheduled to give a lecture to a group of teachers at the University of Calgary. Clearing customs, I was directed to Immigration, where a growing line of anxious or impatient arrivals—mostly dark-skinned, mostly young, I, the glaring, gleaming exception—awaited further examination.

This had become a commonplace for me whenever I traveled to Canada—I was always diverted and delayed, always questioned about my anticipated length of stay and the nature of my business, always double-checked. Whenever I'd ask why I was being subjected to this special treatment, the reply was always the same: "Just a routine check."

It's struck me as odd, though, since I'd never once warranted a second look entering Beijing or Frankfurt, Cape Town or Cairo, Rio or Taipei. Why was it always Canada? Why me? I was never able to get beyond the bureaucratic diversion.

Now I stood before Immigration Officer 1767—a man in his mid-thirties with a stubbly beard, slumping shoulders, and intense eyes—as he peered at his computer screen. Shortly, he rose and excused himself in order to "look some things up" in a separate back room. When he returned, he had several pages of what looked like a computer printout in his hands. He took his seat in the booth, looked up at me, and said, "What's Students for a Democratic Society?" Ah, my dossier at last.

I explained that SDS was a student group devoted to peace and participatory democracy. "Are you still a member?" he asked, and, having never actually resigned, I replied that I was.

"You have quite an arrest record," he went on, and I agreed that, yes, I did, but explained that every arrest was linked to a political demonstration—OK, and one insignificant possession of marijuana charge, but I was innocent!—and that all of my encounters resulted merely in misdemeanors like "disturbing the peace" or "mob action," vague charges designed to cover a multitude of affirmative acts or sins as the case may be. "Almost all," he corrected. "But there is a conviction here from 1969 for assault with a deadly weapon—and that's a felony."

"It couldn't be true," I said. I didn't have any felony convictions whatsoever, in 1969 or any other time.

"My records say otherwise," he said.

"It's a mistake," I replied.

He consulted a large book of regulations and said, "That conviction would bring a ten-year prison term in Canada. I can't admit you."

I began to beg and lobby, plead and beseech, pointing to the Canadian stamps dotting my passport and granting me entry as recently as March, sucking up to national pride and economic self-interest by telling him that I bring my family to Shakespeare at Stratford every year, showing him the publicity flier for my lecture, appealing to what I hoped might be his sense of pity for a sixty-year-old professor stranded at Immigration. "Well," he began tentatively, and I sensed a chink. "Yes? Yes?" "I could call my supervisor at home, and if he agrees I could grant you temporary residence. . . ." Terrific! "And that would cost you a couple hundred dollars." What? Why?

This sounded a lot like extortion to me. I didn't want to pay a bribe or a gift to get into Canada. "All right," he said. "You won't be allowed into Canada today." He handed me a form called "Allowed to Leave Canada" and asked me to sign under, "I hereby voluntarily withdraw my application to enter Canada. . . ." I, of course, refused that too.

After an hour in a holding cell conveniently situated behind Immigration, he fetched me and escorted me back through security and US customs, where agents from both sides of the border shared a collegial laugh. I told him that Canada was always the place I imagined myself escaping *to* if the United States ever plunged into a kind of friendly fascism, and now what would I do? As we made our way to the next plane to the United States, officer 1767 assured me: "I'm not denying entry into Canada on the basis of your membership in Students for a Democratic Society—it's your arrest record." I'm innocent, I almost said, and then I thought of the chorus from the great Canadian singer Leonard Cohen's "The Partisan": "Oh, the wind, the wind is blowing."

I was first on the plane, seen to my seat by 1767, and my passport was returned to me. The agent stood in the galley watching me,

I suppose to be sure I wouldn't shout out some blasphemy or bolt and raise a rumpus in Canada, saw that the door was closed and secured, and waved bye-bye, now from the window, as the plane pulled away. The university must have canceled my talk, but the conference went on anyway. I was detained twice more on attempts to cross the northern border, and as of 2013, I still can't get in to Canada.

Bernardine and I went hand in hand with Sam and Bill and their amazing crew to the Oscars at the Kodak Theatre in weird but hospitable Hollywood. *The Weather Underground* had indeed been nominated for an Academy Award. Unbelievable! When they'd started working on the project years before and had contacted me for an interview, I said, "Sure, of course." I assumed they were like dozens of others who'd stopped by with a camera and a tape recorder and ten questions scribbled on a yellow pad, mostly kids crafting some sort of earnest or envious school history fair project—"Student Protest Then and Now: From the 1960s to Today," "1968—Year of Turmoil," "Antiwar Protest and War Resistance in the United States." It didn't really register until deep into the process that they were making an actual grown-up documentary film. But they were and they did, and it wasn't too bad—not the story I would have told, certainly, but an honest look nonetheless at one instance of what they generically referred to as "hidden history" by a couple of smart and curious guys. And its own curious history—filmed largely before 9/11, edited after 9/11, and released as the government incessantly pounded the drums of war—ensured that it bore a certain conflicted schizophrenia at its heart. But there we all were, at the Oscars, and the ambition to get here was being recalibrated once more: the great news and reward of the nomination, more than bliss a few months before, was replaced with an aching hope for victory!

It was odd and a little creepy seeing myself on the big screen—did I really say that? I must have because there it was, but what was missing? Furthermore, was my acne that bad on one of the days they'd interviewed me? It must have been, but damn it looked out of control on the screen. I reminded myself that I'd written my own version of these events and that this particular story belonged to the filmmakers, not to me and not to Bernardine, and could have as easily been called "Two Smart and Curious Guys Go on an Honest Search for the Weather Underground." They'd talked with hundreds of folks before they'd even turned on the camera, and the film included interviews with allies and enemies, pursuers and pursued. Todd Gitlin was in the Darth Vader role: the camera dangerously close, the face so tight it was about to burst, the choked words spewing forth in a barely controlled stream of spittle and incoherence comparing us as moral partners with Hitler and Stalin and Mao.

The Weather Underground had some stiff competition for an Oscar in the documentary category—*The Fog of War, Capturing the Friedmans*—but being in Hollywood was huge for them in any case, and they kindly invited us along for the party. Bill and Sam and the crew were still happy-exhausted and adrenaline-fueled, stimulated now with skunk and coca leaf and spirits of all types, and really who knows what medications the near-naked waitron, who looked like a shaman from some mysterious mountain, had stashed in her *porte-monnaie* as she circled our table at the upscale pan-Asian bistro the night before the ceremony. No matter, we ordered huge platters of mushroom-filled dumplings, tofu basil scramble with tomato cucumber salad, urban ramen, and five-spice udon. Bill and Sam were intent on performing their anticipated acceptance speeches before our little stunned and stunning audience. Sam, practiced at showing the film to audiences on campuses for months, planned to say, "Rather than the traditional thank-you speech, let's go straight to the Q and A . . . Yes?" pointing to and calling on Bernardine. "The woman in the *fabulous* leather pants from Shanghai Tang there in the first balcony . . ." Bill, holding the statue (a bottle of California merlot at our rehearsal dinner) in his right hand high above his head and raising the power fist with his left, planned to rouse the masses by shouting, "The Weather Underground hoped to make a revolution, not a film; we've made the film, now let's join up to make the revolution!"

Security for the ceremony was crazily ramped up—9/11 and the new normal, I suppose. We each got a rainbow of color-coded wristbands and stickers, hang-tags and lanyards, as well as a blizzard of instructions and a map with a rendezvous point and the maze of closed streets we were to follow toward the Kodak. We passed half a dozen checkpoints before our cars were thoroughly sniffed by trained German shepherds—the dogs were exclusively on explosives detail that day it seemed, and hash or bud got nothing more than a happy drip of drool and a barely perceptible doggy smile. Mirrors were passed under the carriages, and valets drove them off to their undisclosed locations. Assembled on the red carpet, I told Bill and Sam that I felt much safer knowing that after all those showy and elaborate precautions security certified Bernardine Dohrn, of all people, as safe and worthy.

We were on the red carpet for only a few minutes when BJ called—for her being on the red carpet was up there with winning the Nobel or the Super Bowl, appearing on Oprah, or getting your Nobel presented by Oprah at the Super Bowl. And suddenly there she was: Oprah!

I thought the red carpet would be the worst kind of celebrity clusterfuck and the cheapest possible celebration of the most superficial crap in our culture—probably all true, but the lights and the cameras, the cheering crowds and enchanted mountain vibe worked its magic on me, and I felt myself give in. Susan Sarandon seemed genuinely happy to see Bernardine, and so did Tim Robbins, and they had a group hug. When Nicole Kidman dropped her handbag right next to me, I swooped down to help her gather up the contents, saying, "Oops, here's your drugs," and she laughed and teased and poked me in the arm and said, "Don't tell!" I swooned like a teenage boy, or like BJ, and I lingered and stalled and hung back some more.

The Fog of War won the Oscar, and we were all good sports, hugs all around, and clutching our fancy swag bags, we headed back to Chicago.

We did a lot of traveling with the film for a few years and came to admire Bill and Sam more and more. They really wanted their film to raise questions and to provoke discussion, not to be some authoritative last word, and on campuses and in community forums from Maine to California, it did that in spades. Typically a few older people showed up at screenings to reconnect—Grace Paley in New Hampshire, Adrienne Rich in California, Marge Piercy in Massachusetts—or to refight the old battles. But young people couldn't have cared less. They wanted to talk about the US war in Iraq, Guantanamo, Abu Ghraib, and mass incarceration in the United States. Some even wanted to understand that kind of commitment and sacrifice, the angels and the devils that pushed the Weather Underground, the Panthers, SDS, and the Black student movement forward and roiled all of our lives, the lessons we thought we had learned about activism and social justice work.

One night after dinner at a Mexican grill in Greenwich Village, our kids joined us at the Quad Cinema for a short Q and A after a screening of the film. The Quad was a classic art house cinema, the space cramped and the smell of weed heavy in the air, the crowd that night hipsters, poets, painters, students, and freaks—our people. A few minutes into the post-film discussion, a young woman in the audience wondered what it had been like for our kids growing up and being raised by notorious us. I glanced at the kids, and Chesa nodded, winked, and stood up—he'd had a couple of margaritas, but he didn't need that kind of courage because he loved this type of thing anyway.

"You know, whatever hand you're dealt is normal to a little kid," he began. "I mean, what was it like being raised by *your* parents? Normal, right? And maybe a little weird for you looking back at it, or for me if I happened to peek in today." He reminisced about sitting around one afternoon when he was in high school with his cousins and friends—Amilcar, Atariba, Haydee, Thai, Bluejay, and others—and Zayd sighing, "Why couldn't I have been given a normal name like River." River?

"Kids want to be loved and safe and cared for and recognized—we got all that and more. We didn't know anything about them as public people, and why would we?" Chesa described the shock of learning that Bernardine had once been a good friend's partner decades before and then realizing that parents aren't supposed to give their kids a chart of every hookup, and said he doubted he would ever provide such a thing to his own kids.

When we left the theater, Chesa and his friends, now including the woman who'd gotten him on his feet and into the dialogue in the first place, headed to the corner club.

SIX

Palling Around

"This is not a man who sees America as you see it and how I see America," vice presidential candidate Sarah Palin cried out to the agitated crowd during a 2008 campaign rally, referring to then-senator Barack Obama. "We see America as the greatest force for good in this world" and as a "beacon of light and hope for others who seek freedom and democracy." This was how "real Americans" saw things, according to Palin. As for Obama, he's "someone who sees America, it seems, as being so imperfect that he's palling around with terrorists who would target their own country!"

There it was: the punch line that would resonate no matter what else was said or done—*palling around*. It had a special creepy ring to it, for sure.

When Governor Palin—or, as our late friend Studs Terkel called her, "Joe McCarthy in drag"—uttered it that first time (and ever after) the crowd exploded: "Kill him! Kill him!" I couldn't tell for sure whether it was me or Senator Obama who was the target of those chants—perhaps both. I'd been designated a public enemy before. I knew the territory pretty well and accepted the consequences with some equanimity, but now poor Barack Obama as well was forced to play Ibsen's brilliant character, the embattled Dr. Thomas Stockmann, the "enemy of the people." Stockmann was viciously taunted in the public square by a chorus of townspeople bent on delusion and self-deception: Kill the enemy of the people!

There was no way to prepare for what was about to hit me, of course, and at the outset I could barely glimpse it on the far horizon of my imagination—the great speeding locomotive designed to derail Obama would run me and others down as just some unavoidable debris or collateral damage, the inevitable road kill. No one really knew its shape or its power yet, no one could guess at its velocity. I grasped a couple of small things right away, but my family understood a lot more, and they were in fact already gearing up.

At that time, I'd been a professor at the University of Illinois at Chicago for over twenty years and was officially Senior University Scholar and Distinguished Professor of Education—I know, I know, it sounded a bit too lofty to me, too, but I even had official business cards to prove it. I'd written several books—mostly on teaching and learning and education—and I was on the faculty senate and the boards of several national and local organizations. Moving to Chicago from New York in 1987 was a kind of homecoming for us since Bernardine and I had each grown up nearby, and Bernardine had gone to college and law school at the University of Chicago. Hyde Park was the obvious choice for her, and we built our home and raised our three sturdy sons in a little rented coach house there.

When Chesa left home for college and we were on the brink of empty-nesting, Bernardine's father died, and she brought her mother, well into Alzheimer's disease, to live with us. We had found the loveliest and most devoted caregiver ever, and Dorothy Dohrn and Florence Garcia were our steady companions and roommates for almost five years. Dorothy liked to sing at the dinner table—Broadway show tunes and classics from Sinatra mostly—and we were a lively chorus most evenings. When Dorothy passed away in her room in our house, Florence moved out. We were oddly quiet, but not for long. A few months later my dad moved in because of his own advancing Alzheimer's, and thankfully Florence returned for another three years. A lifesaver.

Dad loved playing gin rummy, and Florence learned the game; he was devoted to watching the Cubs, and Florence became a fan; and he was content listening to Fox News at full volume for hours at a time—but that proved to be, for her and all of us, one bridge too far.

One day I came home from work and clicked off Fox News as he slept in his chair. He awoke with a start, looked at me hard, and asked in an accusing voice, "Bill, *what do these gays want?*" I responded a little sharply, "Well, they for sure don't want to marry you," and he laughed and said, "Good! I'm too old!"

My dad, Tom, was a large, public man with a record of accomplishments to fill a book, and he had a big personality to match. Dementia didn't change that. He was an industrialist and a big capitalist, an establishment heavy, civic leader, and energetic cheerleader for all things Chicago, and, of course, in decline those things faded to dust. But he was still charming and talkative and full of good humor.

Sometime after he'd retired in the 1980s, he and I had met for lunch and walked across the Loop toward his train. He seemed to know everyone we passed, and he greeted several by name. When anyone asked, in typical polite greeting, "How are you doing, Tom?" he'd respond heartily: "I'm the best in the world!"

I said to him, "You used to simply say, 'I'm great!' and now it seems you've escalated and ramped it up."

"That's right," he said. "People expect an old man like me to wail and complain, so I try to generate a little hope and a little happiness."

"OK," I said. "But couldn't it be just a bit over the top and a little annoying to hear that you're the *best in the world?* That's a little excessive, no?"

"Fine," he conceded. "I'm also trying to annoy the whiners: Fuck 'em!"

"I'm the best in the world": that was his theme song for the last three years of his life, a message of hope edged with mockery.

Tom was supremely confident, but I never thought he was arrogant—he believed in himself, true, but he didn't think he was better than anyone else. "You're not all-knowing," he said. "The other guy has a point of view, too, and don't be too sure that you're right in all things." He also regularly gave us a bit of advice that he would have more than one occasion to regret in my case: "Always stand up for what you believe."

When Malik graduated from high school, Dad came to the graduation with us. We sat near the front so he could see and hear all the action. The commencement speaker went on too long, of course. There should be an instruction manual for commencement speakers with one big-letter message: PEOPLE CAME TO SEE THEIR KIDS GET THE DIPLOMA, NOT TO HEAR YOU. MAKE IT QUICK! Dad began sighing loudly. I tried to shush him quietly and assured him that the speaker was about to wind up, but it wasn't true, and in any case Dad's complaint turned on the content of the talk, not its length. Finally he turned to me and said in an exaggerated stage whisper, mocking the cliché passing as advice to the graduates: "*Follow your dreams! Follow your dreams!* That can get you in a lot of trouble . . . just look at you!!"

A few days before he passed away, I sat holding Dad's hand for a long while, and as I got up to leave, asked him how he was doing.

"Great," he replied somewhat softly.

"Great?" I asked in mock surprise. This was clearly backsliding!

He smiled slightly and shot back with a weak but determined voice: "I'm the best in the world!"

He had always kidded me for being a "tattooed man." It's true, I got my first in 1963, and I never stopped doodling bits of art on the big living canvas. But there was just a hint of jealousy for the little red heart on my left arm with "Mom" emblazoned across it in script. I'd gotten that one on the day my mother died, and he would say in mock complaint, "Where's 'Dad'?" So the day he passed away at our home, I went back to Dave, my skin artist, and got "Dad" carved prominently on my right arm: "The best in the world."

We were reluctant to see our brilliant friend Florence leave a second time, and I said to Bernardine that the three of us had become such a great elder-care team that maybe we should find some random old person to move in with us. "You're already here," she said, a little meanly I thought, and we laughed about how long in the tooth I really was. OK, but where's my caregiver?

Our three sons monitored news and information from the wide, wide world affirmatively, proactively, and Bernardine and I had ongoing disagreements with them about what to read and why. As a digital immigrant I was particularly slow to even begin to see the propulsive reality exploding all around, let alone know how to negotiate or use it. As digital natives, they knew it all.

Zayd said to me one morning as he packed to return to his home in New York, "You know, I've watched you, and it's kind of sad that you waste an hour or two a day reading the *New York Times* and listening to NPR."

Sad? Was he patronizing me?

"I'm not wasting my time," I said. "Just trying to keep up with what's going on."

He gave me a pitying (yes, *patronizing*) look and said, "If you pay too much attention to them, you actually *don't* know what's going on. Think about Judy Miller."

He was referring to the disgraced *Times* war correspondent who acted like a compliant stenographer for power and whose blind reporting and fawning posture toward government and military sources greased the wheels for the Bush-Cheney-Rumsfeld invasion of Iraq. "She's not a writer with a mind of her own."

Her name had indeed become synonymous with the rotten state of American journalism: no skepticism (unless interviewing a foreign leader out of favor with the State Department) and no follow-up questions (unless involving another inevitable "sex scandal"). Judith Miller and her cohort were a far cry from Mr. Dooley's often-cited observation that a good newspaper reporter ought to "comfort the afflicted and afflict the comfortable," or I. F. Stone's simple reminder that the starting point for any thoughtful political journalist is the knowledge that "*all* governments lie" (Burma, of course, Syria and Russia, but also Israel, Germany, and, yes, the United States), or even the hard-bitten advice that's become less a serious mantra than a self-congratulatory cliché in J-schools everywhere: "If your mother says she loves you, check it out." The degraded state of the profession in Miller and Company's hands was a good deal less lofty. If the Pentagon or the president says they love you, type it up—it's fit for the front page, without a doubt.

Bernardine was easily convinced, and she converted quickly to all-sports AM talk radio, where she became particularly devoted to *Mike and Mike in the Morning* with their high-energy boy banter and macho,

know-it-all posturing. "No pretense," she said, "just diversion, amuse-
ment, distraction—without the faux earnestness, self-importance, or
delusional thinking." But I couldn't see myself sacrificing a ritual I
imagined I shared with millions: waking up with an early cup of coffee
and a pungent reading of the *Times*, two sharp slaps across the face.

"If it makes you feel better, go ahead," Zayd said. "But if you spent
those two hours a day reading Dickens, you'd be much better informed."
Zayd was a playwright; his wife, a poet and novelist. They were two
of the most insightful writers and best-informed people I knew, and
he had a point. I often felt that the *Times* was a self-important, wildly
overdressed, and heavily perfumed toxic waste dump, but one I had to
visit every day just to pick through the remains, like an archeologist
from Mars.

Before he left, Zayd showed us how to set up easy access to better
sources, as well as Google alerts for things we ought to be aware of
instantly. He had alerts set for some of his friends and his whole family, and he set up a file full of every utterance on the web concerning
Bernardine or me.

Because Zayd had a file and had passed some of the juiciest and
most bizarre tidbits on to us, we knew that attacking us had been a
project of the hard, hard Right for years, long before Obama was a glint
in anyone's eye. And of course we had seen the Weather Underground
as fairy tale and emblem resurrected once before, right after the attacks
of 9/11, providing "further evidence," according to the masters of war,
of the imminent danger of violence in our midst and the need to mobilize for permanent combat. And we knew that Bernardine and I could
become a tiny part of some twisted, nutty, deeply dishonest narrative
from the moment Senator Obama entered the Democratic primary in
2007. That's just how I saw it then: tiny . . . twisted and nutty.

There were already a couple of bloggers hyperventilating and flogging the story—"Obama Launches Political Campaign in the Home
Of Radicals," wrote one; "Records Show $200 Donation to Obama
from Weather Underground," said another—and the *National Enquirer*
touched as many bases as possible when it ran a cover story called
"Obama's Secrets" featuring "a chilling murder mystery—the slaying

of a gay choir conductor . . . silenced because of what he knew about Obama"; "Screaming matches with his wife—over other women"; and, of course, "Another ticking time bomb . . . his close friendship with . . . a former member of the violent, hippie-era, anti-American group the Weathermen." Still, no one else seemed to notice.

Senator Obama, after all, was the least likely in a crowded Democratic field, and all the talking heads figured he was putting a toe in the river simply to get the temperature, develop contacts and deepen his experience and party credibility for a more realistic run in 2012 or 2016. He had lots of time—he was young and had nothing to lose by losing. Hillary was the clear favorite—it was her turn, as Espie Reyes kept reminding me—John Edwards and Joe Biden hopeful still, with Chris Dodd and Bill Richardson fading, Dennis Kucinich and Mike Gravel hardly breathing. My dad, a big-capitalist Republican, had loved Obama and had sent him many small checks over the years, but the smart money had Obama in Kucinich-Gravel land then.

Still our kids felt we should be looking ahead, and so when we were all together at a summer gathering in the mountains, we snatched a few opportunities for some forward thinking and contingency planning.

They'd clearly thought some of this through together, which was by now their custom. A couple of years earlier they'd told us that they had combined their savings into a joint account managed by Chesa, a confident investor and college student at the time, and the inescapable image was of the three of them in an all-purpose, fully protected financial escape pod dropping down and veering off just as the inflated Ayers-Dohrn dirigible—the Mother Ship—plowed into a craggy mountain covered in fog and burst into flames. They could at least still attend college.

Malik was a gifted grill chef, and he spent a couple hours after river time most afternoons preparing and marinating food, gathering wood, creating the "perfect fire," and then delivering abundant platters of steaming corn, zucchini, and meat to the table, to everyone's delight. One day in late August, a neighbor brought over a salmon he'd just caught, and Malik seasoned and grilled the big fish and presented it as the centerpiece for our communal dinner. Chesa added lentil soup and curried cauliflower and tomatoes to the meal, and Zayd contributed an elaborate green salad with dried fruits and roasted nuts. It was a long, slow meal; as dusk turned the screen porch dark we lit kerosene lamps, and the talk turned to Obama. No one thought he could possibly break through at this point, but still, "Whether now or four years from now," Malik said, "I can see you guys so easily pushed into the fray." Malik had challenged Barack in basketball years before and was now a talented middle-school teacher in California, a gifted gardener and consummate cook, and someone whose general stance in the world was to cultivate others, take care of strays, support outsiders, encourage the weak, and nourish everyone around him. Now he was looking after us. "You might as well think it through so you don't get surprised down the road."

The consensus from them, in line with Bernardine's steady and consistent basic instinct, was that whatever happened on the web or in the press, we should simply turn away. No comment, no elaboration, no clarification, no response. "Be completely quiet," they said, "and stay calm." "It's harder than it sounds," Zayd added, looking right at me, "especially for you." True, too true: I tend to have a lot on my mind—who doesn't?—and I'm genetically wired to speak up and speak out, and not always with considered judgment. My default position, no matter what, is to *say something*. My dad used to tease us for what he claimed was a genetic trait we all shared: "Often wrong, but never in doubt; routinely embarrassing, but seldom shy." And Bernardine liked to tell people that one of the reasons we'd survived more than a decade on the run was that she'd never actually spelled out for me that we were underground: "He can't keep a secret and he talks too much, so we just kept him in the dark about our predicament." She was kidding—I think.

"You'll get flattened," they now said in unison. "There's simply no sensible path to being heard in the teeth of the howling gale of a presidential campaign."

"I'm not really worried," I said.

Chesa responded, "Whether you're worried or not is beside the point; you're not a worrier, and so you're not the best judge about what to be bothered about. But look: here's this enormous, ravenous electoral creature with neither a heart nor a brain, and when it comes after you, it'll scoop up a lot of other people for no good reason."

"OK, OK. I give up."

We left that summer in full agreement, and over the next months, my brother Rick and several of our closest friends and comrades deepened and extended the conversation, and underlined the basic conclusion: YO, BILL! SHUT THE FUCK UP!

I agreed, truly I did, and I pretty much thought that I'd gotten the message. I felt it unlikely, for example, that I could say anything substantive about the things I cared most deeply about and have it honestly reported—about the continuing American wars of invasion and occupation, for example, or about the racist injustices defining our increasingly barricaded society—but even here they saw backsliding. "Not *unlikely*, Pops," Malik said. "*Impossible*. Try to keep it straight." He was patronizing me again, but, hell, he was also right, because I was being an idiot and keeping everything clear was exhausting me. Everyone—even me—sensed that if the Obama campaign ever got a real head of steam, I'd need some help to hang on to our agreement, and everyone seemed to agree that it would take a village.

After the ABC "debate" and the George Stephanopoulos moment, I got messages from all three guys: "Holy shit, Pops! You're under the bus!" (Malik); "I loved Obama calling you an 'English' professor—brilliant! It's about to get weirder!" (Chesa); "Just hang in there, man—the longer you say nothing, the calmer your world will become. You can do this!" (Zayd).

When I talked with Zayd on the phone the next day, he predicted not only that I would settle into and embrace a practice of quiet reflection, meditation at the eye of the storm, but that all the noise swirling around me would become even more frenzied and more frantic, more incoherent and more out of control, shriller and nuttier. "You'll be sane, and all around you they will be going crazy," he said. He began to sound like my own personal Buddhist advisor, my all-seeing and extrawise Bodhisattva: "Remember: You're watching the roller coaster. Don't get on the roller coaster." Om.

Over the next several days I stayed close to my routine—up before 5:00 a.m., strong coffee, and at least three hours of early morning writing at the big table before the noise of the wider world made its claims on my attention. But some things were beginning to shift without a doubt. I now avoided looking at the media altogether, even the sites that Zayd had recommended—I found the desire to respond and correct the record just too overwhelming, and I wanted to resist that terrible impulse. That was probably on balance a positive thing, but even better, each of our kids now called me at least once every day, "just checking in." We'd always been in regular contact, but this was another bonus, and it had its desired effect. I felt propped up and supported where it counted, and I loved it.

I biked from Hyde Park to the university still, but one day I decided to ride the path along Lake Michigan instead of my usual dash through the South Side, and it instantly became my preferred route. The bike path took a little longer, true, but slowing down was precisely what won me over—the lake was breathtaking and the approaching skyline beautiful, the wind refreshing, the sun on my face warming. As I moved along, breathing in the good air, I began to feel the frenzy outside falling away as a deep tranquility settled in, and I arrived at work filled with calm and inner peace. Several graduate students were cued up to talk to me about their dissertations and class papers during my office hours. Outside was all thunder and lightning, anxiety and challenge, and I felt as if I'd just meditated. It was the end of the world as we know it, and I felt fine.

If somebody had to be thrown into the path of the dark and onrushing train at that moment—if the locomotive of the Lord was set to run someone down—I was in many ways as good a prospect as any, and in better shape than most. True, I'd tried to make a revolution, I had a dubious and hazardous history, and I'd "committed detestable acts forty years ago," as Obama had so delicately put it, which was, after all, kind of the point of the whole messy muddle. But I wasn't overly jumpy or all OCD about it, and I'd lived on. I'd dealt with the legal problems associated with the disorder decades before, and I'd publicly accounted for those dicey times in books and articles and interviews. I'd come under withering media attention and a sustained attack, complete with death threats, seven years earlier. And yet none of that captured how I actually experienced my life, and here I was, still standing, still happily putting one foot in front of the other.

I'd become an unlikely academic at a research university, written about teaching and learning and the requirements of education in a democracy, published several scholarly articles and monographs and books—all the things professors are expected to do—and been recognized, promoted, and steadily rewarded. I was a lot older now, and while my political views were still radical and my activist enthusiasm undiminished, I felt that I'd learned something of the perils of political passion and dedication without either withdrawing my commitments or making idiotic counter-commitments. These were different times with new responsibilities and unique demands, to be sure. But I had a good job and work to do that I thought was important, and I was deeply connected with a sturdy network of brilliant students and a huge community of agitators, activists, dissidents, and outcasts—lepers in a metaphorical sense, or at least folks who'd been forced out of the camp for "having issues"—as well as organizers and engaged colleagues. I had a cast of heroes, sheroes, weirdoes, and queeroes in my life, I knew who my friends were, and I knew I wasn't alone. So under the bus or tied to the railroad tracks, I was feeling OK—pretty great in fact. The best in the world, as my dad would have said.

I was also still trying—with many, many others—to be conscious of and true to that challenge I'd first heard from Paul Potter back at the University of Michigan: *Don't let your life make a mockery of your values.* I didn't take that to mean I could simply memorize a set of rules or make a list and carry it around in my back pocket for a lifetime, sleepwalking step by dogmatic step free of the inconvenience of thinking about what I was doing or rethinking anything I'd done. I took it to be a dynamic test and a living guide, something that I could never achieve nor fully satisfy once and for all, but rather a compass for a complicated world, a standard to be reached for, something to be worked out again and again in the messy process of living.

So I was devoted to leaping out of bed each day determined to work in some small way toward a new world of balance, peace, joy, and justice, knowing that I would end each day having fallen painfully, horribly short. Next day, as dawn spread her rosy red fingers in the dim sky, I'd spring from bed again with my mind reset on freedom. On and on, forever, I guessed.

I was still trying to understand the parameters of a public and engaged person's obligations in troubled times—as well as my *own* obligations in those *specific* times—and I was still trying to fight the good fight, whatever that meant, in whatever ways I could.

I still thought of myself as a revolutionary, but if the test was to have a fully worked-out and internally consistent argument, as well as a set of concrete action steps that could take us from here to there—*there* being some vibrant and viable future characterized by peace and love and joy and justice—then I admittedly and most certainly failed the exam. I had no plan. I did have a lot of tolerance for confusion and contingency, a deep belief in dialogue and open debate, a love of experimentation and spontaneity, a fascination with particularity, an instinct for action, a willingness to dance the dialectic with some abandon, and an abiding faith in ordinary people as agents, actors, and history makers. If a revolutionary is someone who lives with a sense of perpetual uncertainty that typically accompanies social learning, someone trying to make a purposeful and activist life battling the murderous system of oppression and exploitation and opening spaces for more participatory democracy, more peace, and more fair dealing in large and small matters—well, then, OK: I was still a revolutionary.

I knew for sure that it was my own damn life, and that I had to live it for myself without guarantees. I knew that this was my one and only time on earth, that there would be no possible repeat, no second act once I was gone. I knew I'd do my best to write my own story. I was sure I didn't want anyone else to write it for me.

So, come what may, I'd stay quiet and calm, I hoped, do my work and stay close to my loved ones, and just keep on truckin'—like a doodah man.

• • •

Bernardine and I were on the Long Island ferry heading to Michael and Eleanora Kennedy's place for a couple days of needed R and R and R—that last R for reinforcement—when I got a call on my cell phone from Toni Preckwinkle, our city councilperson. "I'm sure you've seen the 'kill him' videos," she began. "I'm really sorry about all this mess." She had talked to Mayor Daley, she said, as well as the police commander in our neighborhood. "Everyone agrees that you should have a little enhanced protection, and with your permission, the Chicago police and the university force will assign patrols to your house." They all felt that a little prudence could go a long way. I'd always assumed they were watching me, but this was from an oddly different angle of regard. "I don't take any of it seriously," I said, "and I don't intend to hide out in my own house."

Actually our street was already pretty snug and sure: beyond Jesse Jackson and Operation Push, beyond the University of Chicago police, the largest private force in the country, and beyond Minister Louis Farrakhan and his elite Fruit of Islam security force—young men with crisp white shirts, skinny bow ties, and close-cropped hair hovering nearby—the Secret Service was just then creating a Green Zone at the Obama residence around the corner. Still, the folks chanting "Kill him!" looked a little dazed, the threats were reaching a fever pitch, and what would it take, after all, to unhinge just one of them? "We'd feel better about it," Toni said. "Thanks, Toni," I said.

Michael and Eleanora provided the perfect retreat for us: long walks on the beach where I picked up tiny specks of sea glass and bleached wood (adding them to the pack of found pennies that I carry with me to repel bad luck); scrumptious, lazy meals on the porch; a constant serenade of breaking waves and ocean breezes. Most important, they provided three days of close friendship and good counsel. They wholeheartedly reinforced the main message: be quiet, turn away from the media, and let things take their own course. "More important," Michael said late one night, "since there's no way to manage most things crashing around your head, your assignment is to be responsibly in charge of yourself. Period. Your integrity and your identity depend on what you choose and what you refuse right here, right now, just this." He was confident that as the madness passed by, our humanity would be rebuilt on having withstood the onslaught without whining or cringing, giving in or backing down.

A few days after Sarah Palin's "palling-around-with-terrorists" rally with its "Kill him!" chorus, we were back in Chicago, and I was hanging out—palling around, I suppose—with a couple of Chicago cops at the neighborhood coffee shop on Fifty-third Street. I'd had a casual, friendly relationship with several police officers in Hyde Park stretching back for years, but as my presence in the campaign pushed forward, our encounters became more animated and more intimate. One morning, chatting about the elections at the coffee shop, one of them—a guy in his thirties with a diamond earring and long dreadlocks—said in a neighborly and cordial way, "Bill, you guys did kill cops way back when, right?"

I thought I'd pass out. "We never had," I said—but I was jolted by the question and utterly astonished at the cordial way he'd asked it. "No, no. We never killed or hurt anyone," I said. "A lot of heated rhetoric, some real destructive vandalism, a lot of pissed-off language and some odd posturing, but, no, never killed a cop."

"Oh," he said. "That's good. A lot of guys in the station house heard you killed a cop, and a bunch of us are reading *Fugitive Days* right now. You think we could set up for you to come and talk about the book at the station house one day?"

"Love to," I said, amazed at the prospect of a *book group* at the *station house* focused on *Fugitive Days*. I had to pinch myself.

Over the next several days and weeks, I ran into one cop and then another and another around the neighborhood, and he or she would corner me for a point of clarification on a passage from *Fugitive Days*. It was utterly surreal for a time.

I had a few faithful haters—guys habitually weighing in on my website or e-mailing me, occasionally even sending snail mail to our home— who became as familiar to me as an old pair of sweat socks. Jack Janski was always close at hand, and still is. His recent comments are typical of our long association: "We're watching you. We know exactly what you are up to, and guess what? We ain't gonna let it happen." "Hell is too good for you anti-American skunks." (I always appreciated Jack for being gender-fair by including Bernardine in most of his rants—thank you.) "You two are dogshit."

Mike Adams had written me several times to tell me, for example, that I was "a filthy subhuman terrorist pig," but he later admitted that "that was a very mean and un-Christian thing to say—even to a terrorist sociopath." Mike decided to repent of his sins by giving me a Christmas gift: a one-year membership in the National Rifle Association with its accompanying subscription to *American Rifleman.* "For years liberals have been denying that Ayers is a terrorist while falsely accusing NRA members of being terrorists," Mike claimed. "Now that Bill's in the NRA, Leftists will have no choice but to admit the following: Bill Ayers is an unrepentant terrorist!" A contradiction with a sense of humor, Mike claimed that the gift was "money well spent in the spirit of reconciliation."

Dan Popa, more rambling than short and snappy Jack, and more humorless than clever Mike, was pretty dependable too: "Don't go totally gutless on me now that you're an old washed-up piece of candy-ass shit. You know exactly what you are and you know Obama as well as anyone, you lying fucker."

The ad hominem attacks expected no real response, I supposed, but I wrote Dan back anyway, trying to reason with him: "Actually, I don't know exactly who or what I am," I said "in part because my self-awareness is as blurry as anyone's, and beyond that I embody a mass of contradictions that I'm in no hurry to resolve—so I'll just have to remain ambiguous, undecipherable, and suspended in the middle of things, just like everybody else."

I couldn't resist a bit of provocation. How could he be so sure that I was a candy-ass, for example, and what kind of candy specifically, hard or soft, and how sweet? Was he offering a sly bit of praise, eh? But my reply only enraged him, and he responded by piling on even more random, happy-go-lucky images: "Your wife has the bad breath of a camel's ass. Was she a man once? You are a lying gutless puke."

"Block those metaphors!" I wrote, and I asked Dan how he knew the smell of a camel's ass exactly and how did that compare, say, to

an elephant's ass or a giraffe's? I added that it was difficult to puke
without a gut.

No matter—he kept coming.

> You are so evil and so is your sick wife. You will both be in Hell
> eventually as the only true path to salvation is Jesus Christ and you
> mock and spit on him. I'll say this for you, Maggot. You are patient
> and you are pretty smart. There is a God. He has lifted His hand
> away from this country, I think deep down you know that, however,
> keep this in mind, there will be blowback from all that you have
> accomplished and done to the kids of this country. You have had
> a great hand in dumbing them down and indoctrinating them and
> there will be no forgiveness for you when you are judged by God for
> you are one of the leaders. It will eventually crumble, and you are
> taking the good down with you, good people, honest, loving people
> are going to die. The blood will be on your hands, Obama's, Con-
> gress, the Supreme Court, the unions, the Communists, the haters
> of all that is good and decent. Fuck you Ayers. There is a place in
> Hell reserved just for you. You will endure 10,000 times what you
> bring on others. Enjoy yourself you sick twisted old smelly SOB
> with your man-looking wife. The light will shine on you cock-
> roaches soon enough.

There were others, though, who were worrisome to me and not at
all funny, partly for what they said but also because they visited only
once, expressed their excessive rage, and retreated quickly to the shadows. *John D. Levin*—"I hope and pray that I will read soon that you
were found murdered, dismembered, and had been horribly tortured
for days before your slow, painful death. God bless anyone who does
it to you." *FBA*—"I hope somebody puts a bullet through your head
you leftist fuck." *Redwingsfan51*—"You should have been executed
for treason a long time ago." *Sniper*—"Watch your back! Your time is
coming!" See what I mean? Sniper sent that letter, postmarked Sacramento, California, to our home and bearing a recent photo of our
front door. Yipes!

Margaret Mead famously said that one should never doubt that a small group of people can change the world—"Indeed, nothing else ever has." This adage, while true, could use a modern amendment: never doubt that one idiot with an e-mail account can change the world—or at least disrupt a lot of lives.

One of my self-appointed tormentors was David Caton, an accountant turned rock-club owner turned memoirist and author of a book about his personal addiction to pornography and ultimate resurrection as a born-again Christian turned right-wing activist as founder, president, and sole employee of the Florida Family Association. While writing me to encourage repentance and a certain path to salvation, he was also waging a one-man jihad against a reality TV show on the Learning Channel called *All-American Muslim*. Because of his intervention, Lowe's Home Improvement and Kayak.com canceled sponsorship of the show—and, of course, covered all the bases by simultaneously issuing statements in favor of tolerance and diversity. What a country!

I'd never actually met anyone face to face from my furiously corresponding Greek chorus. I pictured white, middle-aged loners in terry-cloth robes sitting in Mom's overheated basement rec room fueling up on rum and Coke and fast food, a collision of cigarette butts mingling in a big glass ashtray—until Michael H. stepped from that imagined homogeneous crowd and approached me, video recorder in hand, to introduce himself after a talk I'd given in Denver. Young and soft-spoken, not frothing incoherently, dressed in khakis and button-down blue shirt rather than a black cape or a robe of any kind, he exploded my settled stereotype of the collective howlers. "You claimed you never killed anyone," he said quietly, "but what about the millions you'd planned to kill if your revolution had won?" I responded that I'd never planned to kill a single person—not one, and not hundreds or thousands or millions. "OK, thanks," he said as he slowly swung the camera in a panoramic arc, capturing the entire scene.

And then one morning a man my own age walked into my office on campus off the street and told me in a trembling voice that I deserved to die. He was sweating and red-faced, his veins popping in his neck and forehead. I was shaken but managed to swallow hard and get my own voice steady enough to ask him if he was threatening me. When he said no, I asked him to please leave. He refused, so I shifted direction and invited him to sit down; once in a chair, he became visibly calmer and looked harmless enough. I was cooler, too, and I told him evenly that I was going to call the police. He raised his voice and turned a deeper red. "Don't you mean the pigs?" I said he could call them whatever he liked, but to me, in this situation, I'd just call them the police. We chatted for several minutes until the cops arrived. I didn't want to press any charges, and the police gave him a warning and escorted him off campus.

Attack ads were running on TV in Florida linking Senator Obama to Rashid Khalidi and demonizing him as an anti-Semite with deep ties to the Palestinian Liberation Organization or to Hamas. A reporter interviewed a high official in John McCain's presidential campaign (no, no—not high like that; well, maybe, but I mean high in the hierarchy!) on national television and challenged the stuttering assertion that Obama was affiliated with a bunch of anti-Semites. "Who are Obama's anti-Semitic friends?" asked the reporter. "Rashid Khalidi," said the campaign official. "Who else?" asked the newsman without the slightest impulse to question the assertion that Khalidi was anti-Semitic. "William Ayers," said the McCain man. And without missing a beat the reporter responded: "Ayers isn't an anti-Semite," he said. "He's the terrorist."

Rashid called me, laughing, and wondered if we might change lanes for at least one news cycle. "You be the anti-Semite; I'm sick of it. I'll be the terrorist."

"Oh, come on," I said. "Don't try to wriggle free—you've got your assigned spot. Stay in your lane!"

The demonization had its impacts, even if not exactly in the intended ways. A colleague of Chesa's, a person I'd met several times, told him how sorry she was that I'd been dragged into all this and how unfair it was that I'd become collateral damage of the campaign. She added, "I know Bill killed someone, but that was a long time ago." But I didn't!

As the attacks on me accelerated, Obama's poll numbers inched upward. Maybe people were just becoming disgusted with the gutter tactics; maybe they saw the desperation. Maybe they thought, as I did, that Barack's "connections" to other people, no matter who, did not define the man. Or maybe they liked me—OK, not likely, but maybe. The best news came after Senator Obama was subjected to a steady barrage of attacks for being a "socialist," and a poll discovered that for people under thirty, the word "socialism" had a favorable rating of over 50 percent, while "Republican" garnered less than 40 percent. I imagined some kid in Wyoming hearing the attack ads, Googling "socialism," and reading up on that central social principle, "from each according to his ability, to each according to his need." Hey, that sounds reasonable, even biblical. Sweet! Keep the attacks coming!

Things like this always happen. At the height of the civil rights movement in the South, the White Citizens Council published a notorious photograph of the young Martin Luther King at an activist workshop at the Highlander Folk School in Tennessee with the caption: "King at Communist Training School." Once, when we were reminiscing with Myles Horton, the founder of Highlander, near the end of his life, he told Bernardine and me about a day when he was driving a van load of young people to a demonstration a few hours away when they saw one of these photographs enlarged on a highway billboard. Soon enough they saw another, and as a third billboard loomed in the distance, one of the kids turned to Myles and said, "That's the dumbest advertisement I've ever seen, Myles—it doesn't even tell you who to call or how to get to the school."

When John McCain sat down for an interview with Sean Hannity on Fox, apparently in an attempt to reassure the "base," he was still unaware of the narrative Hannity had been spinning for months. Hannity filled him in. Ayers was an unrepentant "terrorist," he explained: "On 9/11, of all days, he had an article where he bragged about bombing our Pentagon, bombing the Capitol and bombing New York City police headquarters. . . . He said, 'I regret not doing more.'"

McCain couldn't believe it.

Neither could I.

But back on the campaign trail, McCain immediately got on message, and Stephen Colbert, the faux right-wing commentator from

Comedy Central who channels Bill O'Reilly on steroids, followed suit. Colbert ran a clip of Barack Obama at a press conference saying, "Can't we just get over the sixties?" An outraged Stephen responded, "No, Senator, we can't just get over the sixties. It's the gift that keeps on giving. To this day, when our country holds a presidential election, we judge the candidates through the lens of the 1960s; or, for example, the myth that Obama is cozy with William Ayers, a sixties radical who planted a bomb in the Capitol Building and then went on to even more heinous crimes by becoming a college professor."

It was inevitable that McCain would bet the house on his dishonest and largely discredited vision of the sixties. He'd built his political career on being a prisoner of war in Viet Nam after being shot down in a bombing mission over Hanoi. I was a convenient prop on so many levels: an imagined "terrorist" to begin, an unapologetic radical, and a representative of subversive antiwar forces, in sharp contrast to the heroes like McCain who selflessly gave their all to defend the homeland in wartime.

McCain and Palin demanded to "know the full extent" of the Obama-Ayers relationship so that they could root out whether Obama, as Palin put it, "is telling the truth to the American people or not."

In the wake of 9/11, even the left-leaning *Nation* magazine had bent over backwards—sometimes comically, and other times in cringe-worthy ways—to paint themselves as the "good radicals" as opposed to those crazies of the Left (whoever and wherever they might be), who were routinely condemned, demonized, and mostly just ignored. As crude and uncomradely as this tendency always struck me, it mostly warranted a smile or a yawn.

But then they published a piece condemning the dangerous tactics of the Right in the 2008 presidential campaign and managed a bizarre reversal by asserting that the attacks were all "an attempt to make [Obama] appear too radical by calling attention to his tenuous associations with an angry black minister, an un-American education professor and foreign-born Muslims." The tie to Jeremiah Wright was only tenuous if activities like presiding at the wedding of Barack and Michelle, baptizing their kids, sharing a stage at the victory rally when

Obama won his senate seat, and providing the title to his last book are all bits of fluff and nonsense; Rashid Khalidi was born to a secular Palestinian family in New York; and I am a radical, true, but I'm not un-American. They surely meant to protect Obama, and they were certainly correct when they noted that Barack Obama was no radical—but if they'd thought about it they might have gone a step further, endorsing McCain or better yet putting themselves out of business, thereby inoculating their candidate from the charge that the liberal-ish *Nation* liked him at all. I was stunned at first that they accepted the manufactured clichés and the received wisdom about Obama, as well as the outright dishonesty of it all, but insanity was becoming routine. Why not simply say, Wright and Obama were once close—so what? Get over it!

I objected, and the *Nation* published a "clarification" in the back of a later issue addressed to "the irony-impaired"—presumably, that was me. Later, a friend at the *Nation* told me that it was all the fault of a copy editor who'd inadvertently failed to put quotation marks around "un-American" in the first place.

But speaking of irony, while the liberals at the *Nation* and elsewhere were bowing deeply to the nonsense, the independent but irreverent conservative Stanley Fish was firing away, thoughtful and eloquent in resistance. Stanley had left UIC for Florida International University, and I missed our once-frequent campus encounters. But in the midst of the latest flurry, I bumped into him at O'Hare Airport, and we had a chance to get a coffee and catch up.

"Do you know the difference between a terrorist and a liturgist?" he asked as we waited for our coffee. I didn't, no. "A terrorist can still change his mind."

Stanley had followed "the bullshit campaign" against Bernardine and me, and he thought our unwillingness to respond to the attacks was probably wise. "But aren't you bursting to shout something from the top of a tower somewhere?" he asked. "I go back and forth," I said. "Mostly it's just a great comfort to know that I won't have to pick through the wreckage and figure out a sensible response." "I love picking through the wreckage," he said, which was true. "And I'm quite incapable of being quiet." And that was a good thing, too.

A week later Stanley published a piece in the *New York Times* pointing out that the attacks on Senator Obama had resurrected McCarthyism and mixed in a dose of its more recent descendant, swiftboating. The spear point of McCarthyism was always "guilt by association," a term coined by Supreme Court justice William O. Douglas to describe the dangerous and repugnant practice of digging deep into a person's history for the slightest signs of infidelity to the orthodoxy of the day or any different thinking whatsoever, and then demonizing them for any potentially dangerous thoughts they might harbor. *Swiftboating* was the term used to describe the right-wing attacks on John Kerry's military record during his run for the presidency four years earlier. The attacks never tried to document any wrongdoing whatsoever (since there was none) but were aimed rather at "covering the victim with slime enough to cast doubt on his or her integrity," as Stanley wrote. The combination of McCarthyism and swiftboating was, Stanley asserted, "particularly lethal"—witch-hunting in the modern age.

Stanley mocked "the startling revelation . . . that Barack Obama ate dinner at William Ayers's house, served with him on a board and was the honored guest at a reception he organized." He went on to confess to having eaten dinner at our home (on several occasions) and more: "I have had Bill and his wife Bernardine Dohrn to my apartment, was a guest lecturer in a course he taught and joined in a (successful) effort to persuade him to stay at UIC and say no to an offer from Harvard." Of course, Stanley wasn't a politician running for office, but, he offered, "I do write for the *New York Times* and, who knows, this association with former fugitive members of the Weathermen might be enough in the eyes of some to get me canned."

Stanley asked rhetorically:

Did I conspire with Bill Ayers? Did I help him build bombs? Did I aid and abet his evasion (for a time) of justice? Not likely, given that at the time of the events that brought Ayers and Dohrn to public attention, I was a supporter of the Vietnam War. I haven't asked him to absolve me of that sin (of which I have since repented), and he hasn't asked me to forgive him for his (if he has any).

That cheered me enormously.

McCain-Palin campaign literature proclaimed that I didn't regret my Weathermen activities, which, Stanley pointed out helpfully, had absolutely nothing to do with Obama, unless political candidates must be held to a standard where they are asked to repudiate things acquaintances of theirs had *not* said. There were assertions that Obama publically admired my 1997 book on the juvenile justice system (true!), and that Obama and I participated on a panel examining the role of intellectuals in public life (there was a photograph of Obama and me seated under an amusing banner that read, "Are Intellectuals Necessary?" Short answer: all humans are intellectuals, so, yes). But it was all the stuff of McCarthyism and swiftboating, the combined slime lapping at every step. "The suggestion," Stanley wrote, "that something sinister was transpiring on those occasions is backed up by nothing except the four-alarm-bell typography that accompanies this list of entirely innocent, and even praiseworthy, actions." He concluded that he felt "a little dirty just for having repeated a scurrilous rumor even as I rejected it. Apparently Obama's . . . opponents have no such qualms and are happily retailing, and wallowing in, the dirt."

Stanley's writings calmed my alienated heart.

SEVEN

Talking with the Tea Party

Malik noted during the presidential campaign that the supercharged fame that had befallen Barack Obama was in a space all its own—a galaxy far, far away. My experiences with little bits of fringe notoriety and small bursts of public recognition or disrepute over the years were one thing, but this was something else entirely. Even the smallest piece of space dust like me that brushed up against the fiery Obama constellation was destined to become a burning taper in the sky, blazing bright for a nanosecond and fated to be burnt to a crisp.

Malik quoted Dave Chappelle: "Fame is amazin'," he'd said, and Chappelle's comic riff hinged on the difference between being a famous person like himself versus a full-throttle mega-celebrity like Bill Clinton. If Monica Lewinsky had hooked up with Dave she'd still be a private person, he claimed, but just by getting with Clinton, she'd become a living legend.

I became—not Monica, certainly, but for a parallel reason and with a comparable problem—recognizable. I was in Grand Central Station in New York one morning for an early train to Philadelphia quietly sipping coffee and reading the *Times* when a young man who had walked past me staring and done a double-take minutes before began to point at me from the far side of the room and shout at the top of his voice, "There's a terrorist in the waiting room! Right there! It's Bill Ayers, the terrorist! We need help! Terrorist!" I was mortified but also trapped. I tried smiling and shrugging my shoulders, then offering a mildly aggravated but amused look to the other staring passengers, and then shushing him with a friendly don't-be-an-irritating-asshole gesture. I wanted to flee, but why? Where would I go? I hadn't done anything (there I went again, claiming an innocence I could never really earn), and what if he chased me through the station, jeering and heckling? A couple of cops showed up, spoke with him quietly, glanced at me, nodded, whispered, checked his ID, and as the older cop steered him away, the younger one came over to me and said with a smile, "Sure, I recognize you. Sorry about that, but it's New York City. What are you going to do?"

Cab drivers in Washington, Boston, and San Francisco—mostly from Somalia, Ethiopia, or Egypt—were friendly and excited and always wanted to talk, and before we parted insisted on a cell-phone photograph, arm in arm. "I guess I can't be president now," each would say with a laugh.

It was bizarro, to say the least, to be caught up in what you could call a world historical event. I could hardly wait for it to end.

There were a couple of omens early on of a gathering storm that would become more troublesome, dark birds circling above my head and perching in the branches nearby, watching, but they were only understandable as harbingers in hindsight. One came in the form of a letter awaiting me when I returned from summer break signed by three colleagues from the University of Colorado. "This is an unusual letter for us to be writing and for you to receive," they began. They simultaneously informed me that they were organizing a conference to highlight the ideals of progressive education and that because of the troubling and treacherous times we were all enduring, and the disturbing attention focused on me in particular, I would not be welcome at the conference. "We know and deeply respect you and your commitments," they wrote, but "we have to find ways for the public to see progressive education not as radical and threatening but as nurturing and familiar." Therefore, they went on, "we cannot risk a simplistic and dubious association between progressive education and the violent aspects of your past." The letter explained their thinking in some detail and asked that I "understand and possibly appreciate this decision." I'd likely never have heard about the conference had they not written, but here we were. Oh, shit! I said to myself.

When I showed Bernardine the letter she quoted Phil Ochs's brilliant anthem, "Love Me, I'm a Liberal," which chronicles instance after instance of laissez-faire hypocrisy and leftish narcissism. As a kid I marched and protested, says the narrator, and memorized the old union hymns, but now I'm much older and wiser, and I'll have to be turning you in!

I wasn't a liberal—even though I'd earned the dubious honor of being listed by Boycottliberalism.com as one of the "1000 top liberals in America," and I admired lots and lots of the other putative public enemies on that particular blacklist: Harry Belafonte, Spike Lee, Woody Allen, Margaret Cho, Danny Glover, Michael Moore, the Dixie Chicks, and Tim Robbins. And my liberal Colorado colleagues weren't exactly turning me in either, but I knew that I'd have to refuse to "understand and possibly appreciate" their problem. Beyond stubbornness, I felt motivated and energized by the paralysis of the liberals. I got it—from their perspective, they were uncomfortable with the low-level witch hunt lurking in the corner. They disapproved of it, for sure, but also feared it, for damn good reason. Still, asking me to endorse the view that I was now a pariah was asking just a bit too much. Why didn't I just kill myself, as lots of my steady stream of hate mail urged?

My own sense of fairness urged resistance. I knew something of the fatal consequences of a compromise like the one they were asking of me, and where it could possibly end. The proverbial slippery slope heaved into view: a new but no less treacherous twist on blacklisting, an unacknowledged banning, a quiet silencing, and the same old guilt by association, no matter how appealingly dressed up. I would remind them of the invitation by Bard College to Salman Rushdie to join their faculty when the fatwa was issued against him, an instance of principle in action and in the moment when it actually mattered, not remorse and regret after it was all over. To hell with it. I knew what I'd done, and I knew why I'd done it. I'd stand up for it all, and I'd stand up for myself as well.

I replied to my colleagues from the University of Colorado that they had, of course, no obligation to include me in their progressive education conference and certainly not in their deliberations about my suitability to attend. I was in fact tempted to say, with apologies to Groucho Marx, that I wouldn't want to attend any progressive education conference that would have me. But since they'd opened the issue in the way they had, since they'd outlined their thinking on the matter and invited me to understand and possibly appreciate their decision, I felt that I had to respond.

Their desire to position progressive education "not as radical or threatening but as nurturing and familiar," while tempting, struck me as mostly a fool's errand. No one argued that the progressive education movement actually threatened students, teachers, or citizens—rather, it held out the hope of realizing a humane and decent education for all within a revitalized politics and a more authentically democratic society. But progressive education, if it meant anything at all, had to embody a powerful and profound threat to the status quo—a direct challenge, for example, to all the policy initiatives that de-skill and hammer teachers into interchangeable cogs in a bureaucracy, a refusal to bow to all the pressure to reduce teaching to a set of manageable and easily monitored tasks, a rejection of all the imposed labels and all the simple-minded metrics employed to describe student learning and rank youngsters in a hierarchy of winners and losers. It had to be a threat to all that and more. And here was the contradiction laid bare at the heart of the efforts of my Colorado colleagues as well as my own: the humanistic ideal and the democratic injunction insisted that every person was an entire universe, that each could develop as a full and autonomous person engaged with others in a common political and social space and an equality of power; yet the capitalist imperative maintained that profit was at the center of economic, political, and social progress, and developed, then, a culture of competition, elitism, and hierarchy. An education for democracy would always fail as an adjunct to capitalism, just as an education for capitalism would fall short when it came to building either a democratic ethos or a participatory practice. I told my erstwhile friends and comrades that we would have to find ways to engage, then, in the arena of school and education reform even as we struggled toward a world fit for all children. The two were inseparable.

Interestingly, of all the attacks against me from the Right at that moment, the most sensible emanated from Sol Stern, once a liberal but now an apostate claiming to be writing a lengthy biography of me. Stern, a senior fellow with the free-market-loving, conservative Manhattan Institute, pleaded with his soul mates in the blogosphere to get over my dark past and focus on the present, writing on the blog *Eduwonkette*: "Ayers' treachery is not primarily his actions from decades ago, but his activities with schools and children today, principally his advocacy of progressive education—a Trojan Horse that could destroy our civilization." Stern actually read what I wrote and wanted to challenge and refute it; most of the others simply pasted a public enemy label over my face and assumed that was all that needed to be said.

I told my colleagues in Colorado that I had accounted for my actions during the US assaults on Viet Nam and the Black Freedom Movement and paid the price. The only crime I was guilty of now was my alienated mind, and I'd be happy to stand up, tell my story, admit my mistakes, and take responsibility—shoulder to shoulder with everyone else, including war criminals, politicians, soldiers, officers, students, scholars, and all the folks attending their education conference. Absent that, they seemed to say that I had some uniquely dreadful behavior to account for, and on that point I politely disagreed.

I also worried that their attempt to cleanse their conference of the likes of me had no obvious end. They would have to cut out the Marxists and the socialists to start, anyone who wrote critically about capitalism and education, of course, then the militants, the noisy anti-racists, the pushy feminists, and on and on. That struck me as not only unprincipled, deeply cynical, and cowardly; it was suicidal as well, and with lots of miserable historical precedent.

I told them I was not a public enemy and that I would not be complicit in blacklisting myself, and I ended the letter on a lighter note: so invite me already.

There's a lot of wicked history worked up in all of this. In another repressive time, Elizabeth Gurley Flynn was expelled from the ACLU, an organization she cofounded, because of her membership in the Communist Party. There's a lot of fight-back, too, along with principled rejection of the thought police: when the Yippies' Abbie Hoffman and Jerry Rubin were hauled before the fearsome House Committee on Un-American Activities, they dressed up like an original American revolutionary and a Vietnamese freedom fighter, refused to bow down and testify inside the chamber, and helped to laugh that nest of reactionaries out of existence. When several universities were cowed into banning the DuBois Clubs—a handful of students in the youth wing of the Communist Party who were attacked by Richard Nixon for intentionally creating a front group that would dupe people into joining since it rhymed with "Boys Clubs"—I joined up, along with hundreds of members of Students for a Democratic Society, and the ban was overcome. And in the arena of progressive education itself, there's a wonderful story told about its patron saint, John Dewey: when Maxim Gorky visited New York in 1905 and was refused lodging at several hotels because he was traveling with a woman who was not his wife, Professor Dewey and his wife, Evelyn, invited the couple to their home and hosted a reception for Teachers College students "in honor of the non-Mrs. Gorky."

My letter earned a response from the dean of the School of Education herself, now taking full responsibility and explaining that Colorado was in a difficult spot because of all the publicity around Professor Ward Churchill, and that her primary concern was protecting the university and inoculating it from "the claim that violence should be part of the solution," and that my stance might "become the banner" for the school.

I thanked her for her letter and explained that I made no such claim on behalf of violence myself, and that she shouldn't be confused by the media or the mob. Further, if endorsing opposition to violence was the standard and the oath that must be sworn in order to attend the conference or come to the university, she might want to consider some of the other exclusions: both of her US senators, the president and his entire cabinet, ROTC, military recruiters, and on and on. I wondered aloud if all scholars and guests who might attend the gathering were being subjected to the same level of scrutiny and asked to sign the same pledge, and I suggested that if I were really as radioactive as she seemed to imagine, perhaps she should alert my dean and university president, my publishers, and the organizers of dozens of other events I was scheduled to attend and address in the coming months. I told her that she would not be the first, but would be joining a campaign well underway, fueled by Loony Tunes characters like David Horowitz and Sol Stern.

I did get the invitation but no apology, and after all the twisting and turning I felt an obligation to rearrange my schedule in order to attend the conference. It was small and low-key, everyone perfectly polite, with the university-catered lunch drawn from what I could only imagine to be some national food preparation company's menu suggestion for academic gatherings—no zing, no zest, no fiery little something. The sky did not fall, I left no banners, incited no violence, and there's not much else to report really.

Soon enough, the groans of the idiot wind gathered force and focus and became a roaring tempest. I was banned in Boston—Boston University, actually, by order of its little dictator, the chancellor—and canceled in Cambridge. Scheduled lectures were shut down in Sacramento as well as in Urbana-Champaign, Georgia, Texas, Florida, and dozens of other places. Penn State University earned some sort of speed record in my mind: I got an e-mail one morning inviting me to give a talk to a student group; I accepted the request before noon; by 2:00 p.m. that same day—shortly after the administration was informed—my invitation was rescinded.

The rationalizations varied. In Boston, the chancellor at BU didn't want to offend the feelings of the families of police officers killed in the line of duty, an entirely manufactured correlation; in Georgia, the president cited threats to burn down the campus center as the reason I would be banned; and in my sister campus at Urbana-Champaign, the president cited exhaustion from defending me at board meetings and at every Illinois state legislative hearing—all that freedom of speech stuff could really take a toll on a guy!

The US State Department told us repeatedly through press releases and videos that we lived in the freest country on earth, with "hundreds of universities that are the envy of the world." I wasn't sure that the party line was false by every measure, nor could I claim that my experiences with universities and freedom were typical in any way whatsoever. But I wouldn't easily dismiss the view from the bottom of that particular tunnel either—even if it carries with it its own gaps, shadows, and distortions, it casts a unique gloominess on the whole question.

While I was being canceled and blacklisted at home, I had several offers to teach and lecture in England and Germany, Cyprus and Hong Kong—they either didn't think I was particularly toxic, or they didn't care. I agreed to deliver a paper at a curriculum and teaching conference at National Taiwan University and stayed for a week, giving talks at Taiwan Open University and Taiwan Normal as well.

Late on my first night in Taipei, a small group of faculty and students hosted me at a lively restaurant the size of a warehouse pulsing with rock music, where the choice was dumplings or more dumplings, meat or vegetable, savory or sweet dumplings—no menus, just a small army of servers circling the room with huge baskets of steaming portions. We stayed too late and I ate too much, but by the time I got to my room, we had mapped out a plan for the week that was a mixture of work and play, and included a couple of meetings with activists and organizers.

It was 3:00 a.m. in Taipei when I was awakened by my cell phone. I was still a little upside-down in time, but I woke by the third round of ringing. The caller introduced herself as a dean from the University of Nebraska, and she said she was so sorry to disturb me and sorrier still to be the bearer of bad news: a talk we'd contracted almost a year ago for an upcoming research forum on campus was about to be canceled due to threats of violence if I appeared. I heard anguish in her voice, and I thought I heard embarrassment as well, but she pressed on with the dirty assignment she'd been given. She asked if I could please understand that the tension on campus was unprecedented, the frenzy of threats and nuttiness unparalleled, and their ability to provide adequate security in light of it all strained. "OK," I said in a sleepy voice. "And," she continued, "would you be willing to sign your name to a joint letter endorsing the cancellation?" I was fully awake now. "I can't do it," I said, "because I don't think we should cancel the talk. I'm certain the

Nebraska State Police can get me to the podium, and I'll be fine from there." This was all a tempest in a teapot.

"You don't know how bad it's become," she said. "The governor, both US senators, the regents . . . all of them are coming down on us." It was true. I quickly learned that Senator Ben Nelson, a Democrat, had called for the cancellation of my speech, and Governor Dave Heineman, a Republican, had sent a public letter to the regents and the president of the university telling them to immediately rescind my invitation because it was an embarrassment to have "a well-known radical who should never have been invited to the University of Nebraska" on the campus. I wondered if all radicals or only well-known radicals were embarrassing and unwelcome.

"I'm so sorry," I said, "and I don't want you to suffer at all—but I don't want your students or my students, or anyone else, to conclude that the mob can set the limits on speech or on academic freedom. The faculty had the right to invite me, the students had a right to speak with me, and none of us should accept being bullied by some tin-pot politician. I won't sign on to a letter like that, and I don't think you should either. Let the administration do its own weasel work," I said. "I mean, what can they do to you?"

Before I left Taipei, I spent an inspiring day with a multiethnic group of young activists who were organizing undocumented workers, mostly Filipinos, for decent wages and fair treatment, as well as for cultural survival and full recognition of their basic human rights. That evening a couple of dozen workers, children and families in tow, gathered at a community center in a working-class neighborhood to enjoy a red-hot potluck of *ilocos empanada, adobo,* chicken *inasal, suman,* and *halo-halo*. Folk singers performed in Tagalog, while young people in traditional dress delighted the group. I was surprised when, near the end of the party, the principal singer invited me to perform with him in English. "I invite Professor Ayers to the stage," he began, "to join me in a song I'm sure he knows." He explained to the gathering that twenty years earlier he had left the Philippines as a teenager to live with an aunt in Kentucky, where he became an undocumented agricultural worker. Each morning as the van carried the workers to the fields or orchards he would work on his English by memorizing pop music playing on the radio. "My favorite song from those years," he continued, "was a perfect memory of my home in the Philippines." As he strummed his guitar with tears in his eyes the two of us harmonized on John Denver's "Country Roads," and I got tears in my eyes too, marveling at the unlikely but very real globalized world we now inhabited: an undocumented Filipino worker and an outlawed Chicago professor in a community center in Taiwan, singing a classic piece of American kitsch the worker had memorized as a young man in Kentucky and loved because it reminded him of his faraway home in the Philippines.

The Nebraska talk was canceled, their lawyers had jumped in, and the official story—which would be recycled at every blacklisting to come—cited "safety reasons." The Office of [Fairy-Tales and] University Communications went into high gear spinning their fraudulent story: *The University's threat assessment group monitored e-mails and other information UNL received regarding Ayers' scheduled November 15 visit, and identified safety concerns which resulted in the university canceling the event.*

I later learned that the Gilbert M. and Martha H. Hitchcock Foundation in Omaha, which had donated millions in the past, told the university that it would halt all contributions unless the faculty rescinded my invitation. Several other donors indicated that there would be a financial cost if I were allowed to speak. State auditor Mike Foley sent the university a long request for information on my trip, its planning, and how it was being funded. Governor Heineman was reportedly pleased that the university had reconsidered, and he sent a letter to the faculty telling them that there are plenty of other respected educators the university could invite to speak. I wrote an op-ed for an Omaha paper, and I argued that academic freedom was indeed dead the moment the governor, billionaires, or anyone else thought—and then demonstrated—that they could dictate the terms of what is read or said or discussed on a university campus.

Cancellations and abandonment continued apace, and the tempest leapt completely out of the teapot: officials at the University of Wyoming, citing "security threats" and "controversy," canceled two talks I'd been asked to give there, one a public lecture entitled "Trudge Toward Freedom: Moral Commitment and Ethical Action," and the other, a talk to faculty and graduate students called "Teaching and Research in the Public Interest: Solidarity and Identity." One week before I was to travel to Laramie, I was told I had been "disinvited."

A campaign to rescind the invitation had been initiated on right-wing blogs months earlier, accelerating quickly to a wider space where a demonizing storyline dominated all discussion and a wave of hateful messages and death threats hit the University, joined soon enough by a few political leaders and wealthy donors instructing officials in ominous tones to cancel my visit to the campus, or else. This was becoming drearily familiar to me.

A particularly despicable note in that campaign was written by Frank Smith, who lived in Cheyenne and was active in the Wyoming Patriot Alliance: "Maybe someone could take him out and show him the Matthew Sheppard [sic] Commerative [sic] Fence and he could bless it or something." He was referring to Matthew Shepard, the young gay man who was tortured and murdered in 1998, left to die tied to a storm fence outside Laramie.

Republican gubernatorial candidate Ron Micheli released a letter he'd sent to the trustees asking them to rescind the invitation, and Matt Mead, another gubernatorial candidate, said that while he was a self-described "fervent believer in free speech and the free exchange of ideas," allowing me to speak would be "reprehensible." He concluded that I should have "no place lecturing our students."

I told the folks who had invited me how sorry I was that all of this was happening to them, but I thought it would surely pass. Certainly, no matter what a couple of thugs threatened to do, I thought not much would happen. We should stand together and refuse to accede to these kinds of pressures to demonize and mostly to suppress students' right to freely engage in open dialogue. After all, a public university is not the personal fiefdom or the political clubhouse of the governor, and donors can't be permitted to call the shots when it comes to the content or conduct of academic matters. We should not allow ourselves to collapse in fear if a howling mob gathers at the gates with flaming torches in hand; in fact, that's when standing up and pushing back become absolutely necessary. I wouldn't force myself on the university, of course, but I felt that canceling would be terribly unfair to the faculty and students who had invited me, and would send a big message that bullying works. It would be the equivalent of a book burning, and would be one more step down the slippery slope of giving up on the precious ideal of a free university in a free society.

No good. The university posted an announcement of the cancellation of my visit with a long and rambling comment from President Tom Buchanan that began with the obligatory assertion that academic freedom is a core principle of the university, but quickly added that "freedom requires a commensurate dose of responsibility." We are charged to enact free speech and thought, he wrote, "in concert with mutual respect." The heckler's veto had worked perfectly.

I suggested that I show up on campus—no announcement, no security, no fanfare—and stand respectfully in front of the student union with a big sign saying, "Let's Talk." I would engage anyone who happened to walk by and chat about anything that came up.

Those who thought that the university "caved in to external pressure," President Buchanan went on, would be "incorrect":

> While this episode illustrated an opportunity to hear and critically evaluate a variety of ideas thoughtfully, through open, reasoned, and civil debate, it also demonstrates that we must be mindful of the real consequences our actions and decisions have on others.

That twisty sentence qualified him to write for the *Nation*, for while it was impossible to know definitively what he was calling the "episode" that would provide the opportunity to critically evaluate matters—it might have been the public lecture itself or the cancellation of the lecture, it might have been the barbarians at the gates threatening to burn the place down or the foundations and wealthy alumni warning that funds were in the balance—it still had an unmistakable Orwellian ring: we canceled that lecture as an expression of our support for lectures!

And it was eerily similar to the warrior classics: we destroyed that village in order to save it! Work will make you free! War is peace!

One of the truly weird qualities of the Buchanan statement was the hole in its center, the deafening silence concerning why the campaign against me was organized in the first place. I'd been an educator and professor for decades and the hard Right had accelerated the lunacy against thousands of folks—activists and artists, commentators and humorists, academics and theorists—who were, like me, open and outspoken radicals. Wherever possible they'd mounted campaigns exactly like the one in Wyoming. I suppose I was a more convenient target than some. Often university officials stood up on principle and resisted the organized gangs; sometimes they compromised, restricting access to talks and surrounding me with unwanted and unnecessary police protection; and sometimes, as in Nebraska and Wyoming, the university bowed deeply, then turned and ran.

Of course I hadn't been invited to speak about the sixties or any of this, and it's unlikely any of it would have come up without active campaigning and noisy thunder from a tiny crowd of right-wing zealots in the midst of a presidential election. I would have focused my talk in any case on the unique characteristics of education in a democracy, an enterprise that rests on the twin pillars of enlightenment and liberation, knowledge and human freedom. We should all want to wake up and pay attention, to know more, I would have argued, to see more, to experience more in order to do more—to be more competent and powerful and capable in our projects and our pursuits, to be more astute and aware and wide awake, more fully engaged in the world that we inherit, the world we are simultaneously destined to change.

To deny students the right to question the circumstances of their lives and to wonder how they might be otherwise, or to deny them the freedom to read widely and to speak to the broadest range of people, as Buchanan was doing, was to deny democracy itself.

I was contacted by Meg Lanker, an undergraduate who was just back from serving in the military and had been active in opposing the cancellation of my talk in Wyoming. She was a fighter on every level. "I'm going to sue the university in federal court," she told me during our first conversation. "And I'm claiming that it's *my* free speech that's been violated—I have the right to speak to anyone I want to, and right now I want to speak to you." She was young and unafraid, smart and sassy, her dreams being rapidly made and used—no fear, no regret. I liked her immediately.

Meg's approach struck me as quite brilliant—students (and not I) were indeed the injured party. "Inviting you wasn't necessarily an endorsement; I check books out of the library all the time that aren't pre-approved. Let's talk, and who knows, maybe we'll have a big argument. But we have a right to have you here, and they can't stop us."

She contacted David Lane, a marvelous people's lawyer and legal street fighter from Denver, and he filed an injunction against the university. Suddenly, there we were in court before a conservative federal judge. President Buchanan took the stand to complain about security and, when the judge nudged him to remember the First Amendment, said, "But doesn't security trump free speech?" The judge patiently explained that if that were true there would never have been any dissent—including the civil rights movement—in our history. He ruled that the university must accommodate my talk, taking whatever security precautions it felt were prudent. He went so far as to issue a written opinion, giving his ruling the weight of history and legal precedent.

My family thought that for me to travel alone across Wyoming was a bad idea, so Chesa, studying for law school finals, volunteered and became the designated hitter. He flew in to meet me at the Denver airport, where we rented a car and drove together to Laramie. I wasn't sure he added much muscle, but we had a lovely drive together and lunch at a dive outside of town with the lawyers and the dissident students, toured the campus with Meg, sat on benches drinking coffee in the beautiful Dick and Lynne Cheney Plaza, and knocked on President Buchanan's door, but he'd gone home early, so I left him a copy of the US Constitution and the Universal Declaration of Human Rights.

That night, close to 1,100 people braved a blizzard and showed up for my talk. I wanted to think that they all came to hear what I had to say about justice, democracy, and education, but I was realistic enough to know that I'd have likely had an audience of fifty students without all the drama. There were no pickets and no protests, lots of media, and a lovely surprise: Curt Minter, my sister-in-law's father and a retired bishop, as well as the former minister from the United Church of Christ where I'd been confirmed decades before, drove a couple hours to stand in solidarity. I almost didn't recognize Curt because he was dressed in a dark suit with a clerical collar—unusual for him.

"What a great surprise!" I said. "What are you doing here?"

"The Lord moves in mysterious ways," he said with a wink and a smile gesturing with his Bible. "If any of the crazy Christians get out of hand, He wants me to set them straight."

When I was finally introduced, I could practically feel the letdown in the audience—who's that old professor wobbling across the stage, and what happened to the scary terrorist we were expecting?

I wanted my talk that night to stay true to the original invitation, but with modifications fitted to the changed situation. I talked about the principles of education in a democracy, and argued that much of what we call schooling is based too often on obedience and conformity, the hallmarks of every authoritarian regime throughout history—it banishes the unpopular, squirms in the presence of the unorthodox, and hides the unpleasant. There is no space for skepticism, irreverence, or even doubt there. While many students long for an education that is transcendent and powerful, I said, administrators like President Buchanan seemed ever ready to police the boundaries of thought, to see that we stayed on track, reducing education to a kind of glorified clerking that passed along all the received and certified wisdom of the day without doubt or question.

In Wyoming the main victims were truth, honesty, integrity, curiosity, imagination, and finally freedom itself. And the wider but hidden victims would include the high school history teacher in Laramie or the literature teacher in Cheyenne who would immediately get the message: be careful what you say; stay close to the official story; stick to the authorized text; keep quiet with your head down.

I told them that there would be times in their lives when they would have to break the rules in order to stand up for justice and humanity, when there would be no court of last resort beyond their own consciences and free minds, and that it was important to exercise that capacity every day—a little anarchist calisthenics to stay in shape for the big games to come. The young people cheered that line.

I finished by evoking Bertolt Brecht's play *Galileo*, where the great astronomer sets forth into a world dominated by a mighty church and an authoritarian power: "The cities are narrow and so are the brains," he declares recklessly, and he feels himself propelled toward revolution. Not only did Galileo's radical discoveries about the movement of the stars free them from the "crystal vault" that church dogma insistently claimed fastened them to the sky, but his insights suggested something even more dangerous: that we too were embarked on a great voyage, and that we too were free and without the easy support that dogma provided. Here Galileo raised the stakes, and the establishment struck back fiercely. Forced to renounce his life's work under the exquisite pressure of the Inquisition, Galileo denounced what he knew to be true, and was welcomed back into the church and the ranks of the faithful, but exiled from humanity—by his own word. A former student, confronting him in the street, said that many on all sides followed him, "believing that you stood, not only for a particular view of the movement of the stars, but even more for the liberty of teaching—in all fields. Not then for any particular thoughts, but for the right to think at all. Which is in dispute." The link was clear, and the warm response that night encouraging.

A year later the conservative student club at Wyoming invited Ann Coulter to speak as an antidote to whatever radical ideas and left-wing contaminants I'd left around the place. She was paid $20,000—$10,000 from a wealthy anonymous donor (think Dick and Lynne Cheney)—and there wasn't a single threat of cancellation. Meg and her crew resisted their first impulse and decided not to picket the event. Instead they launched a website and built a social network where folks could pledge a set amount of money for the Matthew Shepard Foundation for every minute that Coulter spoke. I pledged $5 a minute. Meg raised a huge banner outside the auditorium that read: "The Ann Coulter Rainbow/Queer Tour—Keep Talkin' Ann!" with the website

listed below. Ann was ninety minutes late, and toward the end of her
talk, referred to Meg's guerilla campaign as she shut up and ended the
fund-raiser at twenty-six minutes. The Matthew Shepard Foundation
made $10,000 that evening.

Keep talkin'!

Meg and the students at Wyoming buoyed my spirits, but the attacks
kept coming and I ached for more people to assemble in my defense.
I'd always maintained a pretty strict no-whine zone around myself—
moaning and wailing and wallowing in self-pity had always seemed to
me to stand in the way of activism, and I tended to think the antidote
to bitching and belly-aching was to get up and do something. Whining struck me as self-defeating in general and pathetic in almost every
instance, but, damn—I began to feel little cracks developing in that
stone wall, and I craved an angel to speak up for me personally. I really did. Like everyone else I can be both tiresomely familiar and also
shockingly unpredictable to myself at times, and now all I desired was
for someone to step up and plead my case: Look, folks, you're mistaken
about this guy; he's a good person, really.

Yes! Yes! Listen to the fantasy person speaking on my behalf—I'm
a good guy!

Pathetic, self-defeating, and desperate.

A putatively radical gathering called the Rouge Forum canceled a
talk I was scheduled to give because one of the other left-wing present-
ers—George Schmidt—said he would refuse to attend if I were there.
"It's you or him," they explained to me, and he was apparently being
unpleasantly adamant.

"Well," I said calmly, "George is the one urging exclusion, not me.
You should tell him there's no way you can participate in a blacklist,
even if it comes from the Left, or you could always invite him to respond to my talk. I can't cancel myself for you."

I was dropped.

But then I got a note from my old comrade Mike Klonsky, and
he included an e-mail thread that cheered me up immeasurably. Mike
and I had been friends for decades, first as student militants and SDS
officers together. When he returned to graduate school I was one of

his professors, and later we'd written on school improvement, edited books, and led a school reform organization together.

Mike had gotten an invitation to keynote an education conference, but the letter included this troubling line: "We had planned to invite Bill Ayers, but concluded that his presence would distract from our work because he's too controversial and too radical now." Mike's note back was written with a flame-thrower: "Shame on you!" he began. "How dare you ask me to scab on Bill Ayers? In fact if you ban Bill, not only will I not give a talk at your gathering, I might picket the place, and I'll certainly advise everyone to boycott your weak-assed conference."

Mike's dad had been a communist organizer, blacklisted during the Red Scare and indicted under the Smith Act; he'd been underground and on the run from the FBI for a time in the 1950s, and Mike instinctively smelled the rats even when heavily scented. I called him to give him some love for being a stand-up guy and a principled friend. "Thanks a lot for defending me," I said.

"Defending you?" he replied. "I wasn't defending you. I was defending myself—I was deeply and personally offended when they said that you were *too radical*, and by implication that I wasn't too radical. I'm as radical as you are, motherfucker." Well, thanks anyway, Mike.

On the one hand, I felt isolated and invisible, cut off and forced into exile, and I wanted to hide. On the other hand, I was determined to resist, not bending an inch. Since the contradiction was alive and as real as dirt, Bernardine advised me to let both sides breathe: "Don't try to settle it, because it's really irresolvable," she said. "You should just work hard to embrace both sides: hold onto the feeling of wanting to hide; clasp the desire to resist. Keep both feelings close." Hugging it rather than running away from it or trying to settle it helped.

Over dinner with the Khalidis, Mona said that she thought that all the finger-pointing and criticism was changing me: "You're more brittle," she said, "not paranoid exactly, but a bit more sensitive."

"Leave the poor guy alone," Rashid said. "He has enough trouble without you piling on."

"No, no," Mona replied. "I'm making a compliment—I like it because you're more receptive and susceptible like this, with a little chink in your confidence. You seem more like me."

We laughed but I, at least, got her point—I was perhaps a little slowed down, a bit more in touch with a knot of contradictory emotions and a little less relentlessly cheery. I was also perhaps a couple of clicks nearer to her experiences of exile and dispossession as a Palestinian, closer as well to the experiences of Kathy and David and millions of other prisoners and formerly incarcerated people—relentlessly demonized and shunned, struggling to find a way forward in the face of hostility and rejection as ordinary people turn away for fear of being identified with the condemned. My situation was not really comparable in terms of intensity or consequences, but it was perhaps qualitatively closer; everything seemed a little magical—even the trembling paranoia. It became a kind of turning point.

Everyone at the table was supportive—we loved each other, and it was the safest place for me to relax into the insanity forcing itself upon me. I didn't choose this, but here it was, and I had to choose who to be in the face of it. Bernardine urged complexity and a human response, Mona vulnerability, Rashid courage. They were all right: what I did— one way or the other—would have consequences, would carry forward. Words and actions would have their unpredictable impact every day and throughout time.

I'd been invited to give a named lecture on urban education at Millersville University in Pennsylvania. When I got a call from a dean there, I was sure we were about to have the same old well-worn conversation regarding opposition, security, "Hope you agree," "so, so sorry," "blah blah blah." But she surprised me: "We are all outraged by the manufactured turmoil that's engulfed us in the wake of the announcement of your upcoming lecture," she began. She was calling to arrange a conference-call between me and a half-dozen top officials to discuss how to respond to the craziness, and even how to "make the controversy a teachable moment."

The conversation a few days later was the most thoughtful and principled I'd known throughout all the crying frenzy. The administration was determined to host me in a safe and orderly environment and hold all scheduled events—informal conversations with small groups of students and alums, a planned semiformal dinner to honor the funder, and the campus-wide lecture—and determined as well to defend academic freedom and give their students and the public a lesson in intellectual courage. The officials assured me that defending the lecture was not a burden to them, but rather it was their duty and their honor. "It's not about you personally," one said. "It's about the mission and the meaning of the university." They then reviewed a letter written to the campus community by the university president, Francine G. McNairy, an African American woman, outlining the purpose of the lecture and the reason it would not be canceled. She wrote, in part:

> A long-accepted value in higher education is that free inquiry is indispensable to the advancement of knowledge. History is replete with examples of ideas that are now precepts of human knowledge that were initially suppressed because their authors were considered heretics or radicals. The focus of the faculty committee, which more than a year ago invited Dr. Ayers to speak, was to advance the dialogue about effective ideas and successful approaches for closing the educational achievement gap between urban students and their non-urban counterparts. This selection was made devoid of political litmus tests for authors. From an objective standpoint, what should matter are which ideas and approaches work and not who develops them. Free inquiry and free speech are critical elements of academic freedom, which thoughtful Americans from our founding fathers to U.S. presidents and Supreme Court justices, more than 200 years later, have judged essential to preparing students to be productive citizens. University administrators have the obligation to support academic freedom in the academy just as public officials are obliged to support free speech in a democratic society. The protection of academic freedom is necessary to afford faculty and students the right to consider and weigh the value of ideas from all sources.

The head of campus police reviewed some of the threats they'd received, many directed at me, of course, and plenty aimed personally and with vile specificity at President McNairy, and outlined a complicated plan that seemed overly elaborate to me, but I figured that they knew better than I, and what the hell.

I was told I'd be picked up at the Harrisburg airport, and as I walked toward baggage claim I searched for my name on one of the little signs held by various drivers. One driver nodded insistently and smiled, and so I nodded and smiled back, but his sign read: "Mr. Bellamy." He gestured in my direction, pushing the sign toward me, and said in a whisper, "Mr. Bellamy, Mr. Bellamy." "I'm not Mr. Bellamy," I said, as he took my elbow, glancing around surreptitiously, and steered me away, speaking softly. "Didn't you get the e-mail?" he asked. "You're Mr. Bellamy." Ah, spycraft, of course!

He dropped me at a hotel they'd reserved, telling me that the room was reserved for "Mr. Bellamy." The clerk who registered me at the front desk asked me to sign in—"Mr. Bellamy"—and then asked for a credit card to put on file for incidentals. Suddenly I was underground again, and I had no ID for "Mr. Bellamy" and no idea what to do—all my ancient underground skills vanished.

I froze.

Next day the campus was locked down—state troopers with bomb-sniffing dogs, sheriff's deputies patrolling with unholstered weapons, city and campus police checking IDs and monitoring the scene. The talk was piped into an overflow auditorium, and while it went off without a hitch, I think Millersville will stay away from radical speakers for a while.

The campaign to demonize and blacklist me was nationally organized, and so picket lines were arranged at every talk I gave. Some were small and sociable, like the one in the tiny town of Arcata, California, where I posed arm in arm with a smiling protestor and her bold red sign "Bill Ayers is a TERRORIST!" And some were large and angry, like the one outside St. Mary's College near Oakland, where Bill O'Reilly had orchestrated and stirred the mob from his perch at Fox News. "There are enemies in our midst," he'd insisted, and I was public enemy number one. St. Mary's was special because Larry Grathwohl, a paid police informant who hung around SDS briefly back in the day, was going to address the crowd. Larry had written a book about the Weather Underground claiming that our apocalyptic plans were to "eliminate 25 million die-hard capitalists." In light of all the fresh publicity and renewed interest in all-things Weather, Larry was dragging himself out of retirement and rebooting his career as a right-wing warrior with several embellishments, including the double fiction that he had once been an "FBI agent" and that he had infiltrated the Weather Underground. Neither was true.

At St. Mary's a man waving an oversized copy of the St. James bible above his head with both hands and quoting the Gospel at the top of his voice rushed toward the podium where I was speaking; in Springfield a couple of people threw tomatoes and eggs; and in Oregon someone was stopped by campus police just short of smacking me in the head with a hard-bound copy of *Atlas Shrugged*. But mostly folks were as friendly as they could be.

In Fresno I had half an hour before I was scheduled to speak to a church group, so I went out to chat with the Tea Party picketers and invited them in. The first two guys I met carried signs saying "Ayers Go Home!" I introduced myself and asked what they had against me. "Oh, nothing," one of them replied gently. "We heard you were friends with Obama, and we can't stand Obama." "Whoa," I said. "That's not fair—guilt by association."

At another event I suggested to a picketer wearing a Ron Paul T-shirt that he and I likely had more in common than he imagined.

"Like what?" he said.

"Like full GLBTQ rights," I said.

"OK, full gay rights—agreed."

"Including the right to marry," I continued.

"No," he said. "The state has no place in the marriage business—none. If for some reason people want to get married, don't ask me why anyone would, well then leave it to their church or magic circle or cult or commune—and keep the government entirely out of it."

I enthusiastically agreed—you've convinced me! "No state-sanctioned marriage whatsoever, gay or straight," I said, "and full equality."

We shook hands, and before I could make a pitch for Medicare for all, a fellow picketer stepped up looking distressed. He was wearing a large wooden cross and carrying a sign that said "Ayers/Obama—The Devil's Workshop," and told my new comrade, "Homosexuality is an abomination!" I urged them to work out their differences on queer rights while I went back inside to speak.

At Georgia Southern University—invited, canceled, and finally re-scheduled—there was a huge police presence and a crazy meandering route through basement tunnels to the stage. As I stepped to the po-dium, a large contingent of Hell's Angels in full regalia and with Tea Party Patriot patches prominently displayed on their arms shambled in and took the first two rows, scowling up at me. I paused as they settled in, welcomed them, and began.

After forty minutes the floor was opened for questions, and first to the microphone was the leader of the Angels, a bony Viet Nam–era vet named Rooster with faded tattoos covering his arms. "I'm surprised to tell you that I agreed with most of what you said," he growled. "But I worry that you're a big-government guy." Rooster wasn't sure why he thought that, but he was concerned. I tried to reassure him. "The main function of any government anywhere is to tax and spend," I said, "and so the only real question is who do you want to tax, how much, and what and where do you want to spend the money? You rode up here on a government-built highway; some of you might even say you took the socialist road. Maybe you thought to yourself as you rolled over those bridges and passed the libraries and sewerage treatment plants and the fresh water canals that that was all money well spent. I know I do. When Mayor Daley sold the Chicago Skyway to a profit-making cor-poration, the tolls skyrocketed and the profiteers still got public money and tax breaks, and most Chicagoans were pretty pissed off. What's so great about profit and greed? Give us back our Skyway!"

"I like that," Rooster said chuckling.

"But," I went on, "maybe as a small-government guy you'll agree with me that we should immediately close down the Pentagon—save a trillion dollars in one stroke." There was a burst of applause.

"Not the Pentagon," Rooster objected.

"So now *you're* the big-government guy," I pointed out.

After I'd signed a bunch of books and the event was officially over, I left the auditorium with my friend and host, the incomparable Professor Ming Fang He, education scholar, survivor of the Cultural Revolution, and self-described "Chinese redneck" ("because I am a sun-burned peasant too"). We found Rooster and his girlfriend, Rose, and a dozen more Hell's Angels waiting for us in the parking lot. I thought they were going to kick the shit out of me, but instead they just wanted to keep talking.

Ming Fang called her friend Min Chuan Yu, chef and owner at Shui Wah Chinese Cuisine, a dim sum place in downtown Statesboro, and wondered if she would be willing to stay open to accommodate some out-of-town scholars. "Come soon," she urged, and we jumped in Ming Fang's car and led the noisy motorcycle gang into town. Perhaps Min Chuan was surprised to see our motley crew file in, but she didn't blink or give a hint of disapproval, bowing politely and welcoming everyone in turn. Each Hell's Angel bowed in response—a sight to see—and soon we settled in to a feast of *har gau*, barbecued pork buns, and crispy calamari "fries" dusted with chili powder. Ming Fang took Rose into the kitchen for a tour while the rest of us ate and argued.

As the dinner was ending, Rooster offered a toast with his water glass: "To a great evening," he said. "You're a good guy, Bill. Why do they write such shit about you?"

"I can only guess," I said as I toasted the anarchist tendencies of the Angels, "but then why do they write all that bullshit about you?"

"Good point—I never believe the crap in the papers anyhow."

Ming Fang toasted Rose, "my new Georgia flower and sister," and insisted on taking the check, treating us all to what she judged to be "the most interesting academic session of all time!"

As the 2008 election careened toward the home stretch, the pressure-cooker that was, after all, our lives got steamier, the shrieking 24/7 whistle grew ever louder, and my head became even dizzier. The Palin-McCain campaign ratcheted up the rhetoric, doubling down on the bet that the Obama-Wright-Khalidi-Ayers connection would destroy the rising superstar, and the Republicans launched multimillion-dollar ad campaigns featuring one or several of the Obama "pals" across the country. The Looney Tune Right stepped up its freelance dealing, and the hate kept escalating.

Fox News ran pictures night after night of our front door with the address prominently displayed. In a couple of weeks' time I got a mountain of identically printed cards in the mail with postmarks from California to New York, each accusing me of murdering a police officer and predicting that "justice" would be served. While the wave of postcards lacked spontaneity—I wondered what kind of far-flung franchise operation ginned up this whole deal—it had its effect. I was weirdly disconcerted and preoccupied, wondering uneasily several times a day about what I might find at home later, and then peering anxiously into my mailbox every afternoon. But the cards—and nothing heavier— kept coming, some with little personalized notes: "Your blasphemy has been noted." "You've rejected Jesus at your eternal peril."

Our house was under siege—reporters from around the country and the world periodically set up camp in the park across the street, trampled the bushes as they occupied our little front yard, interviewed our neighbors, marked our comings and goings, and occasionally rushed up to ask one more unanswerable question. Bernardine ran the gauntlet every day to get to and from work, but I was mostly hunkered down inside working at the dining room table on a comic-book edition of my book *To Teach* with my collaborator, Ryan Alexander-Tanner, the brilliant young Oregon cartoonist who was crashing on our top floor— some version of house arrest but with a resonance. Ryan and I made ourselves focus on the work, and we stayed blissfully unaware of most of what was going on outside except when we ventured out for pizza and candy or coffee to fuel our efforts. Then we would blink our eyes and catch our collective breath as the craziness pushed forward.

For three days, a crew from *The O'Reilly Factor* followed us to the supermarket and the coffee shop, recording our every move. When I gave a talk one night at Shimer College, a tiny local school organized around a Great Books curriculum, they captured the full hour and a half on tape. I was pretty sure they would do something on air with the footage since my lecture hit topics that might provide fodder for their hack attack—democracy and education, the importance of active engagement in civic life, the difficulties of making moral decisions in immoral societies—but I was wrong. A quiet address from me was apparently not the proper optic for them, even if the themes were inherently incendiary and the students led an animated conversation. They needed conflict, they longed for confrontation, they sought red meat. And so every step outside the house invited three of them—camera man, sound man, eager on-air correspondent—to rush urgently toward me, shouting and gesturing as if something of real importance had just occurred that very moment and I was the one person on earth who needed to say something that could make sense of it all. "Mr. Ayers! Professor! One minute! Please! Can you tell us, sir . . . ?" I tried to stay cool, to align my movement with my breath, to meditate on classic silent films, and to go about my business—shopping, scoring the coffee—and avoid ducking my head like a guilty perp or appearing terrified like a turkey at Thanksgiving or bursting into tears like a lost child. "What are you trying to hide?" In that scene and that context, just walking on looks so wrong—seriously, try to stay dignified with the scrum in your face and you'll see how tough it can be.

One day Ryan and I were taking a break from writing, chilling out in the living room, when we heard the crackle of a microphone, and looked out to see a Chicago tour bus idling in front, the tour guide pointing our way and the tourists snapping photos. We were on the tour!

Another day the young man on assignment from Fox tried to push his way through our front door, shouting that if I believed in the First Amendment I had to answer his questions. I wanted to pause, pull out the copy of the Constitution I always carried in my back pocket, and patiently explain the Bill of Rights to the kid, but the scene was way too noisy and a bit too pushy. I told him to get the hell off the porch. That night, Bill O'Reilly, focusing a close-up on the black T-shirt I was wearing with its large red star in the center (Communism! Or Macy's! Or Heineken!), smirked as he said that this well-known socialist (me!) was suddenly a defender of private property (my residence!). I later sent O'Reilly a brief excerpt from Friedrich Engels explaining the difference between personal property and socially produced wealth, but I never heard back.

I increasingly felt the snowballing impact of the public campaign. I was scheduled on the local public radio station regularly for several years, for example, mostly to participate in conversations about education issues, but as the campaign escalated the invitations ceased. After one of my last appearances I hung around for a bit with the host, Steve Edwards, a thoughtful, liberal reporter. He told me that the station got a flood of objections every time I appeared, something he couldn't understand given the content of my positions, and then asked me, "What's it like to be so widely hated in the public mind?" He was perfectly serious and genuinely curious, but I couldn't help laughing out loud.

"Do you really think there's something out there that could sensibly be called 'the public mind,' Steve?" I asked. "And if so, could it possibly be stable or coherent or immutable?"

"No, not really," he agreed. "And you don't seem a likely candidate for the post of public enemy, but it must be weird to be you right now."

"It's not really how I experience my life," I said.

There were parallel campaigns on several campuses to purge my books from schools of education—I heard first from folks at Arizona State and Georgia State, and then from faculty across the country. The campaigns were not universally successful, but they were a troubling trend nonetheless. At little Wheaton College, the Evangelical school outside Chicago famously attended by Billy Graham, an ad hoc committee of alumni formed to investigate why education majors were required to read my blasphemous words and to demand that I be completely purged from the curriculum. That one succeeded.

In any case, the non-invitations made a certain sense to the faculty committees, student assemblies, public programming groups, or conference planners charged with choosing who to include. They granted themselves permission to embrace freedom of expression in general—we don't have any blacklists, they could honestly tell themselves, we don't want to encourage the censors or organize a repression. But the best way to keep the thought police away, the logic unspooled, and to hinder the always unpredictable actions of instinctual anti-intellectualism and tyranny was to organize a reasonable self-censorship and a moderate self-control. Perhaps they figured that there were "plenty of other respected educators one could invite to speak," as the governor of Nebraska so considerately clued-up the professors at "his" university. And, of course, it's true—there are.

I'd instinctively been on the side of demonstrators and dissidents my whole life, habitually with the pickets, but now I suddenly had to cross a picket line or break an order just to hear myself speak. That was weirdly dislocating. The threats and swirling controversy and angry demonstrations seemed upside down. But not wanting to cringe or cower—even when tempted—led me to a new space where all I wanted to do was to engage the demonstrators, an eclectic group of folks whose coherence was largely an illusion orchestrated by a group of billionaires at the top. And once started, I rather loved talking with the Tea Party. Their forces distrusted the government—big deal, so did I. They loved liberty—OK, who doesn't? They didn't hate capitalism, not yet, so talking to them became a project and my mission.

Debbie Meier, a friend and colleague for years and Malik's former New York City elementary school principal, sent me a quick e-mail in the middle of the 2008 presidential campaign. "Why not just apologize?" she asked matter-of-factly. "Get it over with." She'd CC'd several of our school reform pals from around the country.

I immediately hit Reply All: "I'm sorry!"

A few minutes later she wrote a second e-mail: "I don't actually know what I meant by that, so maybe not."

Those back-to-back notes summed up at that moment my own conflicted feelings perfectly: I'm sorry; well, wait, what am I sorry for? Maybe I'm not sorry after all.

Exactly! Contradiction is my only hope!

An endlessly repeating epithet had begun to sound—even to me— like a natural part of my given name: "Unrepentant Domestic Terrorist William Ayers." Who would name their child Unrepentant? And even worse, who would call a kid Unrepentant Ayers, with three middle names? Call me Bill.

I rejected outright the "terrorist" label, and I was bewildered by the constant repetition of "unrepentant." George Stephanopoulos, on that presidential debate night, made a point of saying I'd never apologized for my despicable behavior. Was that even true? I wondered. And if I had apologized, would that have made it all go away? Somehow I doubted it then, and I doubt it even more now.

Why not say you're sorry? I was; I am.

I was happy to discuss anything, and I was able to openly regret lots of things in a range of settings, but somehow stubbornly unwilling to say a single line: I'm sorry I engaged extreme tactics to oppose the war; I'm sorry I destroyed war materials and government property.

I'm not sorry about that, and I can't say with any conviction that I am. Opposing the US invasion of Viet Nam with every fiber of my being is simply not one of my regrets. And as I considered it decades later, I wanted to defend it all—every bombing and each bit of vandalism, every disabled warplane and destructive act, every exposed police killing, each discouraged aggressor and all the cringing, barricaded politicians.

"No Regrets"—the repeated headline taken again and again to be proof that my various wrongdoings had not been adequately recognized, that I'd failed to fess up and that my transgressions, then, were enduring and ongoing—was a theme with legs. It was introduction, conclusion, content, and punch line rolled into one, and it had it all: short and memorable, pithy and hard-hitting, vague and entirely unfathomable.

And so I felt a little trapped: the media chorus demanding a statement of remorse felt to me a bit too close to a gathering horde armed with torches and pitchforks, and the repeating demand for a general admission of guilt seemed impossibly broad. What exactly did the mob expect me to apologize for? I made a short list: being a jerk; destroying draft board files; laughing out loud in church; disrupting the military; my manner; driving too fast and rarely getting a speeding ticket; being born; stopping troop trains; exaggerated claims and inflated rhetoric; dozens of defiant demonstrations; fighting the cops in the streets of Chicago and Washington, DC; talking too much; surrounding the Pentagon; 1968; disabling B-52s headed for Viet Nam; smoking dope;

jail breaks; my subversive outlook; being way too happy; doing anarchist calisthenics at odd times and in inappropriate venues; oh, and yes, there's the matter of vandalism and destruction of property, including a series of high-profile bombings of government and corporate buildings, each a symbol of war and empire, oppression and white supremacy, and each accompanied by an explanatory if rhetorically overheated statement or communiqué. And, if that's not enough, there's the fact that I was born in the suburbs.

Inclined to apologize—sorry, sorry—it would be tough to know where to begin. *Blanket apology:* Sorry! (It sounds so insincere, even to me). *Specific apology:* Sorry I didn't vandalize more war materials (I don't know if that quiets the mob a single decibel).

I read time and again that I was wandering around place to place muttering something incoherent about being "guilty as hell, free as a bird"—unrepentant, triumphant, arrogant. No regrets. What I'd actually written was quite different: "Among my sins—pride and loftiness—a favorite twinkling line . . . guilty as hell, free as a bird." I'd said "my sins" for God's sake, and I'm not a bit religious. What do they want already? Still the stuttering mantra: no regrets!

But there are many, many things to regret, of course, and atonement is sometimes appropriate: the wretched years of the American war in Viet Nam, the desolate decade of serial assassinations of Black leaders, the exhilarating upheaval and the sparkling fight for freedom and peace and justice can't possibly justify everything everywhere. That's too cheap and altogether too trouble-free. Mistakes were made—no, no, no, scratch that cliché with its evasive passive voice. It's the caption of a classic Matt Groening cartoon in which a kid with a guilty look sits alone in the midst of his trashed and torn-up room, the refuge of every rascal weaseling away from an honest accounting or some serious reckoning.

I did adopt a hyperpartisan stance within the movement: you're either with us or you're with the enemy. Every discussion devolved into a clash of creeds; words lost all liberatory potential as they were forged into crude weapons put down as traps to entangle partisans from different factions or other sects. Dialogue disappeared—speaking became more geared toward posturing and performing than persuading—and was replaced with slogans that concealed much more than they revealed.

The Weather canon held that every action must be bent and then directly linked to destroying US imperialism on behalf of a humane future for all the people of the world. My own strict system of received wisdom and right beliefs was as controlling and totalizing as any other. It left me along with several close comrades isolated in a well-lit prison of our own construction with a blinding light bulb hanging from the ceiling by a single strand of wire.

The consequences were dreadful: the movement fractured, deep schisms and fissures ran us through, and all the progressive forces were weakened. I'm sorry for my role in that.

But schismatic sectarianism was the surface symptom of a deeper dis-ease—everyday dogmatism and orthodoxy. No one was free of it, and in fact there was (and is) nothing quite as insistently dogmatic as the rule of common sense—though it's always harder to see one's own dogma than the doctrine, say, of the House Republicans.

In Monty Python's *The Life of Brian*, a reluctant messiah stands on a rampart addressing the masses below: "Look, you've got it all wrong!" he cries. "You don't *need* to follow me. You don't *need* to follow *anybody*! You've got to think for yourselves! You're *all* individuals!" "Yes! We're all individuals!" the masses repeat in unison. "No, no," he says, frustrated. "You're all different!" "Yes, we *are* all different!" "Yes, we *are* all different!" they reply together. One bewildered man in the crowd turns to those around him and says, "I'm not," and the others gang up to reprimand him: "ShhhShhh!"—the easy compliance to the crowd.

Fugitive Days had been perhaps the ultimate non-apology, no matter what was in it, because it provided a snapshot of an excruciating decade by someone—me—who had lived on one extreme edge of it and somehow survived. Of course no one can ever write the *real* story of a life; the real story is the story of life's humiliations, and my memoir was more a story of loss and regret than it was a defense or a justification. Neither manifesto nor history, it was an account of a single soul set down in turbulent times, a brash beginner making his twisty way across a strange landscape without a map, and certainly without the benefit of hindsight.

Michelle Goodman, a dear and admired friend of mine who'd been a mentor for me in graduate school, wrote an agitated note when *Fugitive Days* came out to say that she was not sure what the point of my book was. "Do you think your actions were right?" she asked. Michelle had volunteered to go to Spain during the Civil War and had had a brush with the Communist Party—she knew the painful lash of McCarthyism. I wrote back to say that I tried simply to say what it was like, not to defend anything, but to show how a boy like this got into a place like that. She responded that I "seemed to want it both ways," and I guessed that she was right—I wanted it both ways. Didn't everyone? I wanted to do the heroic thing, and I wanted to survive; I wanted the romance of the outlaw and the moral high ground of the righteous dissident; I wanted to be right but complicated, opinionated but generous, public and private. Every American seemed to want both the good life and a good conscience at the same time. Everyone wanted to be a peaceful person and close their eyes tight to the violence erupting all around and in their names. Yes, I definitely wanted it both ways—I'm sorry; I'm not sorry, just as Deb Meier said.

I was almost sixty years old in 2001, and no one can live that long with their eyes even partially opened without a million everyday regrets: once I walked away from a friend in distress; once I accused the innocent; once I bowed to the guilty. I'm sorry for all of it.

And of course people who lived through the years of war and upheaval were still trying to measure their own contributions—Michelle Goodman referred insistently to the marches and the teach-ins and the letters to Congress she'd sent—against the horror of what we had all witnessed. Many of us recognized how small our contributions to peace really were, and that was its own difficult reckoning.

And I wondered where in all the noise there was any authentic call for a process of truth-telling about the war and the movement for peace and justice—where was the proposal for an honest means to reconciliation and a sincere space of accountability? America, it seemed to me, was in urgent need of some kind of truth and reconciliation process—not because I wanted to see Henry Kissinger, for example, wheeled in front of a magistrate and forced to confront his millions of victims. Well . . . it's tempting, but not the heart of the matter. We needed a process to understand the truth of the past in order to create the possibility of a more balanced future. It was really that simple.

I began to imagine just such a process: a large, lighted stage—the Kennedy Center in Washington or the Kodak Theatre in Hollywood— with a big spiral staircase leading to a central podium. When a name was called, that person—dressed to the nines or making some sly fashion statement—would descend the stairs to a spirited ovation and face the live audience with "millions watching at home." In the spotlight and at the microphone our star would read a list of all of his or her fail- ures to act with integrity, transgressions and offenses, stupid statements and malevolent acts, wrongdoings and misconduct, gaps and omissions and avoidances. Victims would be invited onto the stage to round out the story and to fill in the picture—villagers from all over Viet Nam and Indochina, the parents of Fred Hampton and the families of James Cheney, Diana Oughton, and others. Everyone together would have the opportunity to tell their stories of suffering, and the victimizers would be asked why and how they created that misery. Society would have the opportunity to witness all of it in order to understand the extent and depth of the disaster as a step toward putting it behind us and moving forward. In that setting and standing with Kissinger and McCain, Mc- Namara and Kerry, Bush and Cheney, I'd be happy to say exactly what I did, take full responsibility, and bow deeply. But without any chain of culpability whatsoever, I'll stand on the record, or just stand aside.

The reactionary apostate David Horowitz wrote that if Bernardine and I said we were sorry for everything we'd ever thought or done, and then donned sackcloth and ashes to beg alms on the public high- way, it would be inadequate—there would still be more to account for. To be effective the apology must be enacted every day, its sincerity proved by ongoing symbolic purges, no one of which would ever be fully satisfactory.

Alas, poor David, we knew him well: his parents had been devoted Communist Party members in the 1940s and '50s, and he was a red-diaper baby who became a respected left journalist in the 1960s and '70s. When his parents were gone, David had a rebellion and a rebirth as founder of Radicals for Reagan in the '80s, plunging ever-rightward with the zeal only an apostate can muster. David knew more than most about political apologies and public recantations—his parents had been caught in that nasty web themselves, and now he was a self-appointed avenger.

David tried to launch a campaign to purge colleges and universities of radicals, and appointed himself, of course, chief prosecutor and defender of the faith. He wrote a shabby pamphlet called "America's 100 Most Dangerous Professors" with little profiles and sketches of scholars and academics he deemed treacherous and subversive—poisoning the minds of our youth. It was a completely random register—so many amazing radicals and powerful scholars failed to make the cut—but Bernardine and I were both prominently on the list. I got calls and messages from colleagues across the country for months kidding me and complaining that they'd been overlooked: "I'm sure I was 101!" "Hey, no fair—I'm as radical as you are." "There must be some mistake—I'll send Horowitz my latest book." I told each one that I sympathized with the disappointment at being slighted but reminded them that like every other monarch or ayatollah David's fanaticism was blinding, and being *fidei defensor* was exhausting work—I was certain that they'd be included in a forthcoming edition. Stay the course!

I got a message a few weeks later from a kid who said he'd seen the pamphlet and wanted to set up a debate between David and me, and without much thought I said sure. Over the next days the kid wanted me to get a space at UIC, organize, publicize, and host and pay for the event. It turned out that the fake debate was all part of a larger strategy: get each one of the "100 most dangerous professors"—each flattered beyond measure, naturally narcissistic, and now further addled due to all this media attention—to act as subcontractors and organize a David event under the guise of a debate, amplifying the impact way beyond any merit it might have had on its own. Everyone figured it out quickly, and the debates never materialized.

Naming names during the McCarthy years was the prescribed act of contrition for a youth of radical thought or activity, and people were coerced into providing information when no information was needed—the rift was long past, the names all known and the ghosts all gone, stage right. The ritual was one of expiation, isolation, and realignment—subservience became the essential rite of passage and the price of growing up: "I am not now nor have I ever been . . ." Even when true, the words were mortifying. They spelled the end not only of a dream but of an entire life. The apology in general was uttered, and suddenly someone breathed their last shameful breath. It seemed a particularly dishonorable suicide in the service of power, and I surely didn't want to die like that. I embraced the line of a left-wing union leader hauled before McCarthy: I'd rather be a red to the rats, he'd famously said, than a rat to the reds. That became my security blanket and my mantra.

In any case, the Weather actions were all well known, the legal charges long ago resolved, and I'd faced the consequences with the state and with my parents, my comrades, and my friends. What was there left to do? Those who refused and suffered the lash of McCarthyism—those who "stood on principle"—had a terrible time explaining what the principle was precisely: support for the Communist Party USA? Not exactly. Love of Stalinism? No, definitely not. Opposition to anything the US government does? The importance of never telling on friends? Free speech? I felt the same bind. What did I do? What could I say?

I wanted it both ways.

It was a strange sensation to be assigned a role—in my case, "unrepentant terrorist"—and to be handed a script, only to discover that no editing or improvisation was permitted. There was nothing in *Fugitive Days* that I hadn't said out loud for thirty years, and it surprised me that the book sounded like a departure, but of course 9/11 and the militaristic response of Bush/Cheney had brought the terrorist label back with a vengeance, or created a whole new meaning for an ancient word—something we'd never thought about or imagined before, really (although much of the rest of the world had). Perhaps some modest successes in our professional lives and our "normal-looking family" constituted a kind of implied apology, and then the book by contrast was so, well, so unapologetic. Perhaps, as my student Isabel said to me after class one evening, we were like the punk rock band that suddenly got a record contract—some unstated but assumed agreement was breached. Success was never supposed to be part of the deal. Be a punk! Stay a Weatherman! I will; I am.

EIGHT

Only Dissent Can Save Us

During the heat of the primary battle, Senator Obama had been asked which candidate he thought the Reverend Martin Luther King Jr. would likely support, and he responded without hesitation—Reverend King would not endorse any of us, he said, because King would be in the streets mobilizing an unstoppable movement for justice. That seemed to me exactly right, and the kind of answer only a community organizer could summon. It was a reminder, too, that Lyndon Johnson, who had passed the most far-reaching civil rights legislation since Reconstruction, was never involved in the Black Freedom Movement but was instead responding to a powerful popular social movement for justice erupting from the grassroots; that Franklin Delano Roosevelt was never part of the labor movement but answered to a movement on the ground for workers' dignity and a measure of economic justice; and that Abraham Lincoln never belonged to an abolitionist party but could not ignore or hold back the agitation of free Blacks, the widespread rebellion of enslaved people, and the noble, unstoppable movement from below. Reality forced upon Lincoln the opportunity to declare the freedom of an enslaved people, allowed FDR to make a mark for social justice, and let LBJ to do the right thing when it mattered. Each offered a hint about our task and direction if we would just pay attention.

Bernardine and I—along with lots of friends from our far-flung community of radical activists in Chicago and throughout the land—shared a *Groundhog Day* sense of déjà vu every four years with the approach of another presidential election campaign: the whole country unaware that it was mysteriously trapped in a relentless and cruel time loop, destined to live the same day over and over and over again with the same tiresome outcome. In our case the Tweedledum/Tweedle-dummer nature of the Big Electoral Contest was bad enough, but worse was all the boisterous self-congratulation concerning democracy in action, while the corrosive and undermining effects of big money and big advertising on any sense of real participatory decision making sat stubbornly in plain sight. We identified, naturally enough, with the poor weatherman, played by Bill Murray, who was driven nuts until he prodded himself into action in an attempt to interrupt his insane fate.

As the noisy and colorful election carnival came rolling into town, we wondered how to disrupt *our* stuttering destiny, and we pulled together with our lovely loose formation of community organizers and activists who thought of our work broadly as movement-building. What all of us found most maddening was seeing another rising generation of youth fire up to participate in what they took to be "politics" for the first time in their lives and dive into the electoral fray with energy and enthusiasm, only to emerge in November—win, lose, or draw—a bit jaded but no wiser for the experience. Each of us was engaged in specific grassroots projects—school reform, juvenile justice, labor organizing, environmental affairs, health-care reform, Palestinian rights and solidarity—and we struggled to link the issues, to notice the connections between war and global warming, for example, or the shredding of our civil liberties and the rampant scapegoating of Muslims and Arabs.

We all experienced the corrosive and pervasive ideology of "American exceptionalism"—the concept that the United States was not simply a nation among nations like every other but rather the world's last remaining superpower, the greatest country on earth, and the one "indispensable nation," in Madeline Albright's deathless phrase. No one outside our borders could be expected to buy the hype for a minute, but American exceptionalism was sold relentlessly to Americans as our common-sense birthright: we would never be subject to the rules and laws and standards that apply to others, because we were exceptional! The blinding illusion erased any resemblances between similar sets of facts: we condemned torture, assassinations, invasion and occupation, acts of terrorism, the use of hostages, forced labor, the bombing of civilians, mass deportations, and on and on, if they were the work of "bad guys," while we applauded and condoned those same outrages and atrocities if they were the actions of "our" side—they were now proclaimed necessary operations, and their ethical merits were certified by a bipartisan nationalist-patriot chorus. A point of unity of our small activist formation was to try to act against the orthodoxy of American exceptionalism—the monkey business in our own minds as well as the troubles in the wider world—against our own blind spots and our own ignorance, and we would explore ways to advance authentic dialogue and real reflection.

We knew we couldn't simply will a political or popular social justice movement into being based on the boldness of our actions or the clarity and the rightness of our cause, but we couldn't sit idly by waiting for a movement to be delivered "overnight express" in a brightly wrapped package, either. So our eclectic gaggle, now calling ourselves A Movement Reimagining Change (ARC), met frequently to discuss books, ideas, and plans, and now to imagine how to link youth with grassroots struggles so that whatever young people chose to do around the elections would be grounded in something deeper.

Harish Patel, a twenty-three-year-old student at UIC, was ARC's primary on-the-ground organizer. Wiry and wired, Harish was a marvel of energy and good cheer with the wisdom to admit gaps and needs and the courage to ask question after question. He was a well-known city-wide youth organizer working against the school-to-prison pipeline and the criminalization of youth and mobilizing for better schools and immigrant rights. He exuded self-reliance and confidence, and he knew how to get started, how to keep at it, how to solve problems and improvise on the move. His father had been murdered in India when Harish was just fourteen years old. He was thrust virtually alone into a new life in America, raising himself with little assistance or material resources, and he championed the idea that any justice movement must be a "love movement"—love and beauty scratched out of the ugly concrete and the muck and mud of the world as it is, love powered by anger and hope, passion and energy, thought and feeling, initiative and courage. His enthusiasm was entirely winning for me, and seemingly for everyone in all directions.

Harish was charged with connecting our wondrously weird and far-flung collective of students, teachers, academics, militants, and organizers who were engaged in a huge range of progressive campaigns, projects, drives, interventions, and everyday actions. That was a humongous job in itself, but there was more. Harish was the point person in creating events that pulled together and joined up smaller efforts, finding and building links, creating a common vocabulary, a language of love and solidarity. ARC was our effort to prepare the ground so that when hope and history once again rhymed, the movement would be on the move.

James Thindwa, the lead organizer for Jobs with Justice, was another ARC leader. Tall and handsome with a gorgeous smile and a generous spirit, James had the energy, the magic touch, and the skill set of a successful organizer: the capacity to listen to everyone, the ability to write an op-ed or give an inspiring speech at a rally, the talent to keep a thousand balls in the air at once, and the deep belief that fundamental social change will only come from the self-activity of the "extraordinary ordinary people." James had come to the United States from Rhodesia/Zimbabwe a couple of decades before to attend Berea College in Kentucky, and the anticolonial struggle of his homeland lived deep within him—"activism is in my DNA," he said. For James, community and labor organizing was a calling and an obvious vehicle for justice. All of us mobilized to support James's living wage campaign and rallied at his side when workers occupied Chicago's Republic Windows and Doors factory—we drew a line in the snow—and then moved on to picket Bank of America chanting, "You got bailed out, we got sold out!"

Barbara Ransby, the brilliant historian, exhorted us to develop analysis in order to power a popular movement, as well as a moral vision of an alternative to war and empire, materialism and environmental catastrophe, white supremacy, racism, and poverty. "We need a church of the Left," she would say with a smile, knowing that everyone saw her as an open atheist who insisted that organized religion consistently dropped the ball when it came to ethical action. Her partner, Peter Sporn, a professor of medicine active in the Arab-Jewish Partnership, reminded us to keep Palestinian rights in our consciousness and explicitly in our public advocacy. And Alice Kim, a death penalty abolitionist, pushed us to see mass incarceration as essentially linked to militarism and war and economic crisis.

Whenever our movable feast landed at Alice Kim's for potluck or picnic or backyard barbeque, her little dog Mazy—her "true love"—took center stage, racing from person to person, begging for snacks, performing, cuddling, and chilling out. Even the most unlikely dog-people had to admit she was a sweetie and give up a little Maz-love.

It was at Alice's that we gathered with the remarkable mothers of men on Death Row to celebrate birthdays and mobilize support; it was at Alice's that we got to know several of the exonerated prisoners— Ronnie Kitchens, Darby Tillis, and Mark Clements; and it was at Alice's where we gathered one night with Martina Correa, the crusading sister of Troy Davis, the internationally known Death Row inmate in Georgia, to talk with Troy when he called Martina's cell phone and she put him on speaker, and there he was: Live from Death Row! Several of the men spoke to him with an intimacy that was beyond the rest of us, and Darby pulled out his guitar and sang two songs to Troy. Our young spoken-word artist and friend FM Supreme spit a poem written for him with her partner Deja, and Troy spit a poem right back at them. We hugged, we prayed, we vowed to keep fighting for Troy's life, which we did, even though a few years later the State of Georgia had its way and murdered him anyway.

When Alice applied for a special fellowship for organizers, Ransby and I wrote letters of support, and so did one of the exonerated Death Row inmates. My letter was formal and long, typed on letterhead and designed to impress, but when I saw his down-to-earth letter in her packet I had a new understanding of what grace was. If it hadn't been for Alice Kim, he said, I'd be dead today, murdered by the State of Illinois. "This may not get you the fellowship you're applying for," I told Alice, but it will get you into heaven. "After decades of struggle and defeat and small victories, one letter like that puts an activist life in perspective."

Bernardine and I had worked for months with the coalition to greet the combined NATO and G-8 meetings in Chicago with massive demonstrations and militant resistance focused on opposition to preemptive war and permanent war, nuclear proliferation and threat, the militarization of societies through an unaccountable and shadowy group with a gigantic budget and a great PR front. The coalition was broad and welcoming and included civil rights groups and labor unions, socialists and anarchists, Black Bloc and the Band of Sisters, peace people and vets against the wars, and in every meeting the folks we felt closest to on issue after issue were the vets and the pacifists.

Bernardine attended every planning meeting, fighting to stay engaged and alert (and awake) through the interminable discussions of process, always trying to focus on the substance of why we opposed NATO and the need to reach out and organize more people, and even becoming fond of several of the radicals in spite of the fact that most were operating out of disciplined caucuses that had clearly called some invisible and less generous pre-meetings where the important business had already been conducted, and were now prepared to wait out the less conscious mortals in the room. We'd done that sectarian shit so very long ago, drank the live virus and survived, and now she and I were allergic to the whole thing, but still she persevered and hung in there till the bitter end. We'd worked for years with the vets—men and women, mostly young, of every race, creed, and background—who would lead the march against NATO and everything it stood for, and we remained in awe of their courage and their moral clarity in opposing the US aggression and occupations in Afghanistan and Iraq and elsewhere. The biggest surprise for us was Sister Kathleen of the 8th Day Center for Justice, a tiny, soft-spoken, white-haired nun who sometimes wore shout-y T-shirts: LIVE OUT LOUD! REVEL IN REVOLUTION!

Bernardine and I signed up with Sister Kathleen to be "Peace Guides," a gentler name for what we used to call demonstration marshals, folks prepared to keep order on the route, buffer demonstrators from counterdemonstrators or the police forces if necessary, and maintain the integrity of the march. We attended a three-hour training that she and her colleagues led in a church basement a few weeks before the scheduled action. I'd been through workshops on nonviolent activism and trainings on peaceful resistance dozens of times over forty years, and I knew the drills and protocols pretty well: keep your hands down and don't raise your voice, listen actively, look people in the eye, anticipate problems, and set a tone of calm seriousness and respectful but determined dissent. And have fun! I knew how to de-escalate the rhetoric and how to go limp, how to breathe deeply and administer first aid while awaiting the medics, and how to summon the Lawyer's Guild observers wearing their particularly garish but unmistakable bright-green baseball caps.

Kathleen gave us a set of scenarios to role-play—someone on the march is provoking people to break away to charge the police lines, or the police come charging through our lines attacking us—and we debriefed our choices and decisions thoroughly. The high point for me was when Kathleen demonstrated typical techniques for assisting and creating a calm space of solidarity around someone singled out for attack by the police or the crowd—a noisy anarchist, say, wearing the signature black mask, or an Arab man in a keffiyeh, or anyone for any reason. She said, "Now of course I'm an old white nun, so I'm unlikely to be targeted on the street by anyone." She paused a couple of beats for maximum comedic effect, and added in the voice of a woman surprised by a sudden revelation, "Oh, unless of course the Vatican shows up—then I'll be targeted for sure, and I'm counting on all of you to know what to do!"

On the march itself, Bernardine and I kept drifting over to the Black Bloc because we liked their militancy, and we thought they had the most unifying slogan: "Shit's Fucked Up! Shit's Fucked Up!" Who could quarrel with that? As our friends from the Vets for Peace completed their dignified and moving ceremony, symbolically throwing their war medals back at the commanders who had made them fight and presenting an American flag to the mother of a vet from their group who had recently taken his own life, the bloc began to chant, "Burn that fucking flag!" Bernardine had been a perfect Peace Guide till then, but she lost it with the bloc and flew into the middle of their circle to shut them up: "Don't you tell them what to do! Burn your own fucking flag, but show some respect for these young people." I tried to remind her that we were to keep our voices low and avoid conflict, but to no avail.

We'd lived for decades in a wildly diverse Chicago neighborhood. The film director and Second City veteran Mike Nichols once famously called Hyde Park the most racially integrated neighborhood in the city; then he paused and added a little meanly (but not entirely inaccurately), Black and white, shoulder to shoulder against the poor. Our kids played for years in the dazzling Hyde Park–Kenwood Little League, led by a dynamic core of leaders and coaches, multiracial women and men, and whenever our teams traveled beyond the community borders they were regarded as a marvel—in white parts of town we were seen as a Black team, and in the Black neighborhoods we seemed to be awfully white. People saw whatever they saw through the powerful lens of race, but for parents and kids alike it was an unmistakable point of pride—this was the world we wanted to live in, beyond the world as such.

In spite of one stolen car and three break-ins over the years, I'd always thought that our street was the safest in the city. Minister Louis Farrakhan, of course, lived across the park, and the Fruit of Islam with their standard uniform of dark suits, white shirts, cute little bow ties, and close-cropped hair were an intense and ubiquitous presence. I imagined the FBI and Chicago police were keeping tabs on the minister and his Fruit, as well as on Jesse Jackson, a couple blocks further on. Mayor Harold Washington had lived a couple blocks south, Tim and Zenobia Black and Carole Mosley Braun were nearby, and a rogues' gallery of Chicago politicians and troublemakers was in easy reach. When Barack Obama became Senator Obama and, soon after that, presidential candidate Obama, that virtual Green Zone descended upon us all.

Every time I made the claim of city safety to anyone, Bernardine would remind me that our first Thanksgiving in the house was

interrupted by a frantic couple ringing our doorbell having just been
held up by a couple of teenagers right out front. My mother became
faint at the sight of a bloody nose, and my brother Juan reassured her:
"Mom, it's just the Hyde Park equivalent of your suburban Welcome
Wagon." Furthermore, Bernardine added, "If you're ever mugged, the
Chicago cops, the university police, the FBI and CIA, the Secret Service, and the Fruit might all watch from a safe distance and never lift a
finger—they might blow you a collective kiss good-bye, happy to see
you go." "No, no, not the Fruit," I would say, "the Fruit always nod at
me politely when I bike past them with my friendly wave. The Fruit
are my neighbors and my brothers." "In your dreams," she would say.

Our polling place was in the public school just out the front door
and across the street next to the baseball diamonds, and we had been
the first to vote in every election for several years. But Election Day
2008 would be different. All night, Chicago police and Secret Service
had been checking and rechecking the street, coordinating and deploy-
ing their troops while Streets and Sanitation was sprucing up every
blade of grass, polishing every sign and fire hydrant, and noisily erect-
ing a grandstand for the press right in front of our house—Senator
Barack Obama and Michelle Obama would cast their historic votes in
this remarkable election right here sometime in the next few hours.
The neighborhood was abuzz. When we stepped out into the dark at
5:59 a.m., there was already a crush of people on the street and a festive
line of voters stretching around the block, laughing, sharing coffee and
donuts, and singing. This train don't carry no strangers, and on this day
not one of us would be left behind.

I was pumped: for the second time in my life I was going to vote for
a Democrat for president. I'd campaigned for LBJ in 1964 before I was
old enough to vote or to know better—Johnson had soured me forever
on the whole corrupt mess and illuminated for me the stark limits of
electoral politics—and I'd voted in primaries over the years, notably
for Shirley Chisholm and for Jesse Jackson, but in a general election I
had a devilish time choosing to vote for one of the greatest war parties
ever built in all of history. I typically voted Green or Socialist if either
had a candidate on the ballot, or more often wrote in our son Malik,

who would have been a far better president at the age of fourteen than any of the others. And I always found something on every ballot to support wholeheartedly: I voted for Bruce Wright for judge because he set reasonable bail for poor Black men charged with crimes and was derided by the police association as "Turn 'em loose Bruce." Once I opposed a prison bond initiative that was defeated by a tiny handful of votes only to be reversed by the governor, who magically found money for prison construction, and reversed again when our brother-in-law brought a lawsuit which delayed it for years. I could only stand to vote for a national Democrat once before, in 1972 when I voted against war and for George McGovern. Now I would happily and without any illusions vote for Barack Hussein Obama.

All during the campaign Senator Obama had described himself as a moderate, pragmatic, middle-of-the-road politician. The Right responded in full-throated attack that he was in fact a secret Muslim and a closeted socialist, some kind of Trojan horse and Manchurian candidate rolled into one to destroy the country, while the Left said, in effect, "I think he's winking at me." He wasn't winking, and his self-description turned out to be absolutely accurate, perfectly matching his record in Illinois and in the US Senate if anyone had bothered to look it up. He was super-smart, personable, compassionate, and decent in a thousand ways—all true. He was also a mainstream moderate, as advertised, prepared to sit on the throne of a now-declining empire and command its violent legions.

He was also unique in several ways: an African American who knew many of the inconvenient truths of American history up close; a community organizer who had spent countless days sitting at kitchen tables with poor and working people listening and learning from their experiences and perspectives; a powerful writer of his own unique story; a proud papa; and a global citizen who could brilliantly evoke, for example, a fleeting but meaningful encounter with a migrant worker in Spain, the sense of a shared story and deeper human solidarity embodied in that chance meeting, and describe the traveler as "just another hungry man far away from home, one of the many children of former colonies . . . now breaching the barricades of their former masters, mounting their own ragged, haphazard invasion." That was a stunning piece of writing, from *Dreams from My Father*, as well as a beautiful sentiment reflecting a humane politics that comes straight from the bottom up.

We were besieged by reporters as we went into the school and as we exited, but we just smiled, waved, and kept on truckin'. Election workers were happy to see us and to shake our hands, everyone feeling a kind of collective joy, and even inside the little school gym the folding bleachers had been opened and were filled with press people who shouted questions: "How does it look to you?" "Will you grant an interview tomorrow?"

We hung out on our front porch chatting with friends and neighbors and the Japanese news media until the Obamas arrived in a frenetic swirl of lights and color and noise. The cheering began in anticipation, held a high pitch as they waved and embraced neighborhood folks and walked into the school, and lingered until long after they were gone.

Fox News covered the event with video of Minister Farrakhan voting early, and then a shot of Bernardine and me entering the same polling place, and finally the Obamas coming to vote sometime later. The reporter pointed out the clever sequence and pattern of the parade and then posed the foxy question: "Farrakhan, then Ayers, then Obama . . . coincidence?" I thought, No! It must be a conspiracy! Great investigative reporting: the minister and I had each left voting instructions for the Obamas taped under the tray inside the booth. How else would they know how to vote? And Fox News sniffed it out!

As I was preparing for class later in the day, David Remnick, the editor of the *New Yorker*, rang the doorbell. I'd been pretty solid in my silence for months, but I was suddenly unsure if the injunction had now been lifted. I mean, it wasn't quite *after* the election—there were several hours to go—but we'd already voted, and it was tough to see how anything I might say or do now could sway the outcome or become fodder for the lunatic Right. It suddenly occurred to me: I'm free! I laughed out loud suddenly and did a little spontaneous jig. Ha! I'm free!

And then I wondered, but am I really? Could I now run naked in the streets, all shackles dropped and all bets off? Better not, so instead I called Bernardine. She didn't answer. What to do? I was rusty and unsure, but it was David Remnick for God's sake, and the *New Yorker*, and for a small group of people, me included, that's the pinnacle of something, even though I'm not sure exactly what it's at the top of. Remnick couldn't have been any more nerdy—I can't remember what he looked like at all, youngish middle-aged, I think, khakis and loafers probably, maybe a pocket protector—but I was panting slightly nonetheless, my senses shaky and my vision blurred.

"Could we talk for a few minutes?" he asked.

So we sat on the front steps and talked and talked. He was really smart, needless to say, and low-key, and when he asked if he could take notes and pulled out a notebook and pencil, I said, "Sure, why not, of course you can," and we sat there together, me babbling away. What could I possibly say of interest? No matter, don't think about it—blah, blah, blah. I was off the leash.

Barack Obama won the election, in case anyone missed it. Barack Obama was president of the United States. The satirical *Onion* captured the moment as only it can: "Black Man Given the Worst Job in America." But now when anyone asked to take a picture with me and uttered the old tired joke, "I guess I can't run for president now," I would respond: "What are you talking about? Obama *is* the president—the worst job in America—and who can say I hurt him in the end? Maybe I gave him just the bump he needed."

And it was as if a secret gag order from some undisclosed headquarters was instantly rescinded and an announcement had been sent simultaneously to anyone I'd ever known—the shunning of the past months was suddenly and decidedly over! Colleagues who hadn't glanced in my direction in months stopped by my office for a chat, neighbors waved and offered cheerful greetings, and folks from near and far called me to check in and see how I was doing. Invariably people offered their heartfelt sympathies for the "hammering you took from the Right." Most added that they admired "the dignity and resoluteness" I'd shown through the whole ordeal; everyone was buoyed and relieved, with a generous helping of fellow-feeling. Being welcomed back into the community took some getting used to, but it was also pleasant and satisfying. I was happy the madness had passed, even if temporarily.

But it reminded me of a story a friend of ours from Cape Town, South Africa, had told us years earlier. Vivian had been an underground member of the revolutionary African National Congress during the fight for freedom, and he was simultaneously a leader of the Black Business Association. He'd created a way around some of the restrictions of apartheid with the help of a Jewish friend and colleague. Vivian couldn't operate his jewelry business in an office in a restricted zone, so his colleague—his white cover—took out a lease on an office and signed the papers each year, and Vivian technically became an employee of what was in fact his own business. This arrangement worked for a time, but there came a point when his colleague said it seemed only fair that Vivian pay him a sum for the service of signing the papers. What? Vivian was astonished, argued with his colleague for a time, and then gave in: the papers would be signed for a small fee—a pathetic and corrupting profit from apartheid, Vivian concluded. But, what the hell?

He hardly saw the man again, but shortly after Nelson Mandela's release from prison and his election as president of a free South Africa, Vivian ran into his old colleague on the street. The man embraced him warmly and said, "Isn't it wonderful! We are all free!" Astonished once more, Vivian hugged him back—a bit awkwardly—and marveled at the very human capacity for self-deception. The man had forgotten or suppressed his shabby behavior when it actually mattered.

The gag order was definitely off, and having neither an agent nor much sense, I jumped quickly at the first chance to tell my story. An editor for a national magazine had invited me to do a long personal essay for a ridiculously high fee, and I agreed, but it fell through as soon I wrote a brief op-ed for the *New York Times*. "We wanted an exclusive," he explained.

The *Times* piece was short, and some junior editor gave it an idiotic and impossible headline: "The Real Bill Ayers." Life's too twisty and forward-charging for that, I thought—the *real* me was an open question and a work in progress, a many-splendored thing and a chaotic mash-up. We'll see about the real Ayers, but what the hell—I was happy to speak for myself after being talked about for so long. I was in a hurry, and the *Times* was ready right away.

I explained that all the folks recurring in the weird narrative that dogged the Obama campaign—the "fiery America-hating preacher," the "dangerous Palestinian academic," and the "unrepentant domestic terrorist"—were simply caricatures and fantasies. None of those people actually existed, and flushing out every tie and suggested affiliation with these cartoon characters, which had been big news for months, was nothing but a fool's errand.

As the putative unrepentant terrorist, I'd often felt like Goldstein from George Orwell's *1984*—the public enemy projected onto a large screen in the ritual "two minutes hate" scene when the faithful gathered in a frenzy of fear and loathing, chanting, "Kill him!" In the pre-election frenzy I saw no sensible path to a rational discussion, and so I decided to turn away whenever the microphones were thrust in my face. I sat it out.

But with the election over I wanted to say as plainly as I could that that character wasn't me, not even close.

I sent a note to Sarah Palin then, suggesting that we launch a talk show together called "Palling Around with Sarah and Bill." It was just a joke, but I couldn't resist. Fox News would be good, I said, but I didn't have any contacts there, or anywhere else really. I asked if she could check around for us, kind of be my/our agent. I never heard back.

I went on *Hardball*, a show I'd never seen before—although I've watched like a junkie ever since—and I found Chris Matthews the most fun and entertaining interviewer I'd ever experienced. He ran quickly from one thing to another, throwing out questions helter-skelter, which he mostly answered himself—and that suited me just fine, since I had a cold and a terrible sore throat and was downing cup after cup of Throat Coat tea. He injected little bits of autobiography here and there, and after thoroughly interrogating himself, ended with a judgment: "You're a good guy, Bill Ayers; I think you're a good guy." I figured he prepared for the interview by drinking gallons of espresso, or going off his meds.

I agreed to an interview on *Good Morning America* and flew to New York the night before, staying with my kids in order to make the early morning appointment. I didn't want to get trapped into a silly game of affirming or denying every detail of my relationship with the president-elect—did you meet him at such and such a place? Did you ever have brunch together? Chesa had the smartest answer: "Just say, 'I knew Barack Obama about as well as thousands of other people—I don't believe we ever shared a milk shake with two straws; I mean, we weren't that close—and like millions of others, I wish I knew him much better today.'" That was true.

Barbara Walters and Robin Roberts came by the green room to say hello and to chat—I knew that BJ would absolutely freak out; to her, they were not quite Oprah, but in that league—and they were each lovely. When I later told BJ I'd talked with them, she went nuts and made me relate over and over every detail of our one minute together.

But my on-air interviewer was Chris Cuomo, son of Mario and brother of Andrew, a bit cold and somewhat severe. I realized quickly that he felt compelled somehow to show his audience that he was not seated with a friend—I knew the sad tradition of American journalists assuming a respectful and deferential tone whenever interviewing an ally of the country, every random right-wing Israeli politician, for example, or a dictator like Pervez Musharraf, while an enemy of the state department always got, in effect, an adversarial interrogation and waves of terse toughness. His tone was part of his act, and it changed abruptly when we took a station break. Suddenly, he was kind and relaxed and sympathetic: "I can imagine what you've been going through with these attacks and all the guilt by association," he said. "You know when my dad ran for president, the same thing happened to him—his opponents kept unfairly linking him to the Mafia." Wait a minute, I thought, are you connecting me to your dad, wrongly smeared, or am I in the Mafia role here?

Back on the air he produced a copy of a page from *Prairie Fire*, the manifesto of the Underground, and suggested that I somehow supported Sirhan Sirhan. I said that that was ridiculous and stupid. He asked how well I'd actually known Barack Obama and I said, "I knew Barack Obama about as well as thousands of other people—I don't believe we ever shared a milk shake with two straws; I mean, we weren't that close—and like millions of others, I wish I knew him much better today."

Among the laughable highlights from the lunacy tracking me through the presidential race was a photograph bouncing from blog to blog, conspiracy site to paranoid central—it was an early snapshot of Bernardine and me smiling arm in arm with the caption "Bill Ayers and Obama's mother, 'Ann Dunham': Dreams from Which Father?" Dunham and Bernardine were both born in 1942, it's true, and they were both beautiful and free-spirited women. For a dedicated few, the idea took hold—OMG! We were Barack's parents, not his pals!

The story that I had secretly ghostwritten *Dreams from My Father*, Barack Obama's beautifully constructed memoir had gone wild in a shadowy corner of the blogosphere. A bunch of cranks fed the fire at first, and soon enough more serious analysts signed on and spoke up about the vast, complex conspiracy that I was orchestrating, perhaps even dictating Obama's thoughts. How could I ever prove the negative?

I was walking through Reagan National Airport when a mild-looking middle-aged woman approached me and asked if I were Bill Ayers. "I am," I said. "What's your name?"

"I'm Anne Leary," she replied as we walked along.

"What do you do?"

"I'm a right-wing blogger," she said without hesitation. "And I'd love to ask you one question."

"Sure," I said. "Shoot."

"Did you write *Dreams from My Father*?" she asked, and I laughed out loud.

Here we go, I thought, and then—FLASH!—I had an inspiration. We stopped and I turned to face her. I asked her to please quote me exactly. "Of course I will," she said.

"Yes, yes," I said. "OK. I wrote *Dreams*, every word of it," I said. "Are you getting this down, Anne? I met with Barack Obama maybe three or four times total on this project, and then I just made the whole thing up, ghostwrote the entire book. I doubt that he even proofed it. Now, if you can help me prove that I wrote it, I'll split the royalties with you."

She wrote furiously and smiled broadly. "Thank you! Thank you!" she repeated, shaking my hand. I thought I'd brought a little ray of sunshine into what I imagined must be a slightly dim and arid space, and I felt great.

Anne was true to her word. She posted the interview, and her obscure little site got tons of hits and lots of links, soaring upward on a big traffic-ranking site to number 3 and then number 2 and, finally, number 1! Wow! Anne was big time now in her murky little echo chamber, a real hero for finally getting confirmation on a story they all knew to be true but couldn't prove—until now.

From hero to goat in a matter of days: first Jonah Goldberg, then *National Journal* and Rush Limbaugh, and finally the *Times*, which said that it sounded like "Ayers is jerking some chains." The story suffered a sudden unanticipated reversal, and they began to bicker and dig a bit of a trough for themselves. If *they* said I wrote the book, that was an example of courageous and intrepid investigative journalism; if *I* said I wrote the book, that was just me being a goofball, while making asses out of them. The real story, as Rush saw it, was that I *did* write the book, but by admitting that I did, I was actually cleverly asserting that I *didn't* write the book. Oh, what a tangled web I weave!

I thought the lunacy of authorship was dead and done when I met Jamie Weinstein, a young and eager reporter with the *Daily Caller*. After some harmless chatter, he said, "Listen, I know what you're going to say, but I feel I need to ask you a question, and I'd appreciate an honest answer. Did you write *Dreams?*" I said I did. "No, that's what I mean. I don't want you to make that same joke; I want you to tell the truth—did you write it?" "I did." "No!" Where would this ever end? I wondered.

I wrote to Jamie later and suggested that his insistence demonstrated an irony-challenged temperament. He disagreed: "If I was irony-challenged, I would have accepted your answer . . . at face value. . . . I thought the authorship conspiracy was similarly insane— until I came across Christopher Andersen's portrait of Barack and

Michelle's marriage two weeks ago. Andersen is hardly a right-wing ideologue or conspiracy-monger."

In fact, I'd never read Andersen's book, *Barack and Michelle*, so I didn't know if Jamie had it right, but apparently in it Andersen claims I had a major hand in writing *Dreams*. Jamie went on:

> He [Andersen] claims to have talked to over 200 people close to the president in Chicago and elsewhere. So when I brought it up and you gave me your typical tongue-in-cheek answer, I ignored it and pressed for more . . . My actual question is where could Andersen have possibly gotten the details in the book? You were obviously agitated by the question. There are two possibilities why. One, you have something you are trying to hide. Two, you were annoyed by a question that you felt you have answered and which you considered, perhaps rightly, a wild conspiracy. But my question remains, how did Andersen get it so wrong from his interviews with associates of you and Obama?

I responded that when an earnest and ambitious journalist is knocked for being "irony-challenged" and responds by denying the charge, that's not a rebuttal. It's proof. I'd never heard of the guy he kept referencing, never called him an ideologue or conspiracy theorist, had zero interest in the "inside story" of the Obama marriage and couldn't possibly know his "sources," but that I would think his reporting would take him to Andersen himself. I told Jamie that I was not the least bit agitated by his crazy question.

A self-described deep-thinking intellectual named Jack Cashill set out to prove—independent of my denials or affirmations—that I had indeed written *Dreams*. He sought real evidence through a close reading of texts and a brush with the Internet. He was the great brain who discovered, for example, those infamous maritime references and metaphors in both *Dreams* and *Fugitive Days*, a possible testament to my fraught time as a merchant marine. In any case, it was now clear that I had been the seafaring Odysseus to Obama's father-hungry Telemachus, and *Dreams* the "record of a personal, interior journey—a boy's search for his father." I loved the reflection, and loved imagining my few months on the Atlantic as an epic tale of the human journey.

Cashill found that Rashid Khalidi acknowledged me in his book *Resurrecting Empire*: "Bill was particularly generous in letting me use his family's dining room table to do some writing for the project." Khalidi directed the University of Chicago's Center for International Studies, and at a farewell dinner on the occasion of his departure for Columbia University, Barack Obama toasted him, thanking him and Mona for the many dinners they had shared, as well as for his "consistent reminders to me of my own blind spots and my own biases." But more important, Cashill pointed out, Khalidi didn't need a table—a ha!—no, he needed a mentor, a role I apparently played with a wide range of Hyde Park intellectuals and radical writers.

And he discovered that near the end of my book *A Kind and Just Parent*, I described bicycling through the South Side and identified a few of my notable neighbors: Muhammad Ali, Minister Louis Farrakhan, the poet Gwendolyn Brooks, and the writer Barack Obama. Cashill felt that the "writer" identification was forced and the listing of Obama as prominent utterly absurd at that point.

"The question is often asked why Obama associated with Ayers," Cashill wrote on the website AmericanThinker.com. "The more appropriate question is why the powerful Ayers would associate with the then-obscure Obama . . . My suspicion is that Ayers saw the potential in Obama, and he chose to mold it." Ah, the "powerful Ayers"—it sounded remarkably like the "powerful Oz!"

Here are three samples from his book *Deconstructing Obama* of Cashill's skillful sleuthing on the question of narrative:

AYERS: "The hallmark of writing in the first person is intimacy. . . . But in narrative the universal is revealed through the specific, the general through the particular, the essence through the unique, and necessity is revealed through contingency."

OBAMA: "And so what was a more interior, intimate effort on my part, to understand this struggle and to find my place in

it, has converged with a broader public debate, a debate
in which I am professionally engaged."

AYERS: "The mind works in contradiction, and honesty requires
the writer to reveal disputes with herself on the page."

OBAMA: "Not because that past is particularly painful or perverse
but because it speaks to those aspects of myself that resist
conscious choice and that—on the surface, at least—contradict the world I now occupy."

AYERS: "Narrative writers strive for a personal signature, but
must be aware that the struggle for honesty is constant."

OBAMA: "I was engaged in a fitful interior struggle. I was trying
to raise myself to be a black man in America."

Empirical proof or crackpot confirmation, you decide, but this little exercise is pretty easy to apply almost anywhere, anytime.

Here, for example, is a line from *Politicians, Partisans, and Parasites*, by Tucker Carlson, the libertarian pundit: "Liberals have trouble
believing that anyone who disagrees with them politically could be a
decent person. Once they decide they like you, they assume you must
be a liberal, too—in my case, a closet liberal."

And here's a sentence from *Ayers:* "Some liberals can't help con-
flating intelligence, compassion, and decency with liberal politics. If
you're decent and compassionate they automatically assume you're
a liberal."

OMG! I wrote Tucker Carlson's book too!

When the Public Square, a tiny but wondrous program of the Illinois Humanities Council, organized an online auction to raise needed
funds, Bernardine and I donated two items: choice seats at a Cubs
game and an afternoon at beautiful Wrigley Field with an ardent and
unruly fan—that would be Bernardine—and dinner for six, cooked by
team Ayers-Dohrn. The Public Square was celebrating its tenth anniversary, and we'd been on its advisory board from the start. We'd
already done the dinner thing two dozen times over the years—for a
local baseball camp, a law students' public interest group, immigrant

rights organizing, and a lot of other worthy causes—and we'd typically raised a few hundred dollars. There were many more-attractive items on the Public Square auction list—Alex Kotlowitz was available to edit twenty pages of a nonfiction manuscript, Gordon Quinn to discuss documentary film projects over dinner, and Kevin Coval to write and spit an original poem for the highest bidder. But what the heck, we'd do what we could.

We paid little attention as the auction launched and then inched onward—a hundred dollars, two hundred, and then three—even when a right-wing blogger picked it up and began flogging the Illinois Humanities Council for "supporting terrorism" by giving taxpayer money to us. He was a little off on the concept since *we* were actually donating our money and services to *them*, not the other way around, but this was a rather typical turn for the fact-free, faith-based blogosphere, so onward and upward. No worries.

There was a little button on our dinner item that someone could select and "Buy Instantly" for $2,500, which seemed absurdly out of reach. But in early December the TV celebrity and self-described conservative bad boy, Tucker Carlson, hit the button, and we were his.

I loved it immediately. Carlson was a well-known libertarian political commentator whose signature style for many years was built around a bright bow-tie, a shock of chestnut hair, and an ability to noisily mock anything at hand. He was famously bounced from cohosting *Crossfire* on CNN after an angry on-air confrontation with Jon Stewart of *The Daily Show*. Carlson had criticized Stewart for asking softball questions in a political interview, and Stewart responded that his show was a comedy and added, "It's interesting to hear you talk about my responsibility. . . . I didn't realize that . . . the news organizations look to Comedy Central for their cues on integrity." After Carlson told Stewart, "I think you're more fun on your show," Stewart replied: "You know what's interesting though? You're as big a dick on your show as you are on any show." Carlson went on to found the conservative *Daily Caller*, and surely he had some frat-boy prank up his sleeve—his standard gesture a kind of smug and superior practical joke or an ad hominem put down—but so what? We'd just raised more money for the Public Square in one bid than anyone thought was possible from the entire auction. We won!

Right-wing blogs lit up, some writers tickled with Tucker's entertaining sense of humor, others earnestly saluting his willingness to enter the den of dodgy enemies of the state and sit in close quarters, an unmistakable act of courage and daring in the service of "the cause." But a few took a grimmer view: Don't do it, Tucker, they pled, this will not only legitimize and humanize "two of America's greatest traitors," it will also take the sting out of the steady charge that Obama himself is suspect for the crime of knowing them.

Tucker Carlson got a letter from the IHC: "Congratulations," it began, "You are the winning bidder for The Public Square's 10th anniversary auction item: Dinner for six with Bill Ayers and Bernardine Dohrn. Thank you very much for your payment of $2500 for this item."

The letter went on to offer ten potential dates for the dinner, and to note that "all auction items were donated to the IHC [which] makes no warranties or representations with respect to any item or service sold . . ." and that "views and opinions expressed by individuals attending the dinner do not reflect those of the Illinois Humanities Council, the National Endowment for the Humanities, or the Illinois General Assembly." I laughed out loud imagining the exhausted scrivener bent at his table copying out that carefully crafted, litigation-proof language—does it go far enough? How about the governor or the Joint Chiefs of Staff? But then, I'm no lawyer.

We were besieged by friends clamoring to come to dinner—"I'll serve drinks," wrote one prominent Chicago lawyer. "Or, if you like, I'll wear a little tuxedo and park the cars. Please let me come!"

Everyone saw it as theater, but not everyone was delighted with the impending show. A few friends called to tell us that Carlson and company were "scum" and "vipers," arguing that we should never talk to people like them, ever. We disagreed; talk can be good, we said. Others began distancing themselves from us, wringing their hands the moment they saw themselves mentioned on the right-wing blogs, and instantly, almost instinctively, assuming a defensive crouch.

Things quickly got weirder. Two board members resigned from the IHC—I'm shocked! Shocked! Round up the usual suspects! They complained that the organization was now affiliated with people who "advocate violence," presumably Bernardine and me, not Tucker Carlson or his friends, not the mayor, the governor, the state legislature, the cabinet, or the Joint Chiefs of Staff. The paid stenographers at the *Chicago Tribune* duly reported the two resignations, quoting the outraged quitters and leaving it at that.

In early January the IHC folks suggested I figure things out with Tucker directly from now on—no need to have them act as intermediary: "It's your dinner, and our involvement at this point just complicates things." That seemed sensible to me. We'd scheduled a meeting with top staff and board members, but since the IHC was stepping away, that became irrelevant, and the meeting was canceled.

They'd dissociated formally, but it soon became clear that behind-the-scenes bickering and back channel kibitzing, emergency meetings and heated exchanges continued apace. Some winced and stooped a little deeper, and apparently few were moved to speak up publicly to defend the idea of dialogue and conversation as essential to the culture of democracy generally and to the vitality of the humanities specifically. No one condemned the most knee-jerk instances of demonization and far-fetched guilt by association.

Dinner with Tucker seemed cheery and worthwhile compared to counseling a bunch of cringing liberals. Where is the backbone or the principle? No wonder the tiny group of right-wing flame-throwers with a couple of e-mail accounts feels so disproportionately powerful—liberals seem forever willing to police themselves to the point of forming an orderly line right off a cliff.

I wrote Tucker a quick letter telling him we looked forward to seeing him for dinner in Chicago and what we assumed would be a spirited and enlightening conversation. I saluted him for making such a generous contribution to the Public Square, a tiny program that works mightily to promote public dialogue as an essential way forward.

I mentioned that I'd heard him on the radio kidding around about the dinner with Dennis Miller and saying with a laugh, "When I hear the word 'humanities,' I draw my gun." It was a joke, of course, but I urged him to leave his guns at home.

He promised he would.

A few days later Tucker sent the guest list: Jamie Weinstein, Andrew Breitbart, Matt Labash, Audrey Lowe, and Buckley Carlson. "Entertaining, civil people all of them, guaranteed," he concluded.

Jamie and Matt were his young associates at the *Daily Caller*, Buckley his brother, and Audrey was a random reader who had won the privilege in some kind of contest Tucker had held online. Andrew Breitbart was a founder of *The Huffington Post* and an apostate from the liberal camp—I can picture Arianna Huffington and Andrew passing in the hallway, her fleeing her right-wing past, him retreating from the liberals. He was a self-described "media mogul," the founder of several conservative websites and a practitioner of right-wing guerrilla theater, always playing the role of the grinning and menacing bomb-thrower. His record included active assistance in the demise of ACORN, efforts to damage Planned Parenthood, and the deeply dishonest discrediting of Shirley Sherrod at the Agriculture Department, which led to her being fired (followed by an administration apology and her reinstatement). Breitbart had several screws loose or missing, I thought, but we'd see soon enough, up close and personal. Entertaining and civil! Guaranteed!

A couple of nights before the dinner I was hosting a meet-and-greet coffee at home for a young friend and former student running for the Illinois Senate. (True: he told me he too had aspirations to be president someday—the first Mexican American in the White House—and a coffee at our house seemed like the perfect launching pad!) Bernardine was away for work, so I was on my own. As the event wound down and people began to drift away, an old and dear friend took me aside and told me it was foolish of me to have offered the dinner to the Public Square in the first place—an act of "left adventurism," she called it—and going through with it now would be provocative and stupid.

"What?" I said, my voice rising and cracking. "We've done this dozens of times, so how is this particular dinner donation adventurism?"

"Oh, please," she said, annoyed.

"And we've been on their board for a decade," I continued, "and they asked us to do it, so how is that provocative?"

"But not in this context," she explained. "They're vulnerable, and this is not good for them." I was stunned.

"I'm innocent and I didn't do anything wrong," I said, but that sounded whiny and ridiculous the moment it left my mouth—I'm not "innocent" in the least, and I do wrong things all the time. Still, this dinner just didn't seem like one of my many terrible or even tiny transgressions. I felt rattled and alone.

But this all had a clarifying effect as well. Friends came into sharper focus, well-defined and evident, and those who understood the importance of standing on principle—friends or not—on issues like resisting the grotesque demonization of individuals and whole social groups, or fighting the toxic use of guilt by association in political discourse, also became dazzlingly obvious. Those who were confused or confounded, duped or bamboozled, faded into the background. It occurred to me once more that the good liberals I know would surely do the right thing if zealots began burning young girls as witches in Massachusetts, for example, or if the government said, in a time of fear and threat, "We're rounding up all Japanese Americans and placing them in prison camps." I'm sure they'd all cheered watching the movie *Spartacus* as every slave who'd been lined up on the field stepped forward in solidarity and said, "I am Spartacus," and when in *Point of Order* the courageous Joe Walsh stood up to the bullying Joe McCarthy and, in a voice breaking with emotion, uttered the famous line, "Have you no shame, Senator? At long last, have you no shame?" If only we'd lived in that more perfect time.

It's pretty easy to imagine being a hero from generations gone by—we're all abolitionists and freedom fighters now, all heroes in retrospect—but that settles nothing for today. Several state legislatures want teachers *right here, right now* to compile lists of students with questionable immigration status. Several people *right here, right now* are being interrogated, persecuted, and jailed for giving money or medical supplies to charities in Palestine disapproved of by the State Department. Citizens are legally barred by the US government *right here, right now* from free travel to a single country in the world, that terrifying island ninety miles from Miami. Where is the outrage, right here and right now? Oh, but these things are quite complicated and so very controversial that it's hard to know what to do now—it was all so obvious and a little too easy back then. I mean, McCarthy's name itself was a dead giveaway: McCarthy, McCarthyism . . . who couldn't see that shit coming a mile away?

I shopped; I cooked; I set up for dinner. But it felt mostly like a heavy slog through thick mud. I was cold; I was lonely; I was tired. Not at all the mood or the tone I'd wanted.

Things got better inside my head when Bernardine returned to Chicago. She went right to work, making the carrot-ginger soup, chilling me out, promising fun, and when a wondrous collection of our closest activist friends from A Movement Reimagining Change (ARC) assembled at a friend's beautiful home to help out and serve, mostly to be present at the dinner party, I felt fine. We agreed that we would serve a course and then pull up chairs to chat with our guests, jump up and prepare the next course, ferry dishes in and out, and then pull up chairs for a chat again. There was lots of wine and beer, and we set an elegant table with a place cards depicting six different "great Americans"—Rosa Parks, for example, and Gertrude Stein, as well as Dick Cheney and Sarah Palin—at each place setting, along with a menu printed on card stock they could each keep as a souvenir: Hoisin Ribs and Cucumbers, Carrot-Ginger Soup, White Fish with Black and Red Quinoa, Midwest Farmhouse Cheeses, Apple Pie and Stephen Colbert's AmeriCone Dream Ice Cream. At the bottom of the menu, I'd included two quotations about the humanities: "I just thank my father and mother, my lucky stars, that I had the advantage of an education in the *humanities*," from David McCullough (awarded the Medal of Freedom by George W. Bush); and "When I hear the word *humanities*, I draw my gun," from Tucker Carlson (emphasis mine, in both cases). It was, of course, a joke.

I meditated on Rilke:

Let everything happen to you
Beauty and terror

Just keep going
No feeling is final

And then they arrived. Let the rumpus begin!

Spirited greetings and introductions all around, laughter at the improbability of the whole thing, a flurry of separate conversations as wine was poured and glasses lifted. I proposed a toast to Tucker, thanking him for his generous gift to the Public Square and reminding everyone that this was a dinner party, not an interview or a performance (of course, dinner is always a performance, and this one more than most). Then they were seated at the table, first course served.

Friends had warned us that they would try to create a *gotcha* moment, but not much happened. Tucker and Bernardine gazed out the windows for a time at the Chicago skyline and discovered a shared Swedish background (Christmas cookies!). Jamie Weinstein acted the intrepid cub reporter, notebook in hand, copying the titles of books from the vast bookshelves (Look, Solzhenitsyn! And Vargas Llosa!), questions flying from him in a steady stream, but perhaps his manic, in-your-face manner was the result of jet lag ("I'm just off the plane from Israel," he said half a dozen times. "My third trip!"). Carlson and Breitbart had been on the primary campaign trail, and each expressed deep disdain for the Republican candidates seeking the presidency. When Jamie complained that none was a bona fide conservative, I asked him to define "conservative" for me.

"Small government," he said.

"That's it?" I asked.

"Yes."

It certainly makes thinking easier, if not completely beside the point. I pointed out that Somalia, to take an obvious example, was a small-government paradise.

Tucker told me at one point that his kids went to the same boarding school he'd attended, and asserted that the only difference between his kids' school and a failing Chicago public school was that at the prep school they could fire the bad teachers. I laughed out loud, and he smiled weakly.

Meanwhile, at the other end of the table, Bernardine was saying that the United States should close all its foreign military bases immediately, begin to dismantle the Pentagon, the CIA, and NATO, and save a trillion dollars a year at least—a small-government proposal if ever there was one. The boys weren't buying it at all, clamoring for invasions here, aggression there, violence (normalized, routine, and taken for granted) practically everywhere. Andrew Breitbart, humid and heating up, argued noisily for US military interventions in Iran and Syria and, then, egging himself on, in North Korea and China (!)—on humanitarian grounds, of course—while Bernardine, that notorious poster child for violence, steadfastly urged nuclear disarmament, withdrawal from occupations, peace on earth, goodwill toward all. It was utterly surreal.

I gave each guest a swag bag with candy kisses and one of my books, autographed. Tucker took my comic book about teaching, and I signed it "To my new best friend!" I had bought his book *Politicians, Partisans, and Parasites*, with an epigraph (returned to again and again in the text) from Larry King: "The trick is to care, but not too much. Give a shit—but not really." I asked him to please autograph it for me. He wrote: "Thanks for the fantastic ribs! Please read every word of this—the truth lies herein." Perhaps he was being ironic as well.

As they were leaving, Breitbart told Bernardine that he was thrilled to know her, and he noted that we had at least one thing in common: we were all convenient caricatures in the "lamestream" media.

It was all over in an hour and a half. Andrew Breitbart tweeted from the taxi ferrying them back to their hotel: *Shorthand: Ayers, a gourmand charmer. Dohrn, hot at 70, best behavior. Potemkin dinner. Pampered by their coterie.*

He elaborated in a long radio interview later that night from his hotel bar: "We were exposed to the two most sophisticated dinner party-throwers in the world. . . . This was their battlefield and they couldn't have been more charming. . . . I think I'm going to try and reach out to Bill Ayers and try and figure out if I can maybe do a road trip across the country with him—him and me—and he can show me his America, and I can show him my America, and maybe we can film it and let people decide. Because I've got to be honest with you, I liked being in the room with him, talking with him."

That road trip was a fun if unlikely prospect, but a few days after our dinner it became impossible—Andrew Breitbart collapsed and died outside his home at the age of forty-three, too young.

Life—short or long—always ends in the middle of things.

I was invited to give a keynote speech at an anarchist convention in Greece, and while the rebels who'd organized the event assured me that they would cover my airfare and put me up for a few days at one of their squats, I was still a tad skeptical as the plane touched down in Athens: they were *anarchists*, for Christ's sake. But once I'd cleared customs, all doubt disappeared—two skinny, feral kids, pierced, tattooed, and dressed in vibrant rags with braided and neon-colored hair flying haphazardly from their skulls, bounded toward me wearing big, welcoming smiles. Georges grabbed my backpack and Maria took my arm as we jumped on the bus headed toward one of the dicey districts of Athens.

Seated in the back row, Maria handed over an envelope swollen with a weathered wad of low-denomination euros, "for the plane ticket," she said. It was uncountable on our bouncing bus, but everything was feeling right. "Cool," I said, and stuffed it into my vest pocket. She broke out her military-style pack and pulled up a thermos of thick black Greek coffee and a bag of Arab food, grease darkening the paper sack in a delicate Rorschach, and we dived eagerly into flatbread and falafel, hummus and baba ghanoush. Georges offered portions to our dubious fellow travelers—"We're anarchists!" he proclaimed—and we chattered happily about plans for the week as they pointed out the ancient sights along the way.

"An anarchist convention," I said as we rolled through the city streets. "Isn't that a contradiction in terms—like a fat anarchist?" It sounded like an oxymoron to me, something akin to jumbo shrimp or Justice Scalia. And a keynote speech seemed so unnecessarily hierarchical. "Are you sure you're anarchists?" I teased.

"Don't be fooled," Maria kidded back. "This is all a front for chaos and confusion. You're one of our many props!"

The squat was beautiful: anarcho-graffiti in the entryway and up the narrow stairs, open windows and unlocked doors, assorted chairs in all manner of disrepair in the large commons area, pirated electricity and Internet, big pots of red beans and lentils bubbling away on a small black stove, and a huge, salvaged wooden table overflowing with black bread, apples and cheese, olives, tomatoes, and hard-boiled eggs. I was given a mat and assigned a small back bedroom, which I shared with three other comrades, and situated right next to the toilet (thank you, young anarchists!). I had to give my talk—"Society-in-Motion: Democracy Makes a Tentative Appearance in the Streets of Amerika"—late that night, so I headed off for a nap to shake off the remaining jet lag.

It was already dark when I peeped my eyes open and stumbled out to the common room. "At last!" Maria laughed as she passed me a Greek coffee and a handful of pistachios. "We're late!"

A dozen of us stampeded down the stairs and piled into several cars bound for the Arts College, anarchist headquarters for the week (Do anarchists even have a headquarters? I asked). I was scrunched in the back seat of a rusted-out Soviet-era Zap without springs or shock absorbers. It was a bumpy ride.

My talk, scheduled for 8:00 p.m., didn't get started till 10:00, which seemed fine with everyone else. I was just going with the flow, so it was cool with me too—"Please pass another cup of black coffee," I said. When my time came, I asked for a moment of silent remembrance for fifteen-year-old Alexandros Grigoropoulos, murdered by the police not long before at a spot near where we now assembled. I then channeled the great anarchist thinker Mikhail Bakunin: Freedom without socialism is a license for privilege and injustice; socialism without freedom is slavery and brutality. I spoke of our shared values of peace and participatory democracy, agency and power from below with neither gods nor masters. I offered a modest proposal that Bernardine and I had first suggested at a gathering in Berlin a year before to try to illuminate the fault lines of power and violence: every citizen or resident of a country that has *any* US military presence on its territory must be allowed to vote in US elections. The applause was thunderous and sustained. I ended by saluting the great anarchist tradition in Greece stretching back centuries and sustained by subsequent generations of Greek youth, and reminded them that it was now their moment and their honor to carry it on.

A large group of us left the auditorium after midnight and retreated to a café to keep the conversation going, accompanied by bottles of cheap red wine, an assortment of briny olives, old cheeses, and freshly baked bread. I got back to the squat around 2:00 am and was awake a few hours later to meet Petros, a doctor who had trained in the United States, and catch the fast boat from Piraeus to the faraway island of Paros, where we would spend the day with Manolis Glezos, returning to the anarchist convention late, late that night. Petros was excited to make the introduction: "You and Manolis will love each other," he insisted. "You share some politics." I couldn't wait.

Manolis Glezos was the most respected (or reviled) man in all of Greece and well known throughout Europe for a dazzling act of courage when he was just nineteen: in late May 1941, he and a friend climbed the Acropolis and tore down the Swastika that had flown over Athens since German occupation forces marched into the city a month earlier. Their symbolic action was magnified many times when the Nazis, determined to nip all opposition in the bud lest the virus of resistance spread, offered a reward of Manolis's weight in gold for his capture and sentenced Manolis and his pal to death in absentia. By the time we met, Manolis was ninety years old and a veteran of seventy years of struggle for peace and justice. He'd been imprisoned by the German occupiers, the Italians, the Greek collaborators, and the Regime of the Colonels, adding up to over a decade behind bars; he had been sentenced to death multiple times, charged with espionage, treason, and sabotage, and escaped prison more than once; his fifteen-year-old brother had been executed by the Nazis. He'd been the focus of widespread international protests and "Free Glezos!" campaigns on several occasions over the years, which surely explained why Manolis was still alive and standing at the dock waving happily when we arrived.

His broad smile emerged from his bushy white mustache and drove a deeper crease across his already wrinkled countenance, and his beaming shock of windswept hair stood out against his brown face. He was wearing a loosely fitted, coarse cotton shirt with pants to match, a beige scarf, and a light sports coat buttoned to the top, collar up. We embraced for a long moment, then turned and walked arm in arm— Petros on one side, me on the other, Manolis stepping spryly along in the middle—to a café in the plaza as the two of them caught up on the gossip and the news of the day.

Our walk was slow, for every person we passed—every one, no exception—greeted Manolis and presented a kiss or a handshake or a hug, and he offered an embrace or a word to each in return. It became the customary practice of our day together, and I assumed of his life all the time: he was a flesh-and-blood man, to be sure, but he was simultaneously larger than life, a symbol and an icon. He bore the responsibility gracefully without being in its thrall, responding warmly to everyone he met but remaining as ordinary and earth-bound and humble as anyone I've known.

I asked him about his time in the Greek Parliament. He said that each time he ran, and particularly when he was elected, it was always as part of a larger strategy, a useful tactic for him and his comrades at specific times, but never an end in itself. "I'm interested in people collectively discovering their own power," he said. "That's an entirely different thing from an individual or a party in power."

When we finished our second coffee Manolis led us on a walking tour of the town: up and down the narrow streets, through the white marble gates, in and out of shops and cafes, greeting everyone as we went. The sparkling heavens, bright and blue and clean, matched the luminous Aegean below, and the wind seemed to dance between sky and sea before sweeping over our little patch of rock and trees.

In an Eastern Orthodox Church near the town center, we admired ancient statues and a jumble of holy relics collected in glass-covered boxes while a small tour group assembled on the steps. One tourist glanced in our direction and poked another, who looked over and nudged two more; soon everyone was smiling and waving and craning for a look. The tour guide turned and said, "Oh, hello. There you are." Turning back to her charges, she said, "I see you all recognize our

Manolis Glezos." Spontaneous applause erupted and cameras flashed as Manolis cheerfully went to shake more hands. He welcomed them, and, discovering they were from Spain, told of a time he had visited their homeland—fresh out of prison—at the invitation of Picasso, and said the great artist had done a portrait of him that still hung in Manolis's home. The tourists applauded once more, and we moved on.

Manolis told us about the years when he was the elected president of the Community Council in Aperathou, an experiment in far-reaching participatory democracy. "We governed by consensus," he said, "in a local assembly with forums reminiscent of the period of radical democracy in ancient Greece." They abolished all privileges for elected officials, developed a written constitution, and challenged the idea that "experts" or professional politicians and self-proclaimed leaders were better at running the town's affairs than ordinary people. "Every cook can govern!" was a kind of theme and watchword.

Manolis put his face close to mine and said with conspiratorial conviction, "The biggest obstacle to revolution here—and I'll bet it's true in your country as well—is a serious and often unrecognized lack of confidence." I agreed. Petros was right: we had some politics in common—definitely. "We spend our lives in the presence of mayors and governors and presidents and chiefs of police," Manolis continued, "and then we lose our power of self-reliance, and we doubt that we could live without those authorities. We worship them in spite of ourselves. We may not mean to but we do, and soon enough we embrace our own passivity and become enslaved to a culture of obedience. That's a core of our weakness. That's something you and I must challenge and change."

Before we caught the last boat to Piraeus, Manolis gave me an autographed copy of one of his books, *National Resistance 1940–1945*. I gave him *Fugitive Days*. "I've already read it," he said, "but now I have your autograph!"

Manolis has been arrested by riot police in front of the Parliament building each year since our meeting, still living the activist life, still battling the murderous system of oppression and exploitation, still opening spaces for more participatory democracy, more peace, and more justice. And I still see him in my mind's eye waving cheerfully from the dock—filled with energy and hope.

When I retired from the University of Illinois, the board of trustees voted to deny me emeritus status—an honor initiated by the faculty and advanced on approval from the provost to the chancellor and then to the president and finally to the board. This was a first in the history of the university, and ignited another round of weirdness. Strange times.

I didn't like the sound of it, *emeritus*, except when applied to noxious politicians—George Bush, *emeritus*. Yes! He was gone. And I didn't like *retired* much either, because the cultural construction and the social assumptions all pointed toward the grave.

Christopher Kennedy, head of the board and billionaire chair of Chicago's Merchandise Mart, made an impassioned plea at the end of a public meeting that was quoted in the papers:

> I intend to vote against conferring the honorific title of our University to a man whose body of work includes a book dedicated in part to the man who murdered my father, Robert F. Kennedy. . . . There can be no place in a democracy to celebrate political assassinations or to honor those who do so.

He noted that I had long been a popular teacher at UIC, that I had earned considerable respect among education scholars, but added that since emeritus status is a tribute, "our discussion of this topic does not represent an intervention into the scholarship of the University, nor is it a threat to academic freedom." This last bit struck me as overly defensive and wholly inaccurate.

Kennedy was referring to *Prairie Fire*, the manifesto of the Weather Underground, written decades earlier, and I might have been impressed that Kennedy even knew the book existed except that it, too, had been resurrected in the run-up to the national elections. Sean Hannity and Bill O'Reilly read from it regularly—good stuff mostly— always pointing out that it was "dedicated to Sirhan Sirhan, the man who assassinated Senator Robert F. Kennedy." That wasn't true. The dedication page reads, "to harriet tubman and john brown/to all who continue to fight/and to all political prisoners in the us." This boxed dedication is superimposed over an artist's rendering of wall-to-wall names of people in prison—hundreds and hundreds of them. The force of the piece is that it points to the fact that the United States was already well into creating a massive gulag—and this was way before mass incarceration gripped the country—and it's true that Sirhan Sirhan's name is there, but so are Willy Johnson's and Michael McGann's. Exactly: who the hell are they? And was the artist in any way endorsing Johnson's and McGann's actions, whatever they were? Not likely.

I immediately wrote a letter to Christopher Kennedy expressing surprise that I'd become an issue and noting that I was truly sorry he had found himself in that impossibly difficult situation. I went on,

> I'm also saddened that your loss was once again made present and painful to you and your family. I can only imagine the awfulness of those memories, and as I try to put myself in your place, the sense of anguish and anger seems utterly overwhelming.

I asked to meet with him away from the weight of stereotypes and media creations "to see if we might find some common ground in our shared commitment to the University, to basic democratic principles, and to a belief in the power of redemption and reconciliation."

I told him that I had never praised the man who murdered his father, nor had I ever condoned assassination—"That narrative is categorically false." But I went on to ask him to consider the implications of his action. What are my thousands of students to make of it? And beyond that, what was anyone to make of the board intervening in the academic affairs of the university, making decisions about things they cannot adequately or fully evaluate or judge, and are therefore appropriately the province of the faculty and the officers hired by the board? "But whatever the outcome of this," I said, "I want you to know that I regret the pain that this has rekindled for you. I would welcome an opportunity to talk with you if and when you think that might be worthwhile."

Kennedy sent me a letter back thanking me for my "thoughtful response" and my "kind words and support." He reiterated his point about there being no place in a democracy to celebrate political assassinations and noted that the board decision "was not a personal or political matter, but simply a decision of the board."

Some tricky lawyer—probably Thomas Bearrows—had to have written that last phrase, because merit is the only basis of emeritus status, and he would be hard-pressed to explain my promotion to Distinguished Professor on any other basis. Furthermore, the First Amendment prohibits using political criteria for employment decisions at public colleges, and the role of politics in this unprecedented action is unmistakable.

But Bearrows—who had previously defended me in his role as university counsel—was brought in to counter the Faculty Senate and others who were organized to object. He now endorsed the misrepresentation that I supported political assassinations and repeated the fabrication that I had never expressed any regret for my activities. He escalated the falsification when he asserted that I was a willing participant "in what can only be described as terrorist conduct." I had never been charged, arrested, or convicted of "terrorist conduct."

At that moment a controversy erupted in New York regarding an honorary doctorate for the justly acclaimed playwright Tony Kushner, which had been recommended to the City University of New York board of trustees by the faculty and administration, denied, and then approved in a rapid reversal because of a firestorm of protest. While the facts were different—and I was surely no Tony Kushner—the principles were similar. As the CUNY board chairman, Benno Schmidt Jr., noted, they had "made a mistake of principle, and not merely of policy," and politics and personal opinion should not play a role in these types of things. The board (in that case, as well as the one at UIC) had no capacity to investigate nominees and no stated criteria to evaluate them; the board had never before rejected a nominee in its long history, even though it always had the legal right to do so. The board appeared capricious and arbitrary in its decision.

Being denied emeritus status didn't mean a lot practically: losing my parking permit and my e-mail account—damn! But, really, who cares? Yet when the news hit the media, I immediately got phone calls from folks in parking and communication: "Fuck them," said one older clerk. "You'll get your parking sticker as long as I'm here." And from a young woman computer nerd, "If Kennedy wants to take down your e-mail, let him try. I'll find a way around it. Keep going." And then I got another encouraging note from Espie Reyes: "I returned my emeritus award to Chris Kennedy and told him if you were not worthy, then I wasn't either. I sent him your vitae and told him he owed you an apology." Oh, Espie!

Best of all, a group of friends and faculty hosted a big retirement party on a Saturday night in a funky open space on Sixty-first and Blackstone. The Experimental Station is an innovative South Side social and cultural incubator home to the Blackstone Bicycle Works, B'Gabs Goodies Raw Vegan Deli, the Backstory Café, the 61st Street Farmers Market, the Invisible Institute, the art studios of the renowned Dan Peterman and the dazzling Theaster Gates, and once the *Baffler* magazine. It also hosts events ranging from book launches to theatrical performances to ARC events and rallies. The joint was teeming with a wild mash-up of art, political purpose, and life, while masquerading on the outside as a hulking, abandoned industrial relic.

Hundreds of people—political comrades, university colleagues, family and friends—crowded in, and the potluck tables groaned with plates of fried tofu in dill and basil, yummy homemade tamales, tasty grits with spicy greens, cardamom cake, and sweetened rice squares. Lovable Lisa Lee and her kids made a zillion astonishing cupcakes, each with a strip of paper bearing a quotation from one of my books toothpicked to the top like a delicious exhortation. People loaded up, ate, and talked, and then moved on to the dance floor as DJ Dave kept the party going with a mix of old and new. Bernardine and I swirled through the crowd, warm embraces and surprising homemade tattoos and buttons in every direction: "I pal around with Bernardine and Bill." It was loud and sweaty, lovely and sweet.

Barbara Ransby stopped the music for a moment and invited just a few people to say a word or two to mark the moment—embarrassing but true—and my kids spoke. I choked up a little, and then Rachel

DeWoskin read a poem she'd written for the occasion and I cried. Barbara Ransby presented a plaque to me that read: "The People's Emeritus Award!" That was all I really wanted or needed. Then FM Supreme adapted and spit one of her classic pieces, and everyone joined in on the noisy refrain: "This is the Movement! This is the Movement! So get moving, y'all! Get moving!"

Grant Park, Chicago, November 4, 2008

On the first Tuesday of November 2012, the Obama campaign hosted what they called an election night "watch party" at McCormick Place, a cavernous convention center south of Grant Park, with attendance mostly limited to luminaries and supporters who'd volunteered in Ohio or one of the other "swing states" or volunteers who'd manned the phone banks for the last week of campaigning. They would cheer their man's progress on huge screens, celebrate Barack Obama's reelection, and congratulate one another on a job well done. We weren't invited.

We watched the early returns instead at the home of close comrades, but late in the evening we headed once more to Grant Park—just Bernardine and me this time—to reprise and remember the experiences from four years earlier. There would, of course, be no reliving 2008—that was a one-and-only evening, never to be touched again. Plus, everyone was now at watch parties large and small all over town. But we wanted to tap the ground anyway, so we walked the length of the abandoned park, a cold rain driving off the lake and soaking us to the bone.

In 2008, Grant Park had become a human river in full flood by the time Bernardine and I arrived, people flowing naturally into the gathering stream, moving, churning, surging happily forward, spilling over the shifting banks without incident and then effortlessly remaking the shore. There were children of all ages in hand or tucked into strollers and backpacks, buoyant parents delighted to let them stay up late just this one night in order to witness this precious and perhaps fragile moment. "Eighty years from now I want her to tell her grandchildren she was here," a young man said to us as he posed for a picture with his infant daughter. "She's a part of history, even if she doesn't know it yet."

What had been unimaginable a year, a month, even a day before had become inevitable, and on that special night and in this specific place, unforgettable: an African American president, a community organizer in the White House, a generational shift at last. We sang and we danced, and the enchanted night sparkled in reply. We felt ourselves to be a brand-new, shimmering galaxy, a little bit of heaven on earth.

The crowd was diverse in a thousand ways. I saw a newborn wrapped tight on his mother's chest pushed up next to a small old woman smiling broadly from her wheelchair and waving an oversized American flag in wide arcs above her head. I saw a young Black police officer with a gold earring joined in a circle dance with two gray-haired white women. And on one brightly lit corner, a huge man with a ukulele who beautifully evoked the ghost of Israel Kamakawiwo'ole belted out Iz's version of "Somewhere over the Rainbow"—dreams really do come true—and I burst into tears. What a wonderful world it could be.

We'd stopped by my brother's place hours earlier to watch the first returns. Juan and Judi were lifelong Democratic Party stalwarts, and they'd spent weekends that year with their friends phone-banking and canvassing for Obama in Michigan, Wisconsin, and Indiana. We were tied to multiple screens and they were taking every precinct in those three battlegrounds personally, every vote marking a distinct and intimate victory or defeat. The groans were painful, the cheers joyous, and, as the numbers began to add up, the mood turned giddy.

We had moved on to a large gathering of our closest political allies and comrades at Barbara Ransby and Peter Sporn's place, both longtime peace and justice activists. There was joy here, too, tempered by a sense that this wasn't the end of anything, but rather a new beginning and perhaps an opening of sorts—rising expectations and expanding imaginations, but with more serious work to do tomorrow and the next day and the next. The mood here was more a sigh of relief, less an inclination to dance in the streets.

But we couldn't resist, and before John McCain had conceded we decided that dancing in the streets was exactly what we needed to do, and so we headed for the door with friends in tow: Jacco, a historian from the Netherlands who was staying with us for a few days of jaw-dropping Chicago experiences; Ryan, the brilliant young cartoonist living with us as we collaborated on a comic book about teaching; and Paul, an accomplished Zimbabwean scholar whose irrepressible excitement poured into his cell phone connecting Grant Park to Africa, Europe, and the world.

Zayd called from Harlem, Malik from Berkeley, and Chesa from New Haven.

I'd been a part of large crowds many times before this—demonstrations and rallies, sporting events and the fabulously extravagant Taste of Chicago, also held in Grant Park—but every one of them had been edged with tension or anger or demand or performance, characterized by fighting or drunkenness, gluttony or narcissism. This was unlike anything I'd known before—a huge mobilization sharing a deep sense of unity, satisfaction, and release, closing a door on eight years of fear and loathing, war and divisiveness and looking forward to a world that could be but was not yet. It was oddly serene and sober, and, while there was lots of rejoicing, there was surprisingly little crowing. The dominant tone was a soft purr as people went gently over the moon.

We saw friends and colleagues and former students every step of the way, and we stopped for kisses and hugs and group cell phone photos, the spirit spilling seamlessly over to strangers, with more embraces and more photos. I'd endured snubs and quick expressionless glances for months from some of these same folks, and I'd felt unfairly singled out, but that was then. Now we were all friends again, I guessed, and I felt wave after wave of liberation, like a weight finally being lifted from my neck, an albatross or a yoke I'd forgotten was there because it was with me night and day and I'd grown accustomed to it. Now it was gone, and I felt only lightness and a fugitive memory of a once-solid stone I'd been carrying. A neighbor who had shunned me for months smiled and waved, and maybe I should have felt angry but I didn't, not at all. I felt grateful. I teared up and just let the feelings wash over

me—thankfulness, reprieve, solitude. Bernardine was here, still holding my hand, still dancing, still moving forward.

I surprised myself again and again, bursting into tears all evening
long: first, simply experiencing the connectedness and solidarity as the
animated convergence grew and grew and kept on growing; later when
I ran into two African American high school kids I'd known, their vid-
eocams in hand, filming a curriculum project called "Searching for Democracy;" and much later standing on the exact spot where, forty years
before, at the infamous 1968 Democratic Convention, I'd been beaten
bloody by Chicago's finest and hauled off to jail. I corralled two young
police officers—a Black woman and a Latino man—to pose with me
while Bernardine snapped photos. We all had tears in our eyes.

Barack Obama looked positively Lincolnesque that night, standing
tall with his beautiful family in front of our twinkling starry sky and
our vast blue-black lake. But I'm an entirely untrustworthy witness
here—after all, I'd been inhaling that sparkly, rarified atmosphere for
quite a while by then, and I was prone to being taken over by aliens
the whole day. Luckily Bernardine was right there, nudging me back
to reality.

When the president-elect spoke, the exultation rose in response:

> If there is anyone out there who still doubts that America is a place
> where all things are possible . . . tonight is your answer. . . . It's the
> answer that led those who have been told for so long by so many to
> be cynical, and fearful, and doubtful of what we can achieve to put
> their hands on the arc of history and bend it once more toward the
> hope of a better day.

There was a simple straightforwardness to his talk, and there was
a deep bow to the reality that every community organizer knows well:

> For even as we celebrate tonight, we know the challenges that to-
> morrow will bring are the greatest of our lifetime—two wars, a
> planet in peril, the worst financial crisis in a century. . . . The road
> ahead will be long. Our climb will be steep. We may not get there

in one year or even one term, but America—I have never been more
hopeful than I am tonight that we will get there. I promise you—we
as a people will get there.

Echoes rang out from Amilcar Cabral, the anticolonial African
leader, insisting that the movement tell no lies and claim no easy victories, and from Martin Luther King Jr.—bending the arc of history
toward justice so that "we as a people will get there." Everyone there
heard hard reverberations of the legacy of slavery as well and the struggle for abolition and equality. Everyone saw a symbol of change rise up
in our minds. And everyone felt a pervasive sense that our imaginations
could grow more freely, more powerfully: "This is our moment. This
is our time. Yes we can . . ."

It was a wonderful feeling to breathe in the good air, to breathe out
the bad air, and then just to keep on breathing—wonderful and refreshing. It was great to feel the energy of rising expectations, to hear the
sounds of heavy chains dropping from our minds, to see the shining
faces of hope everywhere.

Barack Obama can't save us, I thought then, but look around: with
some hard work and a little luck, these folks right here just might save
Barack Obama. I wanted nothing more than to embrace that moment,
to hold tight to this fleeting but feasible community, and to store all
this energy away for the tough times to come.

Perhaps that explains why I couldn't summon the get-up-and-go
to leave the park. The Obamas were long gone, the crowd drifting
away, slowly at first and then in big waves, park workers and Streets and
Sanitation cleaning up and breaking down the fences and the scaffold-
ing, and still we held on. Breathe in the good air, breathe out the bad.
Of course we knew the sun would come up tomorrow, reality would
impose its harsh order, and the magic would burn off soon enough,
but not yet, not quite yet. "Let us have this night," I said out loud, a
brief sighting of the world I want to live in—a bit more peaceful and
balanced, with an enlarged sense of participation and possibility, all of
us arm in arm together, recognizing one another as inherently valuable
and fully human beyond class or color or condition. I was on my back

in the grass looking at the stars, Bernardine standing nearby on her cell phone with our far-flung children, when a young cop approached me smiling. "Bill," he said softly, "it's time to go home." He helped me to my feet, asked for a picture of the three of us together, and then walked with us to Michigan Avenue. I knew we might meet one another one day in the future on opposite sides of an angry barricade, but not to-night: "I love you man," I said. "Love you back," he replied. It was two in the morning.

There are a zillion reasons not to write a book: laziness, for starters; insecurity; a recognition that you are incorrigibly self-deceiving and self-justifying, leading to a distaste for interrogating your own ignorance and a sensible aversion to digging too deeply into your own wretched soul; fear of falling short or being exposed for the fraud you surely are; and, of course, the terrible realization that you're neither Hemingway nor Morrison. Add to that vast catalogue one more: once you start writing your book, you will drive the ones you love away with your petty obsessions and your silly distractions. I know; I've indulged the whole set.

As to the relatively few reasons, on the other hand, to persevere in the delicious agony of assembling words on the page, I've long found George Orwell's four-part taxonomy, outlined in his essay "Why I Write," elegantly simple and particularly compelling: all writers, he claims (and he included himself without apology), are motivated in the first place by the most predictable and pervasive sentiment of all: complete conceit and run-away egoism. Guilty! The desire to be talked about and to be remembered after death, to appear clever or to settle scores—it's difficult to deny. And of all the available genres, memoir stands out for its unvarnished narcissism, careening through a brightly lit house of mirrors, entirely out of control.

Include two more possible explanations, fairly straightforward: aesthetic enthusiasm, including searching out the beauty in good prose and "words and their right arrangement," as well as historical impulse, the desire to see things in their true and luminous complexity and preserve them for posterity. Guilty, guilty.

And finally Orwell's number four: "Political purpose—using the word 'political' in the widest possible sense. Desire to push the world in a certain direction, to alter other peoples' idea of the kind of society that they should strive after." That says it all for me: guilty as hell.

The despicable American war in Viet Nam ("Shoot anything that moves!"), combined with the power and promise of the resistance and the courage of the Black Freedom Movement, rocked my world: I had a political purpose, and I knew where I stood. From then on I've tried to live up to that purpose—there had to be something important to say, some aspect of social life to praise or to criticize, some war to end or some injustice to oppose. I plunged into the wreckage headfirst and tried to fight, and to write, my way out. And I was never alone.

I'm most grateful for my everyday comrades in arms in the battles (large and small) for peace and freedom, joy and justice in Chicago: Alice Kim, Barbara Ransby, James Thindwa, David Stovall, Lisa Lee, Therese Quinn, Erica Meiners, Kevin Kumashiro, Martha Biondi, Adam Green, Harish Patel, Tessie Liu, Tom Mitchell, Susan Klonsky, Jessica Disu (FM Supreme), Randolph Stone, Jeff Haas, Prexy Nesbitt, Peter Sporn, Hazel Rochman, Bill Watkins, Simmie Baer, Steve Saltzman, Susan Gzesch, Beth Richie, Kevin Coval, Fred Klonsky, Bruce Boyer, Hymie Rochman, Mike Klonsky, Carol Lee, Haki Madhubuti, Pat Handlin, Jennifer Richardson, Camille Odeh, Cathy Cohen, Jan Susler, Elena Sznajder, Dima Khalidi, Lynette Jackson, Flint Taylor, Daniel Tucker, Monica Murphy, Jamie Kalven, Ann Klonsky, Patsy Evans, Quentin Young, Michelle Lugalia, Iasha Sznajder, Joey Mogul, Julie Biehl, Yoko Noge, Mary Scott Boria, Cynthia Estes, Randolph Stone, Ryan Hollon, Marv Hoffman, Adam Kuranishi, Janise Hurtig, Isabel Nunez, Rosellen Brown, Crystal Laura, Janice Misurell, Bill Schubert, and many others.

In writing this book I've benefited from all kinds of help, including from friends and family who read bits and pieces of the narrative in its various incarnations. Knowing that it was being constructed on nothing more than the chimera of chaos and confusion called *memory*—scandalously fly-by-night, sketchy, and undependable—each nonetheless took his or her precious time to offer advice and helpful perspectives: Malik

Dohrn, Chesa Boudin, Lisa Freccero, Eleanor Stein (twice!), Mona Kha-lidi, Jeff Jones, B. J. Richards, and Kathy Boudin. I'm indebted to each of you. Bernardine Dohrn read every word again and again, caught and corrected each tendency of mine to lurch instinctively toward the ultra-left or, on the other hand, to collapse into the seductive and welcoming arms of the liberal-right, and kept me focused always on the bigger pic-ture. Rick Ayers has been a tireless editor, coconspirator, and sometimes coauthor forever, and his judgments at several turning points were in-valuable. Zayd Dohrn has cheerfully read my attempts to write for close to twenty years, and his perceptive reading, consistent encouragement, and astute interventions were once again indispensable, and Rachel De-Woskin generously weighed in with her incisive comments and brilliant intuition at just the right moment leading to a complete overhaul and reorganization. Of course, none of them is responsible for the deficien-cies, gaps, and foolishness herein—those belong to me alone.

I am again grateful to Helene Atwan, as fine an editor as there is anywhere, whose vision and support made this book possible in the first place, and whose shrewd interferences—knowing when to indulge my ramblings and when to cut the crap and get to work—improved the book immeasurably. My awe and appreciation is boundless, and it extends to the dazzling team she leads at Beacon Press, starting with my first editor there, Andy Hrcyna, and including the brilliant Pam MacColl, the mighty Tom Hallock, and the wondrous magic-maker, Crystal Paul.

And I need to say again how thankful I am for Bernardine, a gift to the world and for forty-three years my partner in crime (I can hear her now: "Please stop saying that, darling"); I am, as always, overwhelmed by my dumb luck. Thanks to our three incomparable sons, Zayd, Malik, and Chesa; to our magnificent-good-fortune daughters-in-law, Rachel and Lisa; and to the coming whirlwinds, Dalin and Lightie and Jacai.

Perhaps the passionate choices, everyday experiences, and conse-quential errors of our fighting past can help illuminate a way forward. In any case, I've never been more hopeful for young activists the world around. For humanity and for the future, we must change ourselves; we can change the world.